Human Gr
& Development
across the Lifespan

3rd Edition

Emma Zara O'Brien

Boru Press Ltd.
The Farmyard
Birdhill
Co. Tipperary

www.borupress.ie

ISBN 978-1-7396232-3-4

Design by Sarah McCoy
Print origination by Jen Patton at Liz White Designs
Illustrations by Andriy Yankovskyy and Derry Dillon
Index by Eileen O'Neill
Printed by GraphyCems, Spain

The paper used in this book is made from wood pulp of managed forests. For every tree felled, at least one tree is planted, thereby renewing natural resources.

A CIP catalogue record for this book is available from the British Library.
For permission to reproduce photographs and artworks, the author and publisher gratefully acknowledge the following:

© Alamy: 36, 39, 47, 49, 52, 57, 68, 73, 118. © Emma Zara O'Brien: 150. © Shutterstock: 8, 10, 21, 24, 35, 41, 56, 78, 80, 91, 93, 94, 99, 108, 123, 129, 130, 132, 134, 137, 141, 160, 164, 170, 171, 173, 176, 178, 199, 207, 208, 212, 220, 221, 227. © Unicef: 160. © World Health Organization: 210. © Youngballymun: 19.

The author and publisher have made every effort to trace all copyright holders, but if any has been inadvertently overlooked we would be pleased to make the necessary arrangement at the first opportunity.

Contents

To Ultan

1

Introduction

In this chapter we will discover:

* The early roots of psychology
* What psychology is
* Different perspectives in psychology
* The goals of psychology
* Lifespan development
* Factors influencing human development
* Key issues in the study of human development
* In Focus: The impact of extreme deprivation on developmental outcomes

Most of us are curious about why people are the way they are and why we are the way we are. What makes some people thrive while others struggle? Psychology offers insights into these question, but also into how we can support people through initiatives and interventions which are based on psychological concepts and research. The question of how we become who we are is not a recent one. As we will see, it has intrigued people for a long time.

THE EARLY ROOTS OF PSYCHOLOGY

History has been characterised by attempts to understand what makes us human, what shapes our thoughts and behaviour. Religion played an early part in attempting to unravel human behaviour through the Christian doctrine of 'original sin' – the idea that we are all born flawed and susceptible to undesirable behaviour. Philosophers added to the debate as the centuries unfolded. John Locke, for instance, suggested that we are born a 'blank slate', or 'tabula rasa', and that our life experiences shape who we become. Jean-Jacques Rousseau, in contrast to the Christian view, believed in the innate goodness of people as we strive to reach our full potential. Of course, these arguments are best left to theologians and philosophers but the study of psychology is not very different in that, put simply, it attempts to gain understanding of humans, their development and behaviours.

WHAT IS PSYCHOLOGY?

Psychology is the study of people; how they think, act, react and interact. Psychology is concerned with all aspects of behaviour and the thoughts, feelings and motivations underlying such behaviour.

In their search for the causes of our diverse forms of behaviour, psychologists take different influences into account:

- biological
- psychological
- social/environmental.

This approach is often referred to as the **biopsychosocial** approach. Psychology is different from psychiatry, which requires a medical degree and examines mental illness.

CHECK YOUR LEARNING

How would you explain what psychology is? Write down your definition and see if it changes the more you learn.

TERMINOLOGY

Terminology can change with each new concept or theory introduced in psychology. It is helpful, early on, to define and clarify the core terms you will encounter in this book. Terminology can be intimidating, so throughout this book we will explain terms in accessible language. The following terms are used repeatedly in psychology:

TERM	DEFINITION
Theory	Describes, explains or predicts certain phenomena
Method	Specifies what to do when faced with certain phenomena
Perspective	A way of viewing or understanding certain experience based on words and principles
Model	A theory or method depicted logically or graphically

Let's look at some perspectives in psychology.

DIFFERENT PERSPECTIVES IN PSYCHOLOGY

In the history of psychology there have been several approaches used to gain a greater understanding of human behaviours, beginning in the early 1800s with introspection.

Introspection

Psychoanalysis

Behaviourism

Humanistic Psychology

Cognitive Psychology

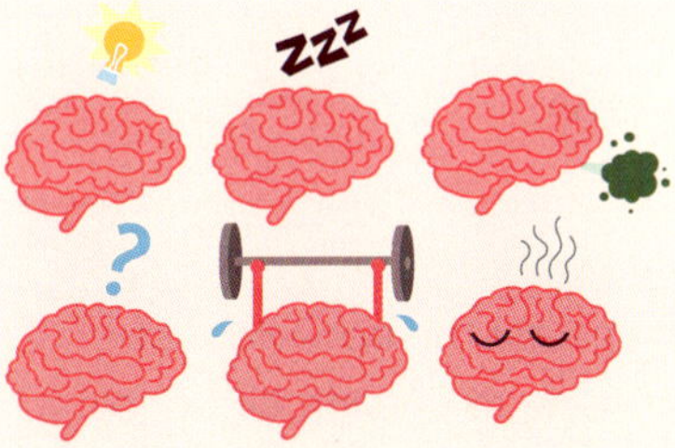

Biological Psychology

Sociocultural Image Theory

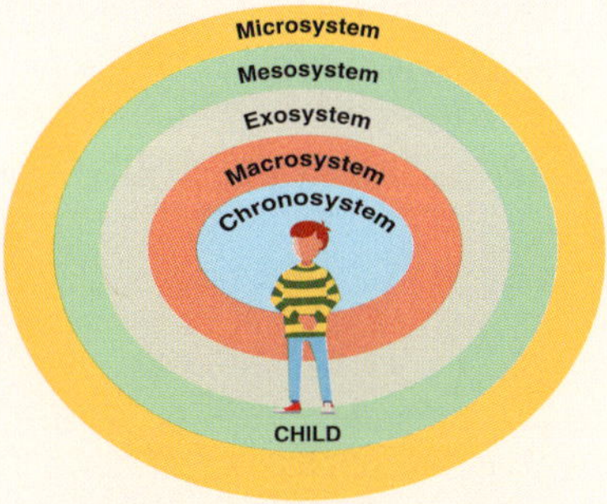

Ecological Systems Theory

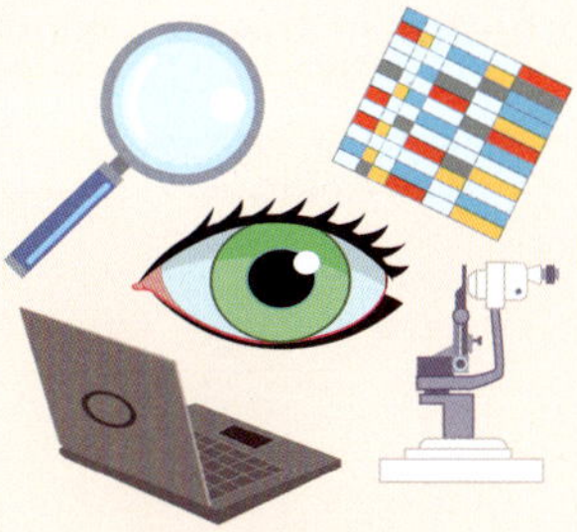

Scientific Theory

INTROSPECTION

This marks the starting point of the field of psychology and it began with the work of William James. As the name suggests, this approach relied on 'inspection'; an individual would be asked to self-report on their feelings and thoughts.

PSYCHOANALYTIC/PSYCHODYNAMIC PERSPECTIVE

Originating in the late 1800s, this movement is best known through the work of Sigmund Freud and psychoanalysis, which we will look at in more depth throughout the book. It placed an emphasis on the 'unconscious' mind, believing that a person only has awareness of a fraction of their thoughts and mental processes. Freud believed that unconscious urges are responsible for behaviour. Techniques such as hypnosis and dream analysis were used to access these unknown recesses of the mind.

BEHAVIOURISM PERSPECTIVE

This approach was very popular in America in the 1920s. Those best known for their work in this field are Skinner and Pavlov. Behaviourists rejected the idea that behaviour is caused by an unconscious part of the mind. They argued that behaviour is observable and often shaped by interaction with the environment. Remember when you were in the schoolyard and the bell would ring? You'd line up to go back into class. This is an example of behaviourism. Your behaviour (lining up on the ringing of a bell) was shaped by your environment (the bell and the teacher). The work of behaviourist psychologists still has some relevance in the area of learning and approaches such as applied behavioural analysis (ABA).

HUMANIST PERSPECTIVE

This approach, it could be argued, was a reaction against the behaviourist picture of humans almost as robots merely responding to outside influence (external stimuli) or the Freudian image of humans driven by our unconscious urges. Humanists such as Carl Rogers and Abraham Maslow promoted the view that within us all is an active desire to reach our full potential, or 'self-actualisation'. Their work has been important in the area of personality and influenced the emergence of person-centred approaches in social care, education and health services.

COGNITIVE PERSPECTIVE

This refers to the changes that occur in thinking, memory, problem-solving and other cognitive mental abilities, including language. It is important to understand that children 'think' differently from adults and it's important that we understand this so as to understand and support children and young people more effectively. Those associated with this perspective are Jean Piaget and Lev Vygotsky. Each took a different approach to understanding the development of cognition (or thinking). Piaget believed our 'thinking' grows or 'matures' as we physically develop, whereas Vygotsky emphasised that all individuals' cognitive development happens as a result of interacting with others and their culture.

The **information processing** approach compares how we all think, and learn to think, as similar to a computer. Information is input (through our senses), processed (memory and representational frameworks called schemas) and then there is an output.

Think about learning a new piece of information. You take it in through your senses (sight, hearing, etc.). You then link it to relevant information (if it exists) and encode it in your memory, where it is stored. Then, when you need to use it, for example in an exam, you retrieve it from memory and use it – this is the 'output'.

BIOLOGICAL PERSPECTIVE

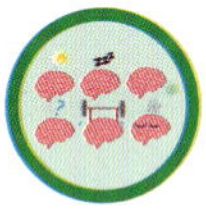

The biological perspective in psychology increasingly offers a gateway into understanding human thinking, behaviour and motivation. 'Biological' can refer to the role of the brain, genes (DNA) or hormones on individuals' psychological functioning. It also includes all other aspects of the physical body. Think about a time when you felt physically unwell. Did it impact on your mood? If it was something you ate, perhaps you recorded in your memory never to eat that food again.

The biological perspective can be found in the nature versus nurture debate, which we will examine later in this chapter. It is pivotal as a perspective in helping us gain greater insight into human development and behaviour.

SOCIOCULTURAL PERSPECTIVE

No man (or woman) is an island. We are social creatures, and this perspective argues that our thoughts and behaviours are influenced by our interactions with others. Importantly, it highlights that we are embedded in the culture we are raised or live in and that this culture in turn influences us. In the past psychology tended to look 'within' the individual to gain a greater understanding without taking account of external influences on them. The sociocultural approach examines how culture is transmitted to its members and investigates the differences and similarities of people from different cultures.

ECOLOGICAL PERSPECTIVE

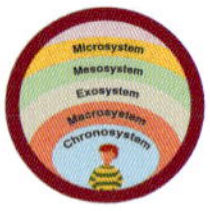

This theory has become very popular among psychologists as it offers a framework for understanding all the different influences (factors) and relationships in people's lives. It looks beyond a person's immediate environment (such as family) to more distant ones like government policies or religion. It shows how all these different layers of influences are present in a person's life. This framework helps us to picture where these factors sit, whether in the person's immediate environment or in a more distant one. When we look at risk and protective factors later in this chapter, think about how the ecological approach allows us to place those factors on a framework so we can gain a better picture of the person and their life.

SCIENTIFIC PERSPECTIVE

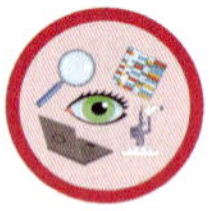

All the approaches we've just looked at come under the umbrella of psychology and represent different fields. The scientific perspective isn't so much a set of ideas or theories about a particular area of human development as an approach used by most psychologists (regardless of their perspective) to research and understand human functioning. At its core is the scientific method, or science of behaviour. Its main focus is to understand the *why* rather than merely observe. Different methods of research (methodology) are used, including statistics and experiments.

This leads us to the **goals** of psychology, which form the backbone of the scientific approach.

THE GOALS OF PSYCHOLOGY

These goals are used by psychologists to identify the main aim of their research. For example, if you are interested in a particular behaviour you would need to decide whether you wish to observe it, understand the causes or predict the behaviour. Your aim or goal will guide you as to which research design or statistical method is best to use.

More recently, some have questioned whether the scientific approach to understanding human functioning can fully capture the complexity of human motivation and behaviour. This has led to newer approaches, one being community psychology, which examines individuals within their social world. Community psychology explores social issues and how they influence individuals, groups and society at large.

While newer approaches continue to increase in popularity, the scientific approach maintains its dominant position in psychology. What is and will remain central to the study of psychology is an interest in exploring human behaviour and functioning from cradle to grave.

LIFESPAN DEVELOPMENT

The study of lifespan development looks at human growth and changes across the lifespan. This includes the study of human growth and development, or **developmental psychology**, which looks at specific areas of development.

The study of **human development** is 'the scientific study of age-related changes in behaviour, thinking, emotion and personality' (Boyd & Bee 2005, p.3).

Developmental psychology looks at how we develop in different areas – physical (including the brain), social, emotional and cognitive (thinking) – and across the lifespan.

Psychologists use different categories as they explore and try to explain fully how humans develop. We shall look at it in two ways: the different periods (categories of age-related changes); and the different domains (or areas) of development.

PERIODS OF DEVELOPMENT

The lifespan can be broken down or categorised into phases or periods. Psychologists use these phases to organise the study of human development. Some periods have clear **biological milestones** with obvious physical changes, meaning that we see them in all people around the world (for example, the physical changes in infancy or adolescence). There are also **social milestones**, which can differ from culture to culture.

Developmental milestones

PERIOD	MILESTONES
Pre-natal Before birth	This is the only period with a very clear biological beginning and end: the moment of conception to the moment of birth.
Infancy 0–2	This period is usually agreed to be between birth and two years of age. Milestones include the ability to communicate and starting to use language.
Early childhood 2–5	Most agree this period to be between two and five years, though some suggest six years of age as the end point. A significant milestone that marks this period is the ability to use language to communicate. In most typically developing children this is expected in early childhood, though it can appear at slightly different ages.
Middle and late childhood 6–11	The ages 6–11 constitute middle and late childhood, although some suggest seven as the starting point for this period. However, there are significant differences between cultures. Some children in Europe start school at six, others (e.g. in Ireland) at four. The start of puberty is seen as the transition point into the next period.

PERIOD	MILESTONES
Adolescence 12–20	Adolescence is usually recognised as beginning with puberty. The starting age of adolescence, however, is not universally agreed: some children have signs of puberty at ages nine or ten; in others it might be 13 or 14. Social milestones include the transition to secondary school. In some states in the USA, teenagers who have committed serious crimes can be prosecuted as adults. This highlights the differences that can exist in how we define and understand this period of development. The major milestone, at least in Western cultures, is related to identity – the teenager tries to figure out 'who they are'.
Early adulthood 20–40	Some policy documents in Ireland define 'young people' as aged between 11 and 23 years. Many people are still in secondary school at 18. So here we can see the blurred line in trying to place age categories across the lifespan. Early adulthood, in general, is marked by the completion of physical maturity. In some cultures, the young person would be expected to complete an 'initiation' ritual to be considered an adult.
Middle adulthood 40–65	There is no significant biological change or milestone that marks the transition from early to middle adulthood. Social milestones and norms are more evident here. For example, in previous decades women generally started having children in early adulthood; nowadays it is more common in older women.
Late adulthood 65+	In the West, late adulthood is often associated with the transition to retirement. Some use sixty years as the start of this period; here, the age of sixty-five has been chosen because for many years that was the age of retirement. There are no clear biological changes or markers in this period. The age at which we conceive late adulthood as beginning will change with our understanding of older age.

CHECK YOUR LEARNING

How many periods of human development are there and how would you define them?

What is the difference between a biological milestone and a social milestone?

In addition to organising categories by age, psychologists also categorise human functioning by areas or domains of development.

DOMAINS OF DEVELOPMENT

The chapters in this book are based on periods of development. Within each chapter we will look at human functioning within the following domains (or areas) of development or change:

* physical
* cognitive
* social
* emotional.

PHYSICAL DEVELOPMENT

This area covers changes that occur in the body and brain, for example height, weight, muscular and skeletal changes. Also included is sensation and perception.

* **Sensation** relates to the organs of sense (vision, hearing, taste, touch and smell), and refers to the awareness of conditions or feelings inside and outside the body.
* **Perception** is how we process the information taken in by our senses.

Motor development and skills are also included. Motor is another term for movement, so this refers to the development of movement and skills such as grasping, walking and manipulating objects.

We will look at these concepts in more depth in Chapter 4.

Within the area of physical or biological development is the brain. The study of the brain within psychology has become increasingly important.

The developments in our ability to look at the living brain with CAT, MRI and fMRI scans has made it possible to witness the central role the brain plays in all aspects of our thinking, feeling and behaviour.

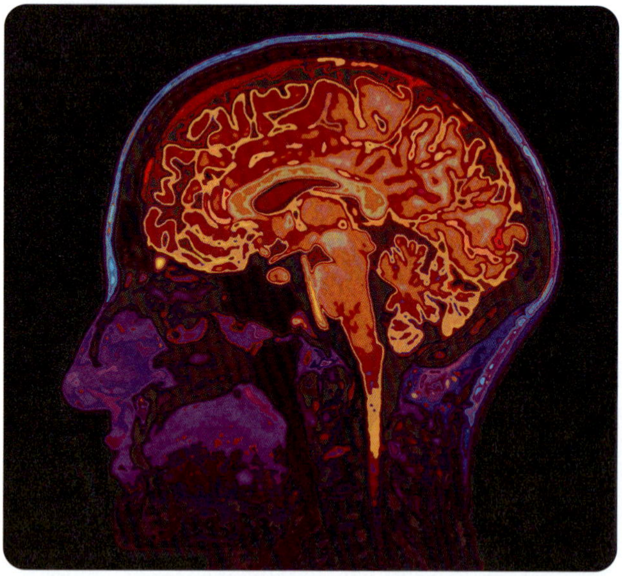

Brain imaging

Think about it

The physical senses are how the body takes in information from its environment. There are five senses; can you name them?

COGNITIVE DEVELOPMENT

At its most basic, cognitive development (sometimes called cognition) refers to thinking. So cognitive development means the development of mental abilities such as memory, problem-solving, learning and language. It is one of the most heavily researched areas in psychology as everything, including feelings and behaviour, has a cognitive component.

For example, cognitive behavioural therapy (CBT) recognises that what and how we think has an impact on how we feel and behave. Therefore, CBT involves changing our 'thinking' or reasoning patterns so as to bring about changes in how we feel or behave.

Think about it

Close your eyes and call to mind a good memory.

How do you think you were able to do that? That's cognitive development – it makes sense of and stores information you encounter as you move through your life.

SOCIAL DEVELOPMENT

Social development includes the emergence and growth of the relationships we have with others. As we saw earlier, many perspectives in psychology place an emphasis on how the interactions and relationships we have with other people can impact on our development. Humans are arguably the most social species. When we are young, adults and older children guide us; in adulthood, relationships become increasingly complex and new relationship types emerge, such as becoming a parent or navigating a workplace setting.

Attachment theory, which we will look at in the next chapter, is one of the most important theories in psychology. It hinges on our 'attachment', or how we develop our relationships with others from birth. Another important concept is socialisation.

Socialisation is the process of learning the skills and attitudes that enable the child or adult to live easily with other members of the community.

Understanding and relating to others are considered some of the most important capacities we need to develop. Our relationships and interaction with others can have a profound influence on the related area of emotional development.

Think about it

What is an important relationship to you?

One of my most influential relationships was with my godmother, Nancy, who I can now see shaped me to be the person I am (well, the good bits anyhow!).

Can you think of a person who had a positive impact on you? What was it about that relationship that was so beneficial?

EMOTIONAL DEVELOPMENT

As already mentioned, we are social creatures. Relationships with others are essential for our development. Their impact, as we will explore throughout this book, can be either positive or negative, but they are always defining. Our emotional development is related to our social relationships. It also encompasses our temperament and personality and sense of self. At its most simple, it relates to how we *feel*. Meggitt (2006) suggests the following definitions.

Emotional development involves the development of feelings:

- The growth of feelings about, and awareness of, oneself
- The development of feelings towards other people
- The development of self-esteem and a self-concept.

So social–emotional development is an integrated approach to understanding how we come to understand ourselves in relation to others and to our own sense of self. It allows us to express our emotions, gain awareness of our feelings and develop meaningful relationships with others. It has a particular significance in childhood but it is an area of development fundamental to us all as we traverse our lives.

Note

Sometimes I think the use of the word 'growth' isn't entirely accurate. I believe the word 'change' is better. When we are young, we are growing, but for some of us at different stages of our life, and for all who make it to late adulthood, decline can occur. As we get older our physical body begins to decline.

Think about it

Name some of the declines that might be seen in older years, both physical and psychological. Can you think of some diseases associated with a decline in performance or function in older age?

FACTORS INFLUENCING HUMAN DEVELOPMENT

People change and develop in many ways, and some changes are more noticeable at different periods in a person's life. For example, the physical changes that occur in infancy are quite remarkable and very obvious in comparison to the physical changes that occur in our thirties. In some people those age-related changes are slowed down or speeded up by lifestyle factors. This area is central to the study of psychology and to unravelling the differences that exist between all individuals. It is at the heart of why we are the way we are.

Think about it

While ageing and physical changes have a very clear impact on our development, are there other factors that can influence our development and life outcomes? Try to name a few.

How many did you come up with? How do we define a 'factor' in psychology?

Factor: an underlying influence that may be responsible for the variations or differences we see in individuals and their outcomes.

Think about it

Identify what factors might be at play in different people and how they could influence outcomes. To get you started, consider factors under the following headings:

* Within the child (including biological, personality)
* In their immediate environment (parents/family, housing, socioeconomic status, peer interactions, community, stimulating environment)
* In the wider environment (culture, government policies, including welfare and economic, discrimination).

Many factors can impact on our development, behaviour and life outcomes. In psychology, 'factors' is another way psychologists categorise and to try to understand human behaviour and functioning. We look at different issues or topics and try to figure out the different 'factors' that impact (for better or worse) on psychological functioning.

As part of that we recognise that factors can be either **protective factors** or **risk factors**, which means they can have a positive or negative impact on a person's development, for example their physical and mental wellbeing.

Risk factors are factors that impact on the person and/or their immediate and distal (distant) environments and that have a potentially negative influence on their development or behaviour.

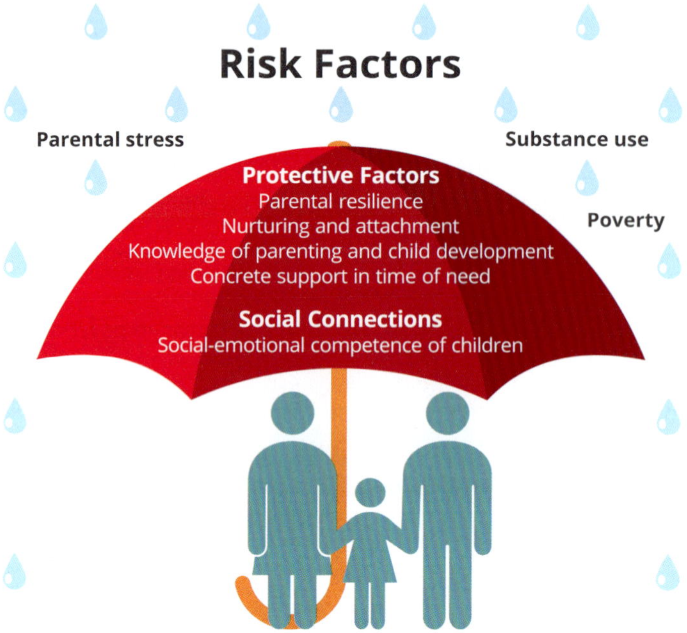

Often where there is one risk factor you are more likely to see others; for example, children born with low birthweight (biological risk) may also be born to mothers with low education levels and who live in poverty (psychosocial risks). This phenomenon is sometimes called **double jeopardy**.

The more risk factors that accumulate, the longer these factors last, and the more severe the factor, the greater the impact on the individual and their development.

Offset against this are **protective factors** that operate in a similar fashion to risk factors. To put it simply, the more protective factors you have, the better 'protected' you are and the more likely you are to enjoy better outcomes.

Intervention programmes such as Young Ballymun and the Incredible Years programme, which we will look at later, operate by targeting individuals who are vulnerable by putting support mechanisms in place. These programmes are protective in and of themselves and their core aims reflects the need to target at-risk populations by increasing protective factors to offset risk factors and thus improve outcomes.

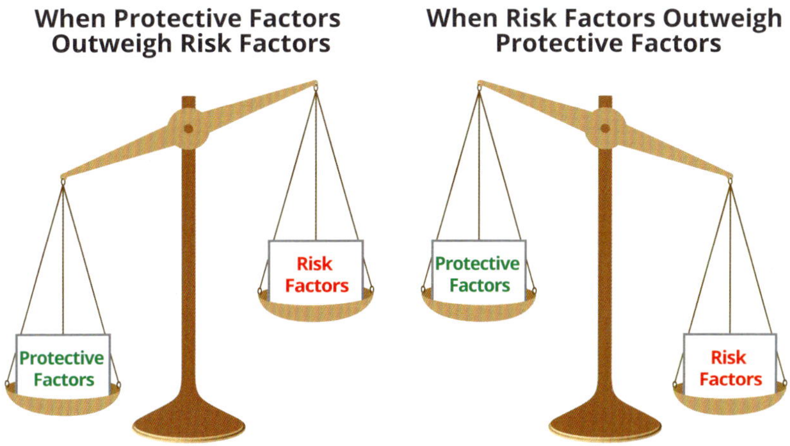

Think about it

Can you think of examples where 'family' as a factor could have either a negative impact on a child's development (parental addiction, perhaps) or a positive one? Does where you live or grow up impact on your development? If so, in what way (physically, socially, etc.)?

Factors that affect our development

Biological	▪ genetic factors	▪ illness	
Psychological	▪ coping style	▪ temperament	▪ personality
Social	▪ family type	▪ parenting style	▪ support networks
Environmental	▪ socioeconomic status	▪ housing	▪ poverty
Cultural	▪ every human group has its own culture		

All these factors interact with each other to influence our development. Throughout this book we shall see how different factors affect a variety of domains of development. An excellent theoretical framework that reflects this interaction and different contexts is Urie Bronfenbrenner's **bio-ecological theory**, which we mentioned above, and which we shall explore in greater depth in Chapter 2.

AN ECOLOGICAL APPROACH

The illustration shows both risk factors and protective factors in children and in different contexts. Some are at family level, others at community level.

RISK AND PROTECTIVE FACTORS

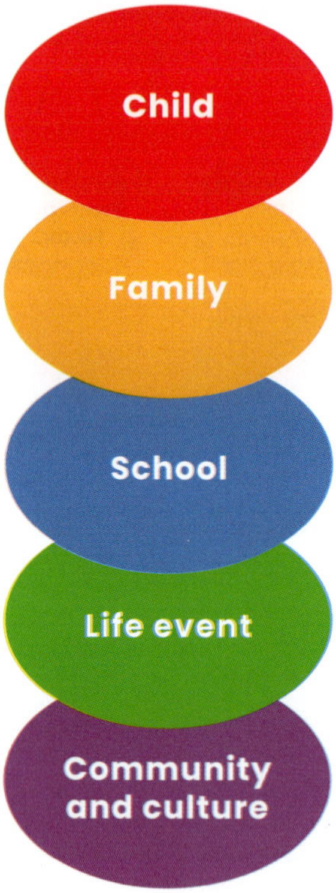

Risk factors

Child:
- Prematurity
- Disability
- Difficult temperament
- Chronic illness
- Poor social skills

Family:
- Teenage mother
- Single parent
- Substance abuse
- Family violence
- Long-term parental unemployment

School:
- School failure
- Deviant peer group
- Bullying
- Inadequate behaviour management

Life event:
- Divorce and family breakup
- Death of a family member
- War or natural disaster

Community and culture:
- Socioeconomic disadvantage
- Urban area
- Lack of support services

Protective factors

Child:
- Social skills
- Empathy
- Above-average intelligence
- Easy temperament

Family:
- Supporting and caring parents
- Small family size
- Responsibility for chores
- Secure and stable family

School:
- Positive school climate
- School norms concerning violence
- Opportunities for achievement

Life event:
- Moving to a new area
- Meeting significant person

Community and culture:
- Access to support services
- Participation in church or community organisation

Source: Adapted from Hanafin and Brooks (2005, p.18)

This illustration focuses on factors that impact on children; some factors might not be as applicable to adults. That reminds us that while there are lots of factors, some are more important at different stages of the lifespan than others. Using what we have learned so far, let's apply these factors to a case study.

CASE STUDY

Layla is three years old and was born 12 weeks premature. She lives in a neighbourhood where there is a lot of poverty and crime. There are not many resources available in the community either. Layla lives with her mum, Molly, and her brother, Jake, who is two years old. Layla and Jake's dad left recently and they haven't seen him since. Her mum cries a lot and seems sad all the time. Molly comes from a close-knit family and Layla looks forward to when her grandmother, especially, calls round. The flat they live in is damp and cold, as Molly struggles to find the money to pay for heating and food now that she is on her own. Layla loves going to the crèche and she is very close to one of the childcare workers. She loves playing with the toys, learning new words and playing with the other children. Molly likes dropping Layla and Jake off at crèche as it gives her a bit of a break as well as the chance to have a chat with the other parents. She has managed to make some new friends.

From this case study, try to identify different factors to go in the table below. Look at the risk factors and protective factors diagram from earlier in the chapter.

AREAS	PROTECTIVE FACTORS	RISK FACTORS
Biological		
Psychological		
Social		
Environmental		

What factors did you choose and why did you pick them? Can you see that for Layla there are factors from *within her* (such as being premature) to ones in her environment (such as the community she lives in).

INDIVIDUAL VARIATION

To end this topic, let's take a look again at individual variation. Recall how there are factors within the person (genetic predisposition) and outside the individual (family setting, poverty, government policies) that all interact and shape a person's development throughout their lifespan. If we apply this approach we begin to understand the differences in human functioning and life outcomes.

These differences or individual variations are accounted for by the interaction of a myriad of factors. Psychologists are very interested in understanding these differences and how they impact on functioning and outcomes in people.

KEY ISSUES IN THE STUDY OF HUMAN DEVELOPMENT

In examining human development, the changes in different domains and across periods of development, certain key questions or issues have arisen. The following are the most hotly debated:

* Nature versus nurture
* Early experiences and later development
* Critical versus sensitive periods.

NATURE VS. NURTURE

We have seen all the different areas and factors that psychology examines in trying to better understand differences. This is particularly interesting when looking at siblings in a family. Why is it that, when they share similar genetic material and are raised in the same family environment and culture, there are differences between them? One answer lies in the unique interactions between **genes and environment**, better known as the **nature versus nurture** debate.

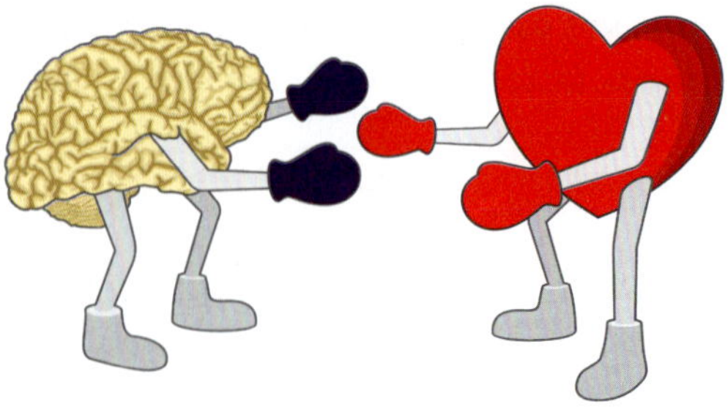

* **Nature** refers to biological processes, genes and our brain as determinants of our behaviour.
* **Nurture** relates to the influence of our environment in our development. The culture we are born into influences how we see ourselves and others and also our behaviour. Other environmental influences are child-rearing practices, education and so on.

The nature–nurture debate is one of the key issues in psychology, particularly in understanding human development. Its origins can be traced to the early philosophers who discussed the nature of humans. Are we 'blank slates', as Locke believed, shaped by those around us and the society we live in? Or, in light of our increasing understanding of genetics and the brain, is biology (nature) more important in understanding who we are? These positions reflect each side of the nature–nurture position.

Think about it

Which do you think is more important in understanding individuals and their behaviour? Take a minute and write down your opinion. Why do you think this? Make a note of some of the reasons. Check back to see if your opinion changes after you've read the book.

In the early twentieth century the 'nature' position dominated, fuelling a belief in the superiority of certain cultures and races. By the 1960s the 'nurture' stance was predominant; it argued for the importance of environment in a person's development and is best illustrated by the explosion of literature on child-rearing practices. Nowadays most agree that it's a bit of both; your DNA and genetics are the building blocks but your environment and relationships with others (nurture) also shape you. Throughout this book we will consider the role of nature and nurture in a variety of topics including attachment and parenting.

To truly gain insights into human development and life outcomes we must strive to understand the roles of both nature and nurture.

CHECK YOUR LEARNING

Explain the nature versus nurture debate in your own words. See if your definition changes as you learn more.

EARLY EXPERIENCES AND LATER DEVELOPMENT

This is another important area and one that is related to the nature–nurture debate.

How do early experiences affect later development? Freud argued that our early experiences have a profound impact on our later development. The debate around early experiences and their impact on later development encompasses all areas of development from cognition and language to relationship-building, personality development and mental illness. It will become clear as we continue to explore more topics throughout the book that most early experiences, for better or worse, shape us. Of course, the debate is *how much* they shape us *and* whether or not the effects of our early experiences can be easily reversed. The debate surrounding this crosses into another contentious issue discussed by psychologists: sensitive versus critical periods of development, which explores the *timing* of development.

CRITICAL VS. SENSITIVE PERIODS OF DEVELOPMENT

Some experiences and the timing of those experiences are pivotal to how we develop. These are known as 'critical and sensitive periods'. Bowlby, as we shall see in Chapter 2, strongly believed that what we experience in our early years is hugely influential in the people we become. More than that, there exists a critical period in which to form attachment relationships and if that period is missed it has a negative impact on the individual.

Certainly there is truth to the importance of early experiences and their timing.

We can see that in the proliferation of intervention programmes aimed at supporting vulnerable families and children, for example Youngballymun.

> *Youngballymun is an area-based Prevention and Early Intervention strategy working to improve outcomes in education, health and mental health for all children, young people and families in Ballymun. We also work with wider partners at national level and in other communities challenged by poverty and disadvantage to disseminate and share the learning from our work.*

YOUNG BALLYMUN
Pioneering Prevention & Early Intervention

We can see from their image a lifespan approach at its heart and from the work they do – a focus on building capacity in both individuals and the community through initiatives aimed to be protective and shape early experiences. (https://youngballymun.org)

Another intervention programme is the Incredible Years programme:

> *Emotional and behavioural problems often start in early childhood and the need for early intervention has been recognised as critical to reducing the onset of conduct problems. The Incredible Years Parent, Teacher and Child Training Series was developed, over the last 30 years, by Professor Carolyn Webster-Stratton of the University of Washington (USA). The programme is specifically designed to prevent and treat emotional and behavioural difficulties (EBD) in children aged 0–12 years. (https://incredibleyears.com)*

These interventions support the role of early experiences in later development and focus on the necessity to support and encourage healthy development.

We are going to look at an issue **In Focus** to explore the debate around sensitive versus critical periods. However, also keep in mind the other two issues of nature versus nurture and early experiences and later development to see if this piece informs your opinion further.

IN FOCUS: THE IMPACT OF EXTREME DEPRIVATION ON DEVELOPMENTAL OUTCOMES

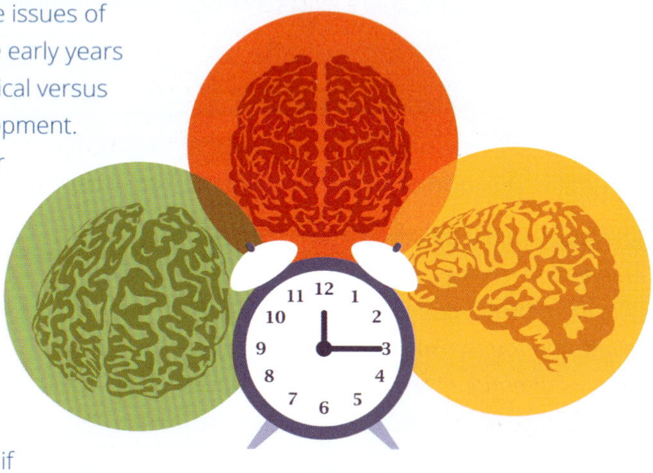

We are going to look at the issues of extreme deprivation in the early years to explore the issue of critical versus sensitive periods of development. Is there a critical period for development such that if development does not occur during this time then the opportunity is lost? Or is there a sensitive period when it is preferable for development to occur but if it does not, development can occur at a later date? This issue relates to many different areas of development from the biological, especially brain development, to acquiring language and developing attachment relationships. The proponents of the critical period, sometimes known as the **first three years** movement, argue that these years are critical in laying down the optimal and best foundations for all areas of development so that the individual will grow and prosper. However, if you accept this position, the issue is what happens to those who miss critical windows of development? Let's look at this issue applied to one area of development – language – to shed more light on this debate. »

David Skuse (1984a, 1984b, 1985) concluded that language appears to be the most vulnerable to deprivation, but much debate surrounds the question of whether there is a critical period for language exposure and/or acquisition. Hall replied to Skuse with the suggestion that 'some exposure to language and communication is essential at a very early stage, even if only for a very brief period' (1985, p.825), while Lenneberg's 'critical age hypothesis' (cited in Curtiss 1977, p.208) states that the critical period runs from two years to puberty.

Skuse refers to Genie, who was confined in total isolation from 20 months until her discovery at 13 years of age. Although intensive language therapy suggested initial promising acquisition, her capacity remained severely limited and she was capable of 'few normal or appropriate acts of communication at 18 years' (Skuse, 1984b: 562).

Meanwhile, Isabelle, who was confined with a deaf-mute mother, developed normal language skills.

Or we could consider the case of the Koluchova twins, grossly deprived and confined from 18 months to nearly 7 years, who went on to develop normally with respect to language (as well as in every other facet of life) (Skuse 1984b).

Think about it

Did the Koluchova twins develop complete language ability due to their early normal language exposure before they were confined? Was it because they had each other for company and developed ways of communicating? Or was it due to their later intensive care in a foster family?

The debate around early versus late experiences is one of the most contentious and hotly debated in psychology.

CONCLUSION

Understanding the 'what' (individual factors) is relatively easy; but 'how' they interact is far more challenging. Factors, as well as critical and sensitive periods of developments and the relationship of early experiences to later development, are all part of the greater debate of nature and nurture.

Finally, a word of caution. It is all too easy to fall into the trap of 'determinism' which suggests that early experiences set in stone our development and behaviour in the future, a pessimistic approach and one I don't subscribe to. Hopefully if there is only one thing you learn, it is that change is possible, for better or worse, so let's try to make it for the better. I hope that the information in this book and the journey it might lead you on will help that happen!

CHECK YOUR LEARNING GOALS!

You should be able to:

1. Identify some of the key ideas suggested by early philosophers about human development.
2. Define what we mean by psychology.
3. Identify and describe the different perspectives in psychology.
4. List the four main goals of psychology and explain their purpose.
5. Explain what we mean by the term 'lifespan development'.
6. Identify how many periods of development there are and list them.
7. Describe the difference between a biological and a social milestone, giving an example of each.
8. Describe what a factor is.
9. Explain the difference between a risk factor and a protective factor and give examples of each.
10. Describe at least two key issues in psychology.

2

Theoretical Perspectives

In this chapter we will discover:

* Social and emotional development theories
  - Sigmund Freud – psychoanalytic theories
  - Erik Erikson – psychosocial theory
  - Attachment theory

* Cognitive development theories
  - Piaget's stage theory of cognitive development
  - Vygotsky's sociocultural theory

* Humanist theories
  - Maslow's hierarchy of needs
  - Rogers's theory of personality and the self

* Ecological theories
  - The bio-ecological theory: Urie Bronfenbrenner

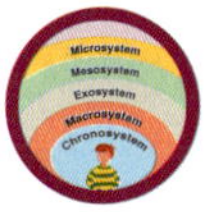

There are many theories that try to explain human development or aspects of it. Theories are generally constructed in an attempt to explain and predict behaviour. We were introduced to some of the different perspectives in psychology in the previous chapter. Here we will meet some theories that fall under some of these perspectives.

We are going to start by exploring the theories of Freud (the 'father of psychology') and Erikson and the theory of attachment. These sit within the realm of social–emotional development, but they also have roots in the **psychoanalytic/psychodynamic** approach, which recognises the role of the unconscious in our behaviour.

We shall consider Piaget's and Vygotsky's theories and the light they shed on how children learn to think.

The humanist and ecological strands attempt to explain human behaviour more holistically. The humanism movement was arguably a reaction to Freud's pessimistic and deterministic outlook on human nature. Maslow and Rogers believed that humans strive to reach their potential but face obstacles that impede their progress. Finally, the 'ecological' strand in psychology, as the name suggests, is interested in the role of 'environment' in development; how external forces, from the immediate (such as parents and siblings) to the distant (such as government policy) influence and shape an individual's development.

SOCIAL AND EMOTIONAL DEVELOPMENT THEORIES

Social and emotional theories relate to the development of our emotional selves and to personality development.

Social development refers not just to our relationships with others and how we construe them, but also to how we see ourselves from the perspective of others.

How we believe we are perceived can be very impactful. One example of this is **social comparison**, where we compare ourselves to another person. Have you ever looked at an image online or on social media and compared yourself to it? (Keep this in mind when we examine the impact of social media in Chapter 7.)

So, as you can see, social development has two aspects.

The three theories we shall look at here fall under the umbrella of social-emotional development, but they offer quite different explanations of this aspect of human development.

SIGMUND FREUD – PSYCHOANALYTIC THEORIES

Sigmund Freud

Sigmund Freud (1856–1939) is considered the founder of the psychoanalytic movement, but what is psychoanalysis and how does it relate to human development?

THE UNCONSIOUS MIND

Freud believed that much of human behaviour, emotions and feelings emanate from the unconscious mind. Our behaviour is merely the tip of the iceberg that is the unconscious mind.

In order to understand behaviour Freud believed that the unconscious mind would need to be accessed through techniques such as word association and dream analysis. We are not aware of this part of our mind, yet Freud believed that it holds powerful urges that have to be satisfied. This creates the impetus for our behaviour.

Freud believed that we only have conscious access to a small part of our mind; the remainder remains unseen by us in our unconscious mind.

Benson (2003, p.49) provides the following explanation of the mind:

Conscious mind (top one-seventh)	The awareness we have when we are awake.
Pre-conscious mind (boundary)	Contains memories of dreams, slips of the tongue, etc. Gives clues about the unconscious from thoughts and actions that appear there. If you have a dream, you are not directly revealing unconscious thoughts but recalling highly coded ideas. This symbolism protects us, so we are not upset or disturbed by what our unconscious is really thinking.
Unconscious mind (six-sevenths)	Contains secret wishes and fears, traumatic memories of the past, etc. All these thoughts are completely hidden and totally unavailable to us. This is necessary for survival – we forget past traumas in order to get on with our lives. We can never see directly into the unconscious.

This has led many to use the analogy of an iceberg as a way of thinking about how Freud saw the 'mind'. Remember, in *Titanic* only the mere tip of the iceberg poked out of the water – its mass was under water and out of sight.

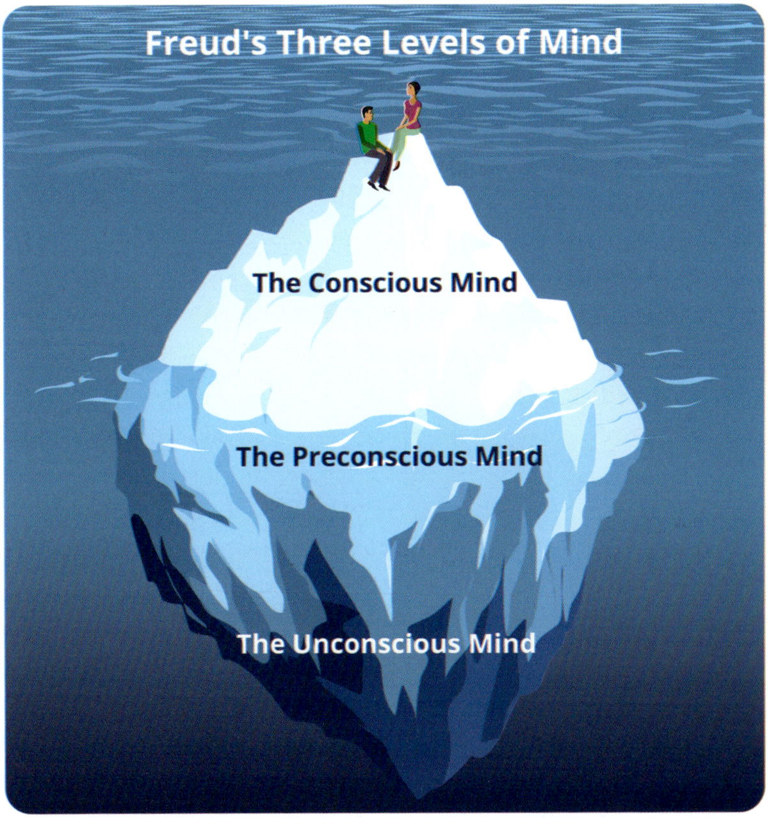

In addition to arguing for the existence of an unconscious mind, Freud suggested that our very personality emerges from the unconscious mind. Let's take a look.

COMPONENTS OF PERSONALITY

According to Freud the personality comprises three components: the id, the ego and the superego.

The **id** is the only structure present at birth and it exists solely in the unconscious mind. Freud (1964, p.106) describes the id as 'a chaos, a cauldron of seething excitations' that 'is filled with energy reaching it from the instincts, but it has no organisation, produces no collective will, but only a striving to bring about the satisfaction of the instinctual pleasure principle'. The **pleasure principle** is solely concerned with instant gratification regardless of any other consideration. In order to control the impulses of the id another aspect of personality develops: the ego.

The **ego** operates primarily at a conscious level and is driven by the **reality principle**, which acts as a check on the id. The ego examines whether it is safe for the id to discharge its impulses and satisfy its instinctual needs.

The last component is the **superego**, which in its basic form is the moral voice of the personality. It endeavours to control the id, particularly with regard to sexual and aggressive needs. The superego grows out of a child's internalisation of their parents' views of morality and is influenced by the cultural norms of the society of which the individual is a member.

The ego stands in the middle between the id and the superego.

Think about it

As we get older we are taught by parents, school and our culture that expectations of us exist and that our needs cannot always be satisfied. For example, stealing is prohibited and frowned upon. Let's say I'm hungry and I go into a shop to buy some food. Then I realise I've forgotten my purse. The id's response would be to take and eat the food – the id is only interested in satisfying my hunger. However, I've been brought up to believe that stealing is wrong, so I put the food back – this is a superego response. The superego develops as we get older and learn more and more of what is acceptable and the rules we must obey (legal and moral).

The ego, which like the superego develops as we get older, mediates between the two extreme responses in this scenario to find an outcome that will satisfy both. The ego solution could be for me to ask my friend to lend me the money so I can buy the food. That way my hunger will be satisfied, keeping the id happy; and I won't have stolen anything, keeping my superego happy (and also my mother!).

Anxiety occurs when the ego confronts either impulses that are threatening to get out of control or external danger.

Anxiety is a painful emotional experience (Hall 1962).

DEFENCE MECHANISMS

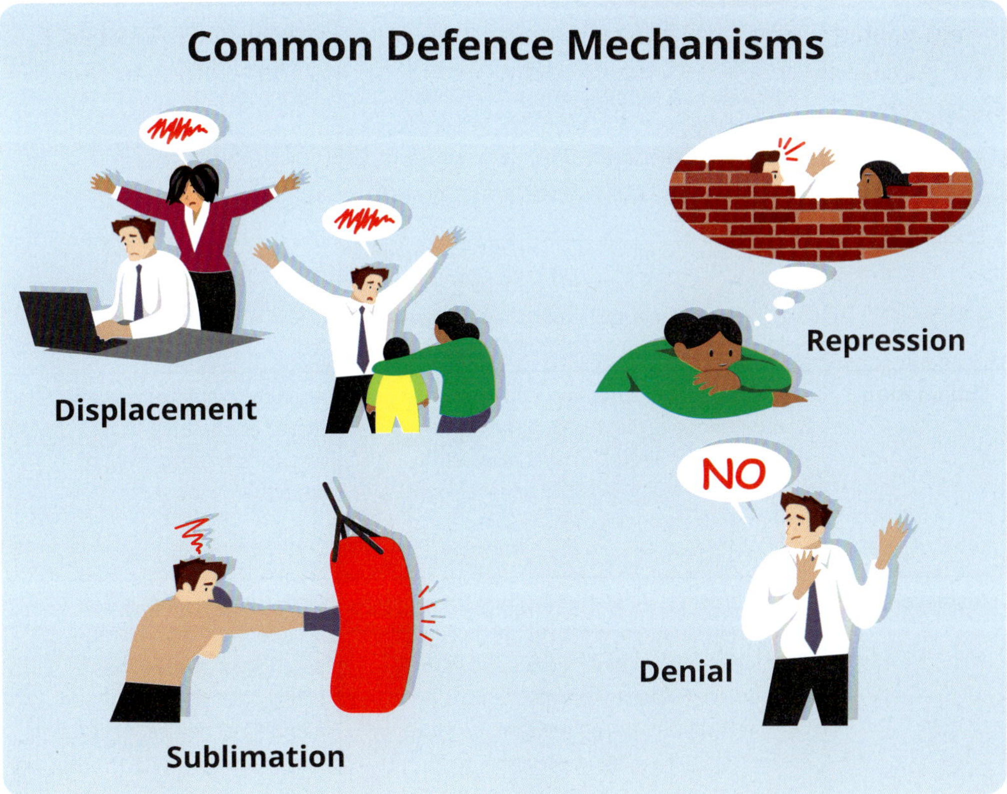

When the ego is unable to produce realistic coping mechanisms in times of anxiety it resorts to what Freud termed **defence mechanisms** to relieve the anxiety in a safe manner by denying, distorting or falsifying reality.

The purpose of defence mechanisms is a developmental one, so they exist early on, being used by the infantile ego to cope with demands and as a protective measure. Freud claimed that defence mechanisms continue after the infant stage if the ego has not developed sufficiently and has remained dependent on the mechanisms.

Defence mechanisms

NAME	DESCRIPTION	EXAMPLE
Repression	One of the most widely known of the defence mechanisms, this was of great interest to Freud. He coined the term to describe unacceptable or painful mental content excluded from awareness. These drives and memories trapped in the unconscious strive for release and occasionally will do so in the form of a slip of the tongue, known colloquially as a 'Freudian slip'.	An individual who was abused as a child develops amnesia about the event.
Denial	The denial of an event or emotions associated with an event that is painful and generating high levels of anxiety. While in repression the individual is rendered unaware of an event, in denial the person is aware but refuses to acknowledge the reality. They deny it in an attempt to avoid acknowledging the extent of the threat. Freud and his supporters contend that denial through a refusal to acknowledge the reality of a situation is a bad thing as it impedes good mental health; they see 'reality orientation' as essential to mental health.	An alcoholic when challenged about their drinking will deny having a problem.
Sublimation	A component of repression, consisting of a repressed impulse released through a desirable form. Freud is never clear as to whether repression is a fully unconscious act or if there is some degree of awareness on the part of the person.	An individual with hostile impulses channels those impulses by becoming a prosecution lawyer.
Displacement	Displacement is a defense mechanism by which individuals cope with acute anxiety by transferring emotions about a stressor onto another. So with this mechanism, a person 'displaces' or redirects the negative feelings from the original source onto an unrelated person or thing they deem to be less threatening.	One example given is that of 'little Hans' whom Freud psychoanalysed. He was a young child who had developed a phobia of horses. It has been suggested that Hans transferred or 'displaced' his fear of his father onto the horses.

Think about it

Steiner (1966) reported that some Jews held in the Treblinka concentration camp, witnessing death on an unimaginable scale, adopted the belief that death did not exist (denial), despite the obvious evidence to the contrary.

Could these people really have coped with the reality of the situation they were in and the fact that they could be next? That is the purpose of the defence mechanism: to protect and enable the individual to cope. Is denial, even in circumstances less dramatic than the Treblinka example, truly a survival mechanism? Should 'reality orientation' perhaps be attempted only with great care, for fear of doing more damage?

Can you think of other situations where defence mechanisms are valuable?

FREUD'S PSYCHOSEXUAL THEORY

While many in psychology accept (to some degree) the existence of an unconscious mind and the concept of the personality as described by Freud (id, ego and superego), another theory developed by Freud has been rejected by all except the most loyal of his followers.

Freud proposed a stage theory suggesting a child must pass through five stages, one after another. At each stage a negative outcome was possible if the child became stuck or 'fixated'.

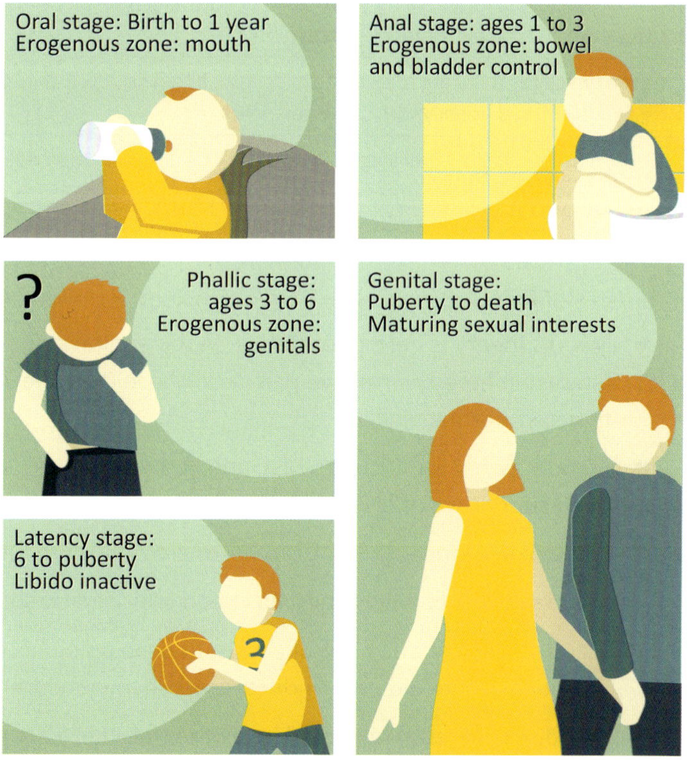

Psychosexual development

The stages of psychosexual development

Oral stage	The mouth is the prime source of pleasure, for survival: the baby instinctively sucks. Through oral satisfaction, the baby develops trust and an optimistic personality. If fixated at this stage the 'personality' may become pessimistic, aggressive and distrusting.
Anal stage	The focus of pleasure shifts to the anus, helping the child become aware of their bowels and how to control them. By taking control of their own bowel movements, the child takes an important step of independence, developing confidence and a sense of when to 'give things up'. However, over-strictness about forcing a child to 'go' or about timing or cleanliness can cause personality problems (Benson 2003). If fixated at this stage, the theory maintains that, for example, the 'personality' may become a hoarder type, refusing to 'give away' anything, or become overly concerned about timekeeping (the idea of 'going regularly').
Phallic stage	Children become aware of their genitals and sexual differences. Consequently, development is different for boys and girls. The main fixation at this stage is the **Oedipus complex**, which applies to males. Each boy, unconsciously, goes through a sequence of stages beginning with the development of a strong desire for his mother, noticing the bond between his parents (i.e. sleeping together), becoming jealous of his father and hating him, then becoming afraid of his father lest he discover his son's true feelings, which results in the final substage of fearing punishment – castration.
Latency stage	During this stage sexual urges remain repressed and children interact and play mostly with same-sex peers.
Genital stage	The final stage of psychosexual development begins at the start of puberty when sexual urges are once again awakened. Adolescents direct their sexual urges onto opposite-sex peers, with the genitals the primary focus of pleasure.

Criticisms of Freud's psychosexual theory include as follows:

- Freud's theory is heteronormative. In the genital stage the resolution of this stage is interest in heteronormative partners. These days the view would not be so limited to heteronormativity.
- Freud's theory is difficult to test, and results from the few tests carried out have not been supportive of his theories.
- Some of the concepts Freud discusses are difficult to test as they cannot be observed.
- Freud's theory of 'penis envy' has been criticised by some feminists as sexist.
- Freud's observations were of adults; in developing his theory of psychosexual development he did not conduct research into children.

Before we dismiss Freud we should be aware that there are elements in his ideas that remain influential today. The concept of some aspect of an 'unconscious' mind is something many accept, though they may disagree on its origins and intricacies, and some defence mechanisms such as denial and repression are accepted.

Arguably the most significant contribution Freud made is his concept of early experience affecting later development, a key issue debated in psychology, as we saw in the previous chapter.

Importantly, Freud was perhaps one of the first lifespan developmentalists as he believed that early experiences could be responsible for behaviour or personality traits in later life.

CHECK YOUR LEARNING

To ensure you are clear on the two theories discussed above, write a summary in your own words of Freud's:

* Theory of personality (id, ego and superego)
* Stage theory of psychosexual development.

Imagine explaining the iceberg analogy of the conscious and unconscious mind. (Imagining explaining concepts and theories to a friend is a good way to check that you fully understand the ideas.)

ERIK ERIKSON – PSYCHOSOCIAL THEORY

Erik Erikson (1902–1994) was born in Germany and became interested in psychology when he met Anna Freud (Sigmund Freud's daughter) who convinced him to study child psychoanalysis in Vienna. While Erikson was influenced by Freud and accepted some of what he said, he believed that Freud's proposition of psychosexual stages was incorrect. Instead, Erikson proposed, individuals develop through **psychosocial** stages. Erikson moved to America and joined Harvard Medical School before moving on to Yale. His first book, *Childhood and Society*, reflected his interest in the role of society and culture in the development of the child.

Erik Erikson suggested that personality develops through the resolution of a series of eight major psychosocial stages occurring throughout an individual's life. Each stage involves a different 'crisis' or conflict between the 'self' (individual) and others, including the outside world, which could result in either a positive or negative outcome.

For example, in the first stage – trust versus mistrust – if the infant is well cared for and their needs met they will develop trust (a positive outcome of this stage). However, if the infant is mistreated or abused a negative outcome of 'mistrust' will occur. Erikson was more positive than Freud as he believed that negative outcomes in one stage could be resolved at a later date.

Erikson was one of the first theorists to see development in a **lifespan context**. His eight psychosocial stages are called the Eight Ages of Man and cover the entire lifespan of the individual.

Erikson's eight psychosocial stages: The Eight Ages of Man

APPROXIMATE AGE PERIOD	STAGE	PSYCHOSOCIAL RELATIONSHIP
Birth–1 year	**Trust vs. Mistrust**	Develop trust in others and the world *or* Suspicion and mistrust
1–2 years	**Autonomy vs. Shame and Doubt**	Sense of self-reliance *or* Feelings of shame about one's capability
3–5 years	**Initiative vs. Guilt**	Ability to start activities *or* Guilt about their feelings
6–12 years	**Industry vs. Inferiority**	Sense of confidence in ability to do things *or* Feeling of inferiority based on reactions of others
12–20 years	**Identity vs. Role confusion**	Develop sense of who you are *or* Confusion as to who you are and role in life
20–40 years	**Intimacy vs. Isolation**	Experience love and form relationships *or* Isolation, shallow relationships
40–65 years	**Generativity vs. Stagnation**	Seek to be productive *or* Lack of growth and boredom
65 years onwards	**Integrity vs. Despair**	Satisfaction with one's life *or* Regret over missed opportunities

Let's look at each stage in a little more detail.

* **Trust vs. Mistrust** (0–1 year): In the first year of life the infant is completely dependent on its caregivers. How well the infant's needs are met and how sensitive the parenting is will determine whether the infant develops trust or mistrust of the world.
* **Autonomy vs. Shame and Doubt** (1–2 years): Children begin to walk and assert their independence. As the term 'autonomy' suggests, children can come to believe in themselves and their abilities through the encouragement and support of their caregivers. If the child's efforts are ridiculed or belittled they will develop a feeling of shame and doubt in their abilities. Toilet training is seen as a key event which can influence the outcome of this stage.
* **Initiative vs. Guilt** (3–5 years): As the child becomes older they exhibit increasing curiosity and interest, initiate play and question more. If this initiative is discouraged or they are held back they will not develop self-initiative and instead will hold back in later life.
* **Industry vs. Inferiority** (6–12 years): During this time the child begins to attend school and they interact more with peers. If praised in their efforts they develop a sense of industry and feel good about what they have achieved, which encourages the feeling that they can fulfil their goals. If they repeatedly fail or are not praised when they try, a sense of inferiority will develop.
* **Identity vs. Role Confusion** (12–20 years): This relates to the adolescent period of life when the teenager is establishing their identity, their sense of who they are and their role in life. They are becoming more independent and their peers are increasingly important to them. If they can reconcile these issues they will develop a feeling of identity; if not, role confusion will occur.
* **Intimacy vs. Isolation** (20–40 years): This period is marked by the desire to establish relationships with others. Successful completion leads to a sense of security and intimacy. Avoidance of intimacy or an inability to establish a secure relationship leads to feelings of isolation.
* **Generativity vs. Stagnation** (40–65 years): During this period we settle down in a relationship and begin having children. People also establish their careers. A sense of community and being part of the bigger picture become important. If we do not achieve these objectives the resulting feeling is one of stagnation.
* **Integrity vs. Despair** (65 years onwards): In older age, people slow down and begin to reflect on their lives. If the individual feels they have had a successful life, a sense of integrity prevails. If the person believes their life to have been unproductive a feeling of despair occurs.

The major strength of Erikson's theory is it allows us to view the entire lifespan and consider how our personality is shaped as we move through it. However, there are some criticisms of his theory:

* When you look at the stages, particularly from adolescence onwards, do you feel they reflect our norms and the ways we live our lives today? Many people, for example, don't start families until much later in life. Young people tend to live in the family home for much longer than in the past. Older people retire later than when Erikson wrote this theory.
* Erikson's theory is one of the first stage theories that crosses the entire lifespan. The idea inherent in stage theories – that you must pass through one stage before you can move to the next – is increasingly rejected.

CHECK YOUR LEARNING

To ensure you are clear on Erikson's psychosocial theory, write down a summary of it in your own words, including its strengths and weaknesses.

Also make a note of whether you agree with his understanding of each of our life stages – are there parts of it that 'make sense'? If you are critical, write down your reasons.

Without doubt, Freud's suggestion that we place some of our experiences, particularly early ones, within our unconscious has remained popular though not as he conceptualized it. This idea of a psychodynamic approach can be seen in Erikson's psychosocial theory and we are to witness it in the following theory. Attachment theory is one of the most important theories in psychology, remaining popular and being heavily researched, with findings supporting its existence.

ATTACHMENT THEORY

LINK

In Chapter 1 we reviewed three key debates in psychology. Attachment theory is relevant to all of them. Refresh your knowledge of these debates and as you continue to read about attachment theory see where you can find evidence to support or refute them.

Attachment is 'a long-enduring, emotionally meaningful tie to a particular individual' (Schaffer 1996).

Attachment is recognised as one of the most important concepts in psychology and as such has been heavily researched. Our ability to form secure and meaningful relationships not just with our parents/caregivers but also with others later in life is considered a touchstone for healthy and happy functioning. Difficulties in this realm can have immediate and long-term consequences for the individual.

Shaver and Mikulincer (2010, p.168) outline the following benefits of secure attachment during different phases of life:

* A safe haven in times of threats or stresses
* A secure base for exploration and personal development.

To begin with, we will look at the origins of attachment theory, how ethology and psychoanalysis shaped the emerging theory, and Bowlby's pivotal role in formulating the importance of this early relationship and its impact. Mary Ainsworth's work in developing Bowlby's ideas into a testable assessment tool and subsequent attachment styles will also be considered. We will look at the different categories of attachment, how they are observable and behaviours that promote attachment.

Let's begin by tracing the history and development of attachment theory.

INFLUENCES ON ATTACHMENT THEORY

Ethology

Ethology is the study of animal behaviour. Psychologists look at animal behaviour to gain insight into human behaviours.

The term **imprinting** was coined by Konrad Lorenz and relates to the behaviour he observed in geese. When they hatched they automatically attached to the first moving object they encountered. Lorenz found that when the geese hatched they attached to him even though he was not one of their species. Thus, Lorenz believed that 'imprinting' is instinctual and cannot be reversed.

Harry Harlow studied the effects of **maternal d eprivation** in rhesus monkeys. He removed newborn monkeys from their mothers and raised them in isolation without contact with other monkeys. The baby monkeys had access to two 'mothers' in their cage. One was made of wire mesh and had a bottle attached so the monkey could feed from it. The other was a cloth figure covered in soft, tactile material but offered no opportunity for the monkey to feed. Harlow noted that when the baby monkeys were given the choice between a mesh wire figure with a feeding bottle and a figure covered in soft material, the monkeys chose to cling to the soft material rather than the wire figure. Previously it was believed that the motivation for mammals to attach to a parent was for the purpose of feeding. However, Harlow's study indicated that monkeys sought 'comfort contact' and that social reasons were as important as, if not more important than, feeding.

When the monkeys were re-introduced to the troupe they were frightened, exhibited anxious behaviours and had difficulty socialising with other monkeys. This suggested that their early experiences created difficulties for them later in their social relationships with others.

Psychoanalysis

As we've seen, the psychoanalytic or psychodynamic approach emphasises the role of the unconscious in the formation of our personalities and behaviour.

* **Mother–child relationship:** Freud stressed the importance of the mother–child relationship. Many psychoanalysts believed that **early experiences could affect a person in later life**.
* **Object relations:** A famous psychoanalyst, Melanie Klein, developed the **object relations** approach, which suggested that the 'loss' of an object could have a potentially negative effect. For example, to an infant an object could be their mother, and the loss of the mother (perhaps through death or separation) could in turn lead to negative outcomes for the child in later life.

JOHN BOWLBY AND MATERNAL DEPRIVATION

John Bowlby (1907–1990) was the first to devise the basic tenets of this theory. Bowlby was working in a home for children with behavioural problems. The children had disrupted relationships with their families and it struck Bowlby that these difficulties might hold the key to their emotional and behavioural disturbances. His time there prompted him to train as a child psychiatrist. Bowlby received training at the British Psychoanalytic Institute (BPS), where he was supervised by Klein.

Bowlby agreed with Klein's view that early experiences shaped an individual in later life. He also supported Klein's **object relations** approach and the potentially negative effect of the loss of an 'object'. However, unlike Klein, Bowlby believed that **actual** family experiences were important and possibly the cause of emotional problems experienced by the children he had worked with. Bowlby also came to believe that relationship problems between parent and child continued to be passed down through the generations. Thus, in order to help the child a practitioner should look at and help the parent.

Heavily influenced by the work of ethologists such as Lorenz and Harlow, Bowlby came to believe that there is an instinctual aspect to the development of a bond between mother and child and that there is a critical period for its development.

Harlow's research suggested that feeding alone, or the satisfaction of hunger, are not necessarily the primary motivation for bonding and that more social needs are at play. You will see how these beliefs came to shape Bowlby's attachment theory.

Bowlby theorised that:

Maternal deprivation is where a child experiences a disruption in their relationship with their mother (through separation or death), which has a negative impact on the child.

Bowlby believed that there is one fundamental attachment relationship and that this is between mother and child – what is termed **monotropism**. Further, he believed that there is a critical period between six months and three years of age when attachment must be maintained.

Bowlby's work is not without its critics:

- **Monotropism:** Research indicates that infants form several important attachment relationships with figures other than their mother (e.g. fathers, grandparents and siblings).
- **Negative outcomes:** Bowlby emphasised that if a child experiences difficulties in their attachment relationship this could have disastrous outcomes in later life. Michael Rutter has rejected this bleak view, pointing out that all children experience separation at some point (e.g. going to school) and that we need to differentiate between different situations.
- **Role of the mother:** Feminists have criticised Bowlby's insistence that the mother must remain at home with the children to prevent the child suffering due to her absence. There has been suggestions that Bowlby's research coincided with the return of male soldiers after World War II and the desire of governments to encourage women to give up their jobs to the returning soldiers. By suggesting that children were being negatively impacted by their mother's absence, it was envisaged that women would not wish to work outside the home.

MARY AINSWORTH AND THE STRANGE SITUATION: HOW TO ASSESS ATTACHMENT

Mary Ainsworth joined Bowlby's research team when she came to Britain. Whereas Bowlby formulated ideas surrounding the nature of the attachment relationship, Ainsworth developed a way of testing the attachment relationship. This would become known as the **strange situation** experiment and it led to the identification of four classification patterns.

Ainsworth conducted a huge amount of 'naturalistic' observations of the behaviour of mothers and their infants in Uganda and in America. From these observations she developed a way of testing the quality of the attachment relationship through the strange situation.

This involve placing a mother and her child in a room where their behaviour is observed. The child should use the mother as a secure 'base' from which to explore. During the experiment a 'stranger' will enter the room twice: when the mother is present and when the baby has been left alone. The baby's reaction to the return of the mother is used to gauge what attachment pattern exists between mother and baby.

The reactions of the infants form the classification of attachment styles.

Attachment classifications

Type A – Insecure/ Avoidant	Babies exhibited an avoidance of interactions with the mother on her return. The baby either completely ignored the mother or displayed avoidance behaviours such as turning away or avoiding eye contact. During separation the baby did not display distress, or the distress seemed related to being left alone rather than due to the mother's absence.
Type B – Secure	Babies classified as securely attached actively sought interaction and contact with the mother, especially during the reunion episode. If the baby showed distress during the separation episode this was judged to be solely related to the absence of the mother.
Type C – Ambivalent/ Resistant	These babies were extremely upset when the mother left. On reunion with the mother the baby seemed to want to be near her yet 'resisted' her efforts to comfort them. If the mother picked them up they displayed significant angry behaviour and tried to struggle free.
(Fourth classification later added:) Type D – Disorganised	This category relates to babies who displayed 'disorganised' or disoriented patterns of behaviour that could not be classified under the other categories.

Of the four attachment types, disorganised attachment appears to be predictive of psychopathology in later life, an issue which we will explore in Chapter 4.

INTERNAL WORKING MODEL

Bowlby believed that the child represents its relationship with its mother internally, and it is thought that this model serves as a sort of template for future relationships.

Internal working models are 'cognitive structures embodying the memories of day-to-day interactions with the attachment figure. They may be "schemas" or "event scripts" that guide the child's interactions and the expectations and affective experiences associated with them' (Smith et al. 2003, p.98).

In Chapter 4 we will look at attachment theory in young children and particularly how these early attachment experiences can have an impact on later development, leaving some at higher risk of mental health challenges.

COGNITIVE DEVELOPMENT THEORIES

Cognitive development refers to the changes that occur in cognitive abilities, for example thinking, memory and problem-solving.

One of the most famous and important theorists in the field of cognitive development is Jean Piaget and his work is still influential in psychology, education and child development.

PIAGET'S STAGE THEORY OF COGNITIVE DEVELOPMENT

Jean Piaget (1896–1980) was born in Switzerland. After completing his PhD, he developed an interest in psychoanalysis and travelled to France to work in a boys' institution which had been founded by Alfred Binet. Binet is best known for his work in developing intelligence tests and Piaget worked on standardising these tests. It was through his work on the tests that Piaget came to the conclusion that young children think differently from adults. He noticed that many of the children were giving the same 'wrong' answer.

Jean Piaget

This work and Piaget's observations prompted him to develop a theory of cognitive development. Piaget's theory is a **stage theory**, meaning that the individual must pass through one stage before they can progress to the next. Piaget suggested that children pass through **four stages** of cognitive development from infancy to adolescence.

Interestingly, Piaget was a forerunner of **naturalistic observation**, which is now a popular research method. This approach to collecting data relies on observing individuals in their natural environment, rather than in a laboratory. Piaget and his wife Valentine observed their three children from infancy and kept detailed journals noting their intellectual development.

Piaget can be daunting to understand, especially his terminology, but don't let that discourage you. What Piaget is trying to do is outline how he believes children organise the information that they receive in their daily lives.

Before we look at the stages of his theory it's helpful to understand how Piaget believed learning occurs.

He used the term **schemas** to describe 'internal frameworks' that the mind builds as it comes into contact with more and more information. It's the equivalent of structures that can hold and make sense of incoming information. For example, as the infant gathers more and more information the schemas become more sophisticated.

A **schema** is an internal framework that organises incoming information, thought and action.

Piaget believed that in order for learning to occur the child must experience a sense of 'disequilibration', which simply means an imbalance.

When an individual has an experience that does not fit their existing thinking, they become dissatisfied with their original thinking and a state of **disequilibration** or imbalance occurs.

Because the new piece of information won't fit, the child must adapt in order to process the new piece of information. This can be done in two ways: through assimilation and through accommodation.

Assimilation is when the person fits incoming information or experience into an existing schema.

Accommodation is when an existing schema changes to incorporate new experiences.

So what does that actually mean? Let's consider the following:

When is a fox not a dog?

A young child who sees a fox for the first time might call it a 'doggie'. Here the child is trying to make sense of this new experience by applying an existing 'doggie' schema to the fox, which has four legs and a tail. This make sense because a dog also has four legs and a tail – this is **assimilation**.

Yet as we get older we come to understand that a fox and a dog are not the same and this causes us to change our schema. This process is called **accommodation**.

CHECK YOUR LEARNING

When a very young child sees a picture of a fox, which of these, according to what you've just read, is most likely to happen?

Tick the box you think applies and explain why you chose that answer	**ASSIMILATION**	**ACCOMMODATION**

This, according to Piaget, is the *process of how we learn*. Following his observations of children he argued that in childhood we pass through four stages as our thinking capacities emerge and develop. As with the other stage theories we have come across, Piaget says you must complete one stage before you can move onto the next. So let's take a look at his theory of how we develop thinking and mental capacities as we mature.

Piaget's stage theory of cognitive development

AGE	STAGE	CHARACTERISTICS
0–2 years	Sensorimotor	▪ The baby knows about the world through movement and sensory information ▪ She learns to differentiate herself from her environment ▪ Develops first schemas ▪ Achieves object permanence ▪ Emergence of symbolic thought ▪ The capacity to form internal mental representations emerges
2–7 years	Preoperational	▪ Symbolic thinking emerges as the child use symbols/images to represent objects and problem-solve ▪ The child begins to understand classification of objects ▪ Child is egocentric ▪ Child focuses on just one aspect of a task ▪ Animism – the child believes inanimate objects have consciousness ▪ Pretend play is a feature of this stage »

AGE	STAGE	CHARACTERISTICS
7–11 years	Concrete operational	▪ The child understands conservation of mass, length, weight and volume ▪ Decentring – the child becomes less egocentric, taking more easily the perspectives of others ▪ Reversibility is a feature – the child learns that some things that have been changed can be returned to their original state. ▪ Child can classify and order, as well as organise objects into series ▪ Child is still tied to the immediate experience but within these limitations can perform logical mental operations
12+ years	Formal operational	▪ Abstract thinking marks this period as the individual is now able to manipulate ideas in their head. ▪ Inductive and deductive reasoning emerges, enabling the formulation and testing of hypotheses

Source: Adapted from Cowie and Smith, *Understanding Children's Development* (3rd edn, 2003 p.336)

Many of the chapters in this book follow ages or periods of development. Within each of these we will look in more depth at some of the theories introduced here. For each of Piaget's stages the key concepts outlined in the table above will be explored and discussed further. For the moment, his stages are introduced below.

SENSORIMOTOR STAGE (0 TO 2 YEARS)

'**Sensori**' relates to the senses or sensation – taste, touch, smell, vision and hearing. '**Motor**' means movement.

During this period, learning is accumulated through the senses and movement. Have you ever noticed how young babies are forever putting things in their mouth? This is because they are using this sense to explore the new world they inhabit.

As the infant begins to crawl they often head straight for the kitchen presses, much to the consternation of their parents; this reflects the child's attempts to use their new-found movement to further explore their environment. The infant is hungry for new experiences and information that will form the basis of their developing schemas.

By the end of this stage infants will have acquired object permanence.

Object permanence is an important concept that refers to the understanding that objects continue to exist even when we can no longer see them.

Before Object Permanence

After Object Permanence

A simple test for object permanence is to allow the child to see a toy and then place the toy under a blanket. If the child seeks the toy out it is an indication that they understand that the toy continued to exist even when they could not see it. This ability comes towards the end of this stage.

PREOPERATIONAL STAGE (2–7 YEARS)

One of the most notable features of this stage is that the child is **egocentric**. If you break the word up it gives a clue to its meaning: ego means 'self'; centric refers to the centre of things. So egocentric means self-centred.

In the context of cognitive development, **egocentric** means that the child thinks that everyone else sees the world through their eyes. They do not understand that other people might see or think about things differently and this is reflected in their thinking.

One test that allows psychologists to see egocentricity in the child is Piaget's Three Mountains task, which observes a child's ability to take the perspective of another. We will look at this in more depth in Chapter 5.

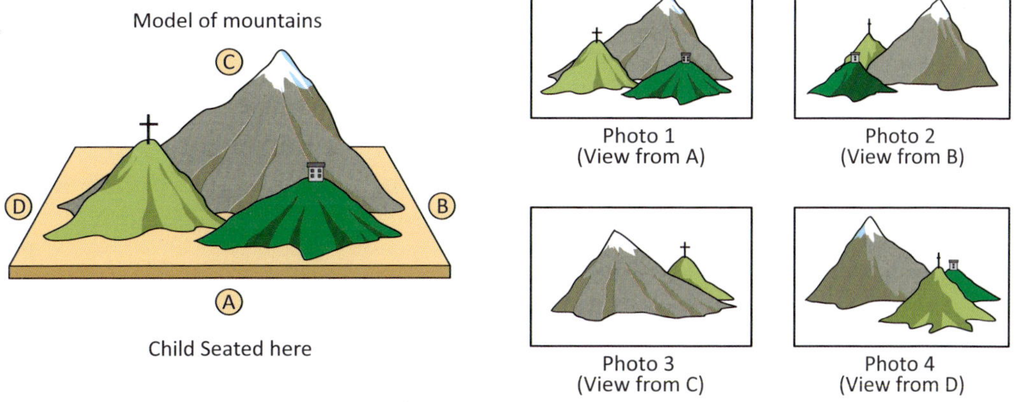

Think about it

Being able to understand or take the perspective of another person is considered central to our social and emotional development.

When was the last time you were able to take the perspective of another? For me, it was recently: my son came home from school and I could see he was stressed. I asked him was he okay and he explained that he was stressed about his exams. I was able to recognise that my son was stressed (even when I wasn't stressed myself) and was able to put myself in his shoes and see things from his perspective. Having grown out of egocentric thinking in childhood, I am able to understand that others have their own thoughts.

(Remember: Taking the perspective of another is different from sharing attitudes or opinions. It is the ability to see things from another person's point of view.)

What's your example? Write it down.

Another feature of this stage is **symbolic thinking**. As the child begins to acquire language (which is, of course, made up of symbols – such as letters, words and images) they can use this newly developed ability to enhance their thinking. The child now can use words and images (symbols) to represent objects. For example, when a toddler sees a dog they might exclaim 'woof woof'. They are using that noise to represent a dog.

Pretend play is another beneficiary of symbolic thinking. For example, a stick is transformed into a sword.

An interesting aspect of this stage is **animism**. Have you ever smacked a 'bold' table that a young child has just run in to? Children at this age ascribe consciousness to inanimate objects, so the table now becomes a naughty, bold table that is responsible for their knock on the head!

CONCRETE OPERATIONAL STAGE (7–11 YEARS)

This is the third stage in Piaget's theory of cognitive development.

The main features of this stage are:

* Conservation: the understanding that quantity, volume and length remain the same
* Reversibility: the understanding that numbers or objects can be altered and then returned to their original state
* Decentring: children become less egocentric.

Children learn through concrete or 'real' objects. Piaget believed that the acquisition of **conservation** was an important developmental milestone (see Chapter 6, page 144 for a diagram of conservation). While there are many types of conservation (length, mass and weight), let's look at conservation of liquid. Have you ever seen an argument breaking out at a children's party because one child seems to have more juice than another? However hard you try to explain that although the glasses are different shapes the amount of liquid in each is the same, the child refuses to accept this. This is because the child lacks an understanding of the concept of conservation.

Another goal that is reached at the conclusion of this phase is **reversibility** and it is needed to enable the child to grasp conservation. Reversibility is the ability to mentally undo an action, for example in solving maths questions. I need to be able to work forward but when I see I've made a mistake, I need to be able to reverse back through the steps I took.

A final feature is **decentring**. Decentring occurs during this period. The child becomes less egocentric in their thinking and able to take the perspective of others.

FORMAL OPERATIONAL STAGE (12 YEARS ONWARDS)

This final stage is marked by the acquisition of **abstract thinking** as the individual is now able to manipulate ideas in their head. Up to this stage the child can only think about things that are 'real' or concrete. According to Piaget they are unable to reason about make-believe problems or situations. Now they can begin to think more logically and they can consider hypotheses or explanations. Inductive and deductive reasoning emerges during this stage, enabling further formulation and testing of hypotheses. We will delve further into these concepts in Chapter 7.

CHECK YOUR LEARNING

List the four stages of Piaget's cognitive theory and one feature of each stage.

In addition to his stage theory of cognitive development, Piaget also developed a theory of play which aligns with his cognitive stages. From his observations of children he believed that play is central to the emergence and enhancement of their developing cognitive capacities. He famously said, 'Play is the work of childhood.'

Think about it

What do you think Piaget meant by 'Play is the work of childhood'? Read the following section on his theory of play and write down some examples that support his quote.

PIAGET AND PLAY

Piaget conceived that the development of play is broken into three stages: the mastery, play and game stages.

Stages of play

PLAY STAGE	AGE	PIAGETIAN STAGE	TYPE OF PLAY
Mastery stage	1–2 years	Sensorimotor	▪ Plays alone ▪ Features of play include repetition and mastering behaviours through imitation
Play stage	3–6 years	Preoperational	▪ In the early years the children are too egocentric to play with others; play is either alone or parallel ▪ Use of symbolic thinking in play; objects and actions are used symbolically ▪ Egocentrism begins to ease towards the end of this stage
Game stage	7+ years	Concrete operational	▪ No longer egocentric ▪ Children begin to play together, especially in a co-operative manner ▪ Language is used in establishing rules and roles for games

Play is increasingly understood as fundamental to children's acquisition of mental capacities and cognitive development – it's a way for them to learn and to make sense of the world around them.

Piaget is arguably one of the most influential thinkers in psychology and his ideas and conceptualisation of cognitive development has been popular since he first developed them.

CRITICISMS OF PIAGET

However, he is not without his detractors. Some criticisms of his work are:

* He underestimated children's abilities. Researchers have shown that children demonstrate many of the key features of his stages at much earlier ages then Piaget suggests.
* As we have seen previously, many have criticised the concept of stage theories. Miller (2002) says there is inadequate support for Piaget's notion of stages, which lies at the heart of his work.
* Piaget is a maturational theorist. When Piaget speaks of 'maturing' he is referring to the biological growth of the individual, especially their brain. For this reason, Piaget gave little attention to the influence of other people on a child's cognitive development.

VYGOTSKY'S SOCIOCULTURAL THEORY

Lev Vygotsky

In psychology some theories have elements of different perspectives and Lev Vygotsky's work is an example of that. Lev Vygotsky (1896–1934) was a cognitive theorist, but he is sometimes described as a sociocultural theorist. This is because Vygotsky emphasised the role of 'others' in the development of learning. Unlike Piaget, Vygotsky believed that **social interactions** are a powerful influence in a child's cognitive development. Another influence is the culture they are raised in, and because he emphasised these influences Vygotsky is sometimes described as a sociocultural theorist. However, his focus was on the acquisition of cognition and for that reason he is most often placed under the cognitive perspective.

While Piaget and Vygotsky both developed concepts and theories explaining cognitive development, they differed in what they believed influences the acquisition of cognition. Piaget's approach implies that social and cultural influences are secondary to biological processes, whereas for Vygotsky it is in our social interactions that we acquire our cognition, including language.

Vygotsky was Russian and although he was born in the same year as Piaget it is only in recent years that his writings have come to the attention of the West. Vygotsky died at a young age and in the years before his death he had been under pressure from the Russian government to modify his beliefs. After his death his theories and ideas were dismissed by the Russian government and it is only because his students kept his work alive that we in the West have come to know his work.

His main idea can be summarised as 'Through others we become ourselves' (Vygotsky 1978). Key points from his theory are:

- Children learn from others (including other children)
- The importance of play in the development of learning
- Language plays a central role in mental development
- Language and development build on each other
- Development cannot be separated from its social context.

Like Piaget, Vygotsky emphasised the importance of **play**. Piaget emphasised the child as a solitary learner, in that when they play they discover new ideas for themselves. Vygotsky, on the other hand, believed that children learn through their interactions with others who introduce them to new concepts and ideas.

ZONE OF PROXIMAL DEVELOPMENT

The **zone of proximal development** (ZPD) is the distance between what a person can achieve on their own and what they could achieve with the intervention or help of another.

Vygotsky was interested in the role others could play as a **scaffold**, building a bridge to help the child reach their full potential development.

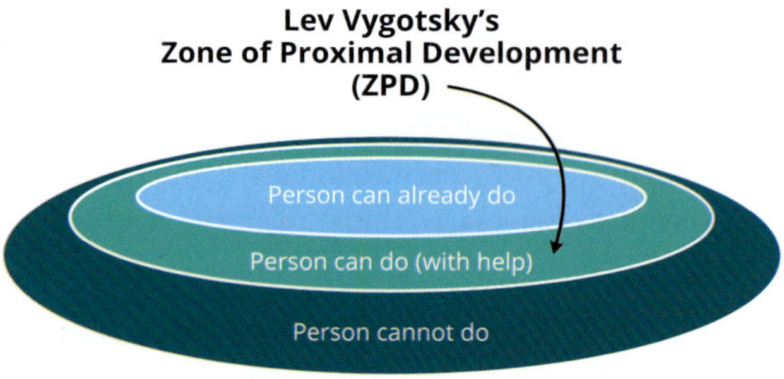

For example, as an adult I started going to Irish classes as I was not as fluent in Irish as I wished to be. My tutor ('other') observed the level of Irish I did have and recognised what I could achieve with her help and so she devised a learning plan to enable me to reach my potential. The trick for the tutor was to make sure that it was challenging enough while ensuring it was not so far beyond my ability that I could not do it, even with their help. As we've seen, Vygotsky felt that it is through interaction with others (teachers or peers) that children learn. This applies to an adult trying to brush up on their Irish as much as to a young child learning about different animals from an early years practitioner.

Think about it

Can you recall times when you were young and a more knowledgeable other (an older sibling, peer, parent or teacher) helped you to learn or figure out something new?

Do you think you learned more quickly with their help?

Have you done the same for others?

RELATIONSHIP BETWEEN LANGUAGE AND THOUGHT

Vygotsky believed that language represents an opportunity for social interaction and learning. Further, the shared experience that language brings is necessary for the development of cognitive ability. When children begin to talk it opens a window into their minds and we can begin to understand their thought processes.

Think about it

Imagine trying to explain something to another person without using language or any symbols. How would you be able to communicate your thoughts?

CULTURAL CONTEXT

The following two aspects have been highlighted by Miller (2002) as weaknesses in Vygotsky's theory, highlighting the vagueness of the theory and the fact that it is untestable:

CRITICISMS OF VYGOTSKY

The following two aspects have been highlighted by Miller (2002) as weaknesses in Vygotsky's theory, highlighting the vagueness of the theory and the fact that it is untestable:

- Vagueness of the concept of the zone of proximal development: Knowing the width of children's zones does not provide an accurate picture of their learning ability, learning style, current level of development compared to other children of the same age, and degree of motivation. It's hard to 'quantify' what this looks like.
- Measuring cultural-historical contexts: While most psychologists agree that social, cultural and historical contexts are important to understanding development in children, Vygotsky doesn't set a clear-enough framework for understanding these contexts or specific parent–child interactions and how they can be measured in relation to children's learning.

Think about it

We can see that both criticisms reflect a more 'scientific' approach popular in psychology, that phenomena are observable and, more important, measurable.

Which do you think is more 'scientific', Piaget's or Vygotsky's theory? Why?

CHECK YOUR LEARNING

Identify the main aspects of Vygotsky's theory and outline a criticism.

This brings us to the end of the section on developmental theorists, which has outlined the range and depth of knowledge that the theorists we discussed have attempted to explain. The common thread running through the theories of proponents of developmental theory is an emphasis on **change over time**.

HUMANIST THEORIES

Humanism, also known as the 'third force' in psychology, marked a new departure in the unfolding story of psychology. The Freudian perspective, it could be argued, took a relatively negative view of human nature. Humanism, on the other hand, took a more positive view of human nature, grounded somewhat in the Renaissance tradition, which celebrated the greatness and beauty of humankind.

Humanism: An individual's ultimate goal is to reach their full potential ('self-actualisation'). Obstacles (both internal and external) block an individual's path to reaching their full potential.

Abraham Maslow and Carl Rogers were to epitomise this viewpoint and are influential founding figures in the field of humanistic psychology. Both men were interested in the concept of self-actualisation.

Self-actualisation, at its most fundamental, equates with supreme self-expression and reaching one's potential.

Before looking at Maslow and Rogers, let's explore a little further what is meant by the term **self-actualisation**, which is central to the humanist perspective.

SELF-ACTUALISATION

Is self-actualisation a state of being or a developmental process? Leclerc *et al.* (1998, p.73) are clear that it is a developmental process: 'this aspect is clearly emphasized by Maslow in his definition of self-actualization as the "full use and exploitation of talents, capacities and potentialities" (Maslow 1970, p.150).'

This highlights the idea of a continuous development of the individual's potential being a central aspect of self-actualisation. The same idea of a **developmental process** is also present in Rogers's definition of self-actualisation: 'the inherent tendency of the organism to develop all its capacities in ways that serve to maintain or enhance the organism'. (LeClerc et al. (1998, p. 73))

So if self-actualisation is a developmental process, reaching our full potential is something done over the passage of time as we continue to grow and develop. This is comparable to the other theories we have looked at in the realm of cognitive and socio-emotional development – we grow and change over a period of time. The term shines a light on the development of the 'self' or 'personality'.

Though both Maslow and Rogers are humanistic in their perspective, the direction and application of their work are seen in different fields: Maslow's ideas are often found in the field of motivation; Rogers is best known for his work on 'self' and within psychotherapy.

MASLOW'S HIERARCHY OF NEEDS

Abraham Maslow

According to Pearson and Podeschi (1999), central to the work of Abraham Maslow (1908–1970) are **four intertwining concepts**:

- The idea of self
- We are capable of growth
- We are responsible for what we become
- We are capable of influencing social progress.

These core beliefs form his model known as the '**hierarchy of needs**'.

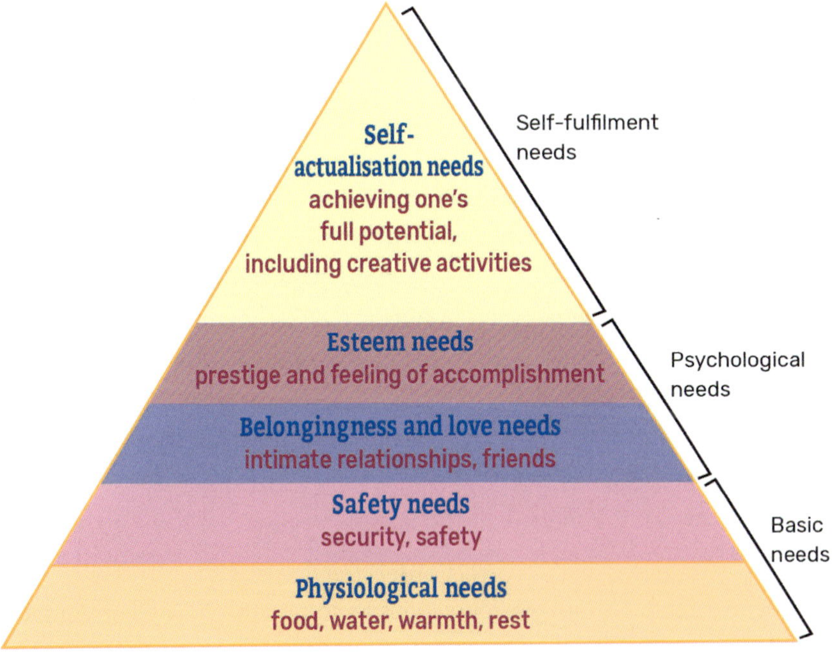

Maslow's Hierarchy of Needs

This is a framework for understanding human motivation. Maslow published his hierarchy of needs in a paper entitled 'A theory of human motivation' (1943). He begins the hierarchy with basic physiological needs (food, water, etc.) progressing through to more complex psychological needs such as security and esteem.

The needs at one level must be at least partially satisfied before those at the next level become important determinants of action. When food or safety become difficult to obtain, higher needs are less relevant to the individual, whose attention is geared towards meeting the more basic needs they are lacking.

IN FOCUS: MASLOW'S WORK AND ITS IMPLICATION FOR SUPPORTING OTHERS

Does Maslow's hierarchy of needs have relevance for those who support others?

Best *et al.* (2008) applied Maslow's idea to supporting those with addiction issues. They argue for the real relevance of Maslow's hierarchy of needs to care planning, provision and practice with clients.

Two major implications of the hierarchy of needs model for the delivery of treatment are:

1. That lower-level interventions must come before higher-order ones
2. That higher-order needs are unlikely to emerge in the initial contact stages.

What does this mean?

The *first implication* is that it's essential to ensure the client's physiological needs are met before signing them up for a training course, for example. If someone is homeless their need for both physiological and safety needs must be met first before progressing up the hierarchy.

The *second implication* is that when we are working with clients our approach should be based on, and guided by, the client's emerging pattern of needs.

Finally, Maslow's hierarchy of needs provides a way of looking at individuals' case studies, etc. and identifying what needs are being met, or not met. This offers a roadmap for identifying areas for intervention and insight into developmental aspects that have not been met in the past.

CHECK YOUR LEARNING

See if you can write down (in the correct order) the five levels of the hierarchy of needs. How would you explain Maslow's ideas to someone who was not familiar with them?

ROGERS'S THEORY OF PERSONALITY AND THE SELF

Carl Rogers (1902–1987) is best known for his contribution to the development of psychotherapy, especially his pivotal role in recognising the influence of the client–therapist relationship.

Here we are going to examine another aspect of his work: the **self**. Rogers's work emphasised the individual's subjective or private experience of the world.

Carl Rogers

The **self** is the 'I' or 'me' and includes awareness of 'what I am'. Ideas, perceptions and values all form the structure of self.

This perceived self is the reference point for the individual's perception of the world and behaviour. Self-concept and self-esteem are related concepts that are informed by the individual's sense of self. According to Rogers, the sense of self is a central measure for self-evaluation. Individuals with a strong, positive self-concept will view the world differently from people with a weak or negative self-concept. Rogers believed that self-concept does not always reflect reality; for example, a highly successful person may privately view themselves as a failure.

The self-concept of a well-adjusted person is flexible and can change to integrate new experiences and ideas.

The other 'self' that exists is the **ideal self**, which represents the person one wishes to be.

Should a significant gap exist between our 'ideal' self and our 'perceived' self, this can result in an unhappy individual and psychological challenges. The diagram below captures Rogers's conceptualisation of this. On the right we can see that the ideal and perceived self are well aligned – Rogers uses the word 'congruence' to capture this alignment. On the left we can see a gulf between the person's self-image and their ideal self. Rogers labelled this lack of alignment 'incongruence'.

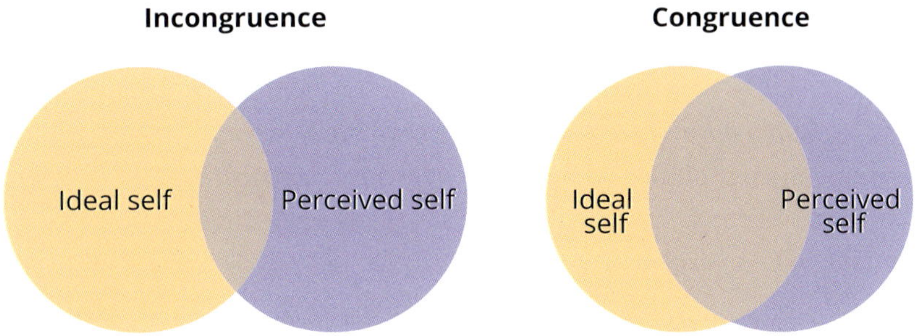

In Rogers's view, to achieve 'congruence' or the alignment of perceived and ideal self involves having supportive individuals around you. Parents, teachers and other authority figures inevitably play a significant role in self-esteem. Psychological challenges are often a result of having to push down or distort our inner needs in an effort to satisfy the perceived standards of such dependency figures.

From Rogers's perspective, continuing awareness of authentic inner desires is essential to healthy development and self-actualisation.

COMPARING AND CONTRASTING MASLOW AND ROGERS

Gross (2009, p.745) compares Maslow and Rogers in their shared positive evaluation of personal growth (self-actualisation), commenting:

> *Maslow's theory is commonly referred to as a '**psychology of being**' (self-actualization is an end in itself and lies at the peak of his hierarchy of needs).*
>
> *Rogers' is a '**psychology of becoming**' (it's the process of becoming a 'fully functioning person' that's of major importance and interest).*

CHECK YOUR LEARNING

Write a summary of Rogers's concepts of the self. What is the ideal self versus the perceived self? What happens when these are 'incongruent'?

CONTRIBUTIONS OF HUMANIST PSYCHOLOGY

Humanism, or the third force in psychology, has been sidelined by the dominance of the scientific approach. Elkins (2009) claims that the humanist psychology of Maslow and Rogers has faded away due to the dominance of the scientific approach, despite the fact that research from psychotherapy clearly supports humanist ideas and concepts.

Elkins (2009) provides a list of contributions which he feels humanistic psychology has made:

> *The humanistic movement was primarily responsible for changing society's perception of psychotherapy from a 'medical treatment for mental illness' into a vehicle for personal growth and a source of support and guidance during difficult times.*
>
> *Humanistic scholars have written extensively about the limitation of the scientific approach in understanding psychological functioning. They have demonstrated the importance of taking other non-scientific based perspectives, such as more qualitative approaches in understanding human experiences.*
>
> *The humanistic movement was largely responsible for turning America into a 'therapeutic culture' and helping enlarge the field of psychology from a small guild of about 7,000 in 1950 into a profession of more than 100,000 today.*
>
> *Rogers's Person-Centered Approach (PCA) has been the focus of hundreds of research studies that overwhelmingly have confirmed the effectiveness of his 'necessary and sufficient' conditions of therapy – empathy, congruence, and unconditional positive regard.*
>
> *Humanistic psychology has had a significant impact on other fields such as education, nursing, social work, organisational development, and so on. (pp. 282–4)*

ECOLOGICAL THEORIES

THE BIO-ECOLOGICAL THEORY: URIE BRONFENBRENNER (1917–2005)

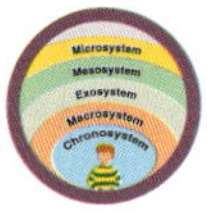

This theory looks at a child's development in the context of the system of relationships that form his or her environment. You can see from Bronfenbrenner's theoretical model that there are several systems that impact on the individual child's development. The really clever aspect of this approach is that it encompasses:

- The inner workings of the person (biological)
- The immediate environment of the child (parents, siblings)
- More distant influences at the outer circle (e.g. social welfare payments).

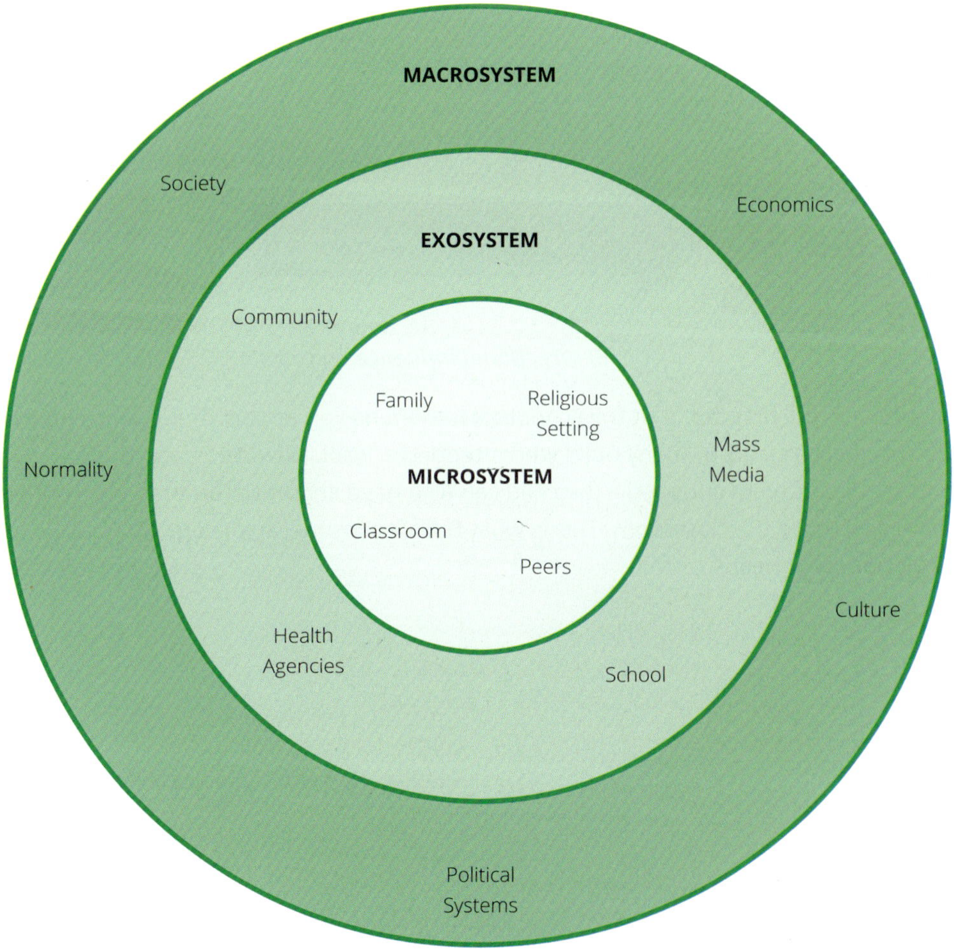

Bronfenbrenner's bio-ecological theory system

We'll look at each of the 'circles' in the child's environment.

MICROSYSTEM

This circle comprises the child's immediate environment and includes family, school/teachers, peers and neighbourhood. Thus anything and anyone the child interacts directly with or has a relationship with can be included in this circle. Not only do these influences impact on the child, the child also impacts on their immediate environment.

Relationships at this level have a two-way impact. Bronfenbrenner would call this a **bi-directional** influence.

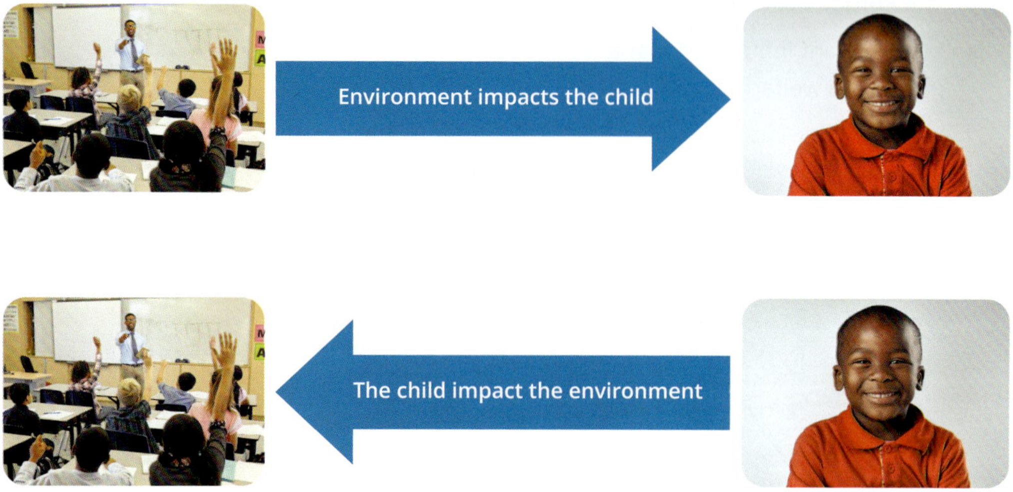

Bi-directional influence

You can see in the diagram that the school/classroom has an impact or influence on the child. This makes sense to many of us who attended school. However – and this is important and often overlooked – the child can also have an impact on their environment, i.e. in this example the classroom. This is what Bronfenbrenner's concept of **bi-directionality** means.

Think about it

Can you identify other environments in a child's life? Remember, an environment is not just a physical space – it can also include people.

MESOSYSTEM

This can be a little trickier to understand. It refers to connections or relationships between different microsystems (for example, linkages between home and school).

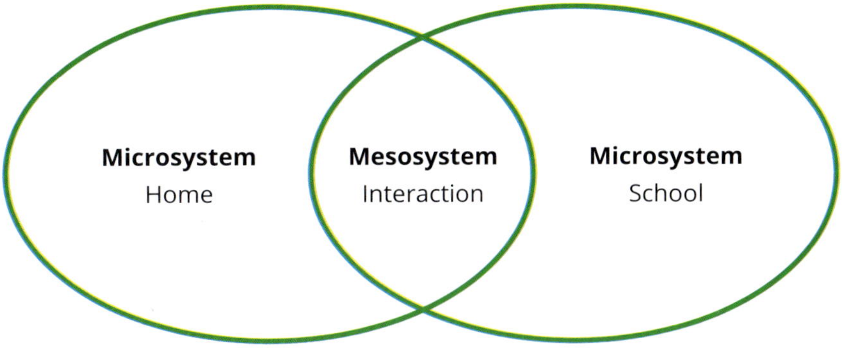

If a child has a difficult relationship with their parents this can influence their interactions with peers (linkage between two microsystems, in this case parents and peers).

EXOSYSTEM

While the child does not have an active role or is not in immediate contact with this system, the exosystem can nonetheless affect what the child experiences in their immediate context.

For example, work problems can affect the relationship between parents and also the child. If the father is promoted in work this might mean he spends less time at home, leading to arguments with his wife and less time spent with his child. So the child is inadvertently impacted on by the workplace of their father. The education system, government agencies and mass media are influences that are seen in the exosystem.

MACROSYSTEM

This system is the culture and belief patterns of the people/society in which the child lives.

CHRONOSYSTEM

This relates to changing sociohistorical circumstances. Put simply, each generation may have different experiences as time passes. Before the equal marriage referendum in Ireland in 2015, gay people could not legally marry, but now same-sex marriage is available. This is one example of a change that have occurred with the passage of time.

Think about it

Can you think of other changes that have occurred over the passage of time? Think about changes in the rights of different groups, for example women, or changes in attitude, perhaps in the area of disability and how that has changed access to education and employment. On your own (or in discussion with another), how many examples can you think of? Jot them down.

Initially Bronfenbrenner's theory was a strongly ecological one, meaning that it emphasised the impact of nurture or environmental influences. He later modified his theory to include the biological aspect of the child, reflecting the current view that both a child's biology and their environment interact in the development of the child. (Recall the nature versus nurture debate in Chapter 1, page 16.)

This modified theory is referred to as Bronfenbrenner's bio-ecological theory. If you look at the model you will see that aspects such as the child's sex, age and health are included in influencing development.

CHECK YOUR LEARNING

Revisit the case study in Chapter 1 (page XX) where you first applied Bronfenbrenner's bio-ecological theory. See if you are able to identify more influences in the case study and apply the correct label to them (microsystem, exosystem, etc). Use the blank here below to check if you are able to label each 'system' correctly. Then use it as a guide in placing different aspects of the case study in Chapter 1 within each 'system'.

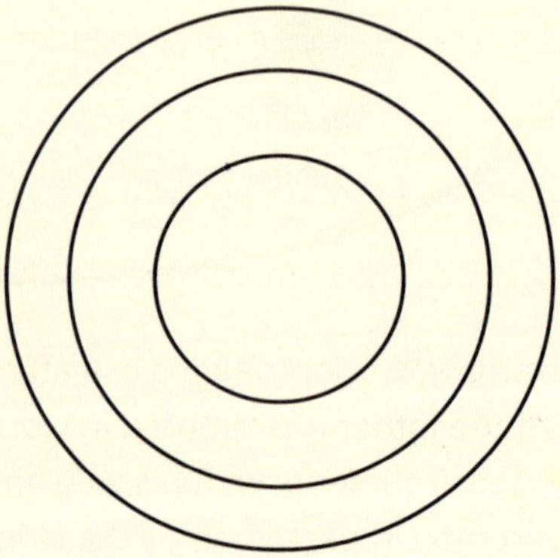

CHECK YOUR LEARNING GOALS!

You should be able to:

1. Name Freud's theory of personality and explain its three elements.
2. Summarise what is meant by the 'iceberg' analogy.
3. List the five stages of Freud's psychosexual theory and two criticisms of it.
4. Explain the purpose of defence mechanisms and describe three of them.
5. List all eight stages in Erikson's psychosocial theory and summarise them in your own words.
6. Explain the key issue on which Erikson disagreed with Freud.
7. Name two criticisms of Erikson's theory.
8. Define the term 'attachment'.
9. Outline the 'maternal deprivation' theory.
10. Explain naturalistic observation.
11. Explain the strange situation, including the four attachment patterns that were observed.
12. Explain what is meant by the term 'cognitive development'.
13. Summarise how we learn, according to Piaget, making reference to assimilation and accommodation.
14. Explain 'naturalistic observation'.
15. Outline the age range that applies to the sensorimotor stage.
16. Describe, in your own words, all four stages of Piaget's theory of cognitive development.
17. Describe how to test for object permanence.
18. List and summarise Piaget's stages of play.
19. Explain two criticisms of Piaget's work.
20. Explain why Vygotsky is sometimes referred to as a sociocultural theorist.
21. Outline what is meant by the zone of proximal development (ZPD).
22. Explain how Vygotsky differs from Piaget in how they believe children acquire cognition. Which of them do you agree with and why?

»

23. Explain humanism as the 'third force' in psychology and why it is referred to as that.

24. Define humanism in your own words.

25. Explain what is meant by the term 'self-actualisation'.

26. List (in the correct order) the five levels of Maslow's hierarchy of needs.

27. Summarise each of the stages.

28. Differentiate between the 'ideal self' and the 'perceived self'.

29. Explain what Rogers means by the term 'congruent'.

30. Give two reasons why humanism is not more dominant in psychology.

31. Outline the major contributions of humanistic psychology.

32. Draw a diagram of the five different levels of 'systems' in Bronfenbrenner's bio-ecological theory.

33. Name some of the elements you might see in the microsystem.

34. Explain what is meant by 'bi-directionality'.

35. Name the system that represents the interactions or linkages between two microsystems.

36. Identify and describe the different perspectives in psychology.

37. List the four main goals of psychology.

38. Explain what is meant by the term 'lifespan development'.

39. List the periods of development.

40. Describe the difference between a biological and a social milestone, giving an example of each.

41. Define a 'factor'.

42. Explain the difference between a risk factor and a protective factor and give examples of both.

43. Describe at least two key issues in psychology

3

Conception, Prenatal Development and Birth

In this chapter we will discover:

* Conception
  - Fertilisation/conception
  - Chromosomes and genes
  - Genetic inheritance
  - Chromosomal conditions
* Prenatal development
  - Stages of prenatal development
  - Hazards during the prenatal period
  - Teratogens
  - In Focus: Stress and the developing brain
* Birth
  - The stages of labour
  - Assessment and screening of newborns
  - Birth statistics and trends
  - In Focus: Low birthweight and social inequality

In this chapter we will start on the journey of understanding human functioning and behaviour: how we become who we are. Often when people think of human growth and development they think of it starting at the moment a baby is born, but that's not the case at all. As we will see, much of our foundations are laid during the period covered in this chapter. None more so, arguably, than at the moment of conception when the embryo forms with the genetic material of the biological parents.

CONCEPTION

We will begin by exploring the processes that occur at conception and the possible impact they can have on a person's development *after* birth.

FERTILISATION/CONCEPTION

The menstrual cycle occurs in females of reproductive age. At the beginning of the cycle an egg (**ovum**) begins to develop in the ovary. This egg is released and travels down the Fallopian tube.

Fertilisation occurs when a women's ovum or egg is penetrated or fertilised by a man's sperm. The fertilised egg is called a **zygote**.

A continual process of cell division then occurs until this mass of cells attaches itself to the uterus of the mother, approximately 10–14 days after fertilisation. The man's sperm and the woman's egg each contain hereditary information in the form of **chromosomes**.

CHROMOSOMES AND GENES

A **chromosome** is a tightly coiled molecule of deoxyribonucleic acid (DNA) that consists of smaller segments called **genes**. Genes are like your body's instruction manual; they affect your looks, health and how your body works.

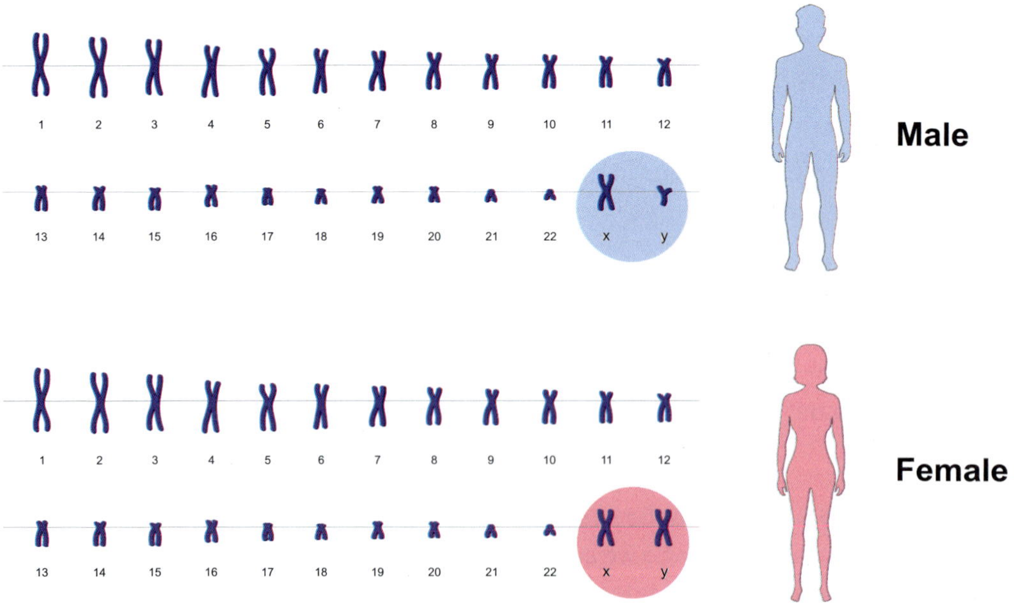

Chromosomes

The zygote contains **23 pairs of chromosomes**, 23 single chromosomes from the sperm and 23 chromosomes from the egg (in total 46 chromosomes, or 23 pairs). Thus, in the fertilised egg each pair of chromosomes contains one chromosome from each parent. Out of the 23 pairs of chromosomes, it is the final pair (the 23rd) that determine a person's sex.

* In males the 23rd pair consists of an X and a Y chromosome.
* In females the 23rd pair consists of two X chromosomes.

There are approximately 25,000 genes contained on the 46 chromosomes in each cell in a human body. This means that one chromosome contains thousands of genes. We inherit our genetic make-up from our parents through the transmission of their genes during conception.

* **Genotype:** The sum total of our genetic make-up, the specific genetic make-up of the individual. Our genotype is present from conception and never changes.
* **Phenotype:** The observable characteristics that are produced by that genetic make-up. Phenotypes can be affected by other genes and by the environment (such as climate, diet and lifestyle).

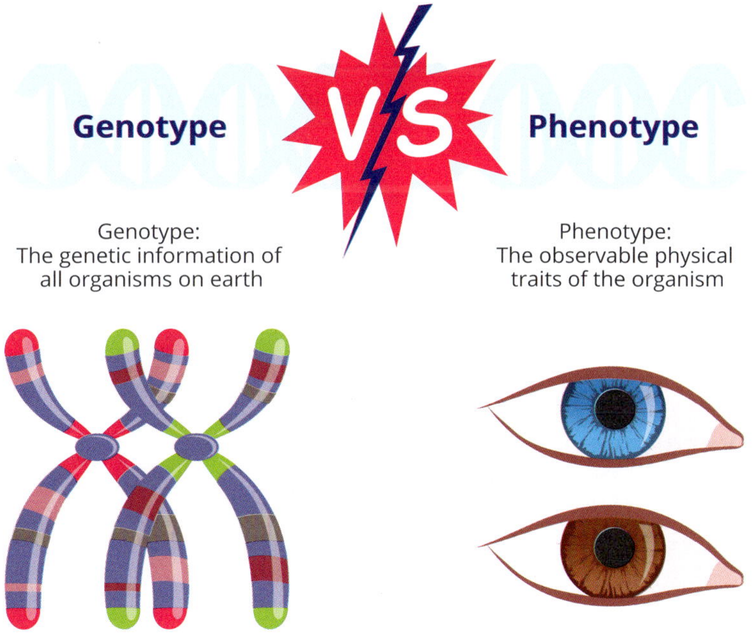

Put simply, the **genotype** is the genetic make-up and the **phenotype** is the things we observe in a person such as eye or hair colour.

Many kinds of variation are influenced by both genetic and environmental factors. Though our genes govern what characteristics we inherit, our environment can affect how these inherited characteristics develop or are shaped.

Think about it

An individual may have inherited a genetic tendency to be tall but a poor diet during childhood will cause poor growth.

LINK

Can you think of any of the key issues in Chapter 1 that are relevant here? How about the nature versus nurture debate? Is genetic inheritance nature or nurture?

What factors in an individual's environment, other than poor nutrition, might impact on their development?

GENETIC INHERITANCE

We've seen that each human has 23 pairs of chromosomes and at conception we inherit one from our mother and one from our father, making a pair. Genes are segments within the chromosome that act as your body's instruction manual. "Allele" is the word that we use to describe a version of a gene. As we can see in the image below, some genes are dominant and some recessive.

Dominant
Allele which controls the characteristic whenever it is present.
BB or Bb

Recessive
Allele whose characteristics only show up when it is present on both chromosomes.
bb

Let's look at hair colour to see what this means.

Brown hair is regulated by a dominant gene, blond hair by a recessive one. My father has brown hair and my mother has blonde hair. I have brown hair yet my brother has blond hair. How is this possible?

If at conception the gene for brown hair is present, the child will have brown hair because it is the dominant gene and 'overpowers' the recessive blond hair gene. Just because my father has brown hair doesn't mean he doesn't also carry the blond hair gene (his mother was blonde). Thus at the moment of my brother's conception my mother and father both passed down the recessive blond gene and this is why my brother has blond hair.

Genetic inheritance is like playing the lottery: you never know the mix of numbers you might end up with at each draw – similar to genetic inheritance at each conception. So conception is literally a lottery!

However, not all our genetic inheritance is a lottery. Some people will inherit genetic conditions and illnesses. The concept of **dominant** and **recessive** genes is important here. Let's take a look.

RECESSIVE INHERITANCE

If two parents are both carriers of a genetic condition with a recessive inheritance pattern, there is a one in four chance that each child will be affected. So, on average, one-quarter of their children will be affected. There is also a one in two chance that each child will be an unaffected carrier, like the parents.

Examples of genetic conditions that show a recessive pattern of inheritance are cystic fibrosis, sickle cell disease, Tay-Sachs disease and phenylketonuria (PKU).

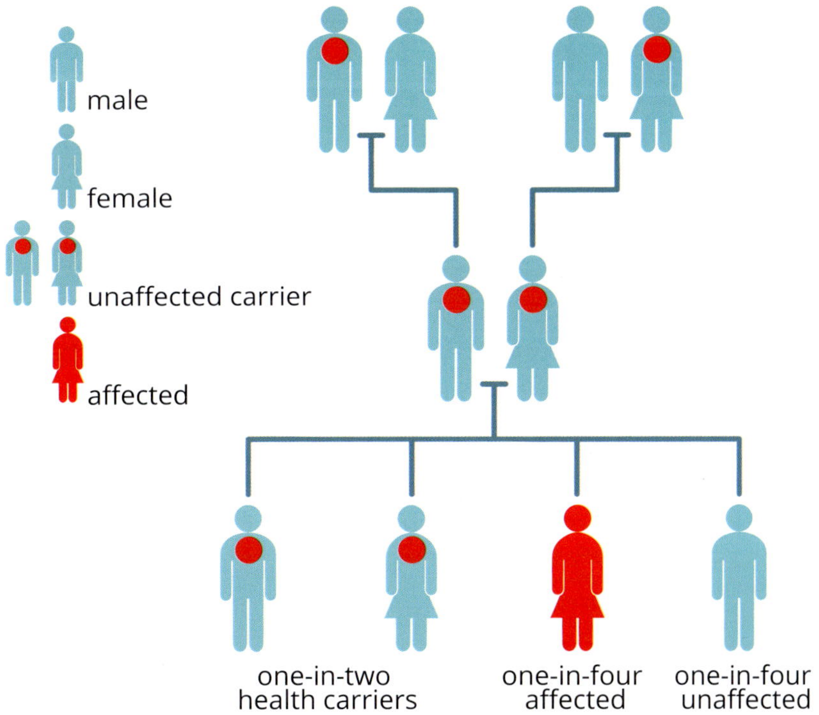

Recessive gene inheritance pattern

DOMINANT INHERITANCE

If one parent is affected by a genetic condition with a dominant inheritance pattern, every child has a one-in-two chance of being affected. So, on average, half their children will be affected and half their children will not be affected and will not pass on the condition. However, as chance determines inheritance, it is also possible that all or none of their children will be affected.

Examples of genetic conditions that show a dominant pattern of inheritance include Huntington's disease.

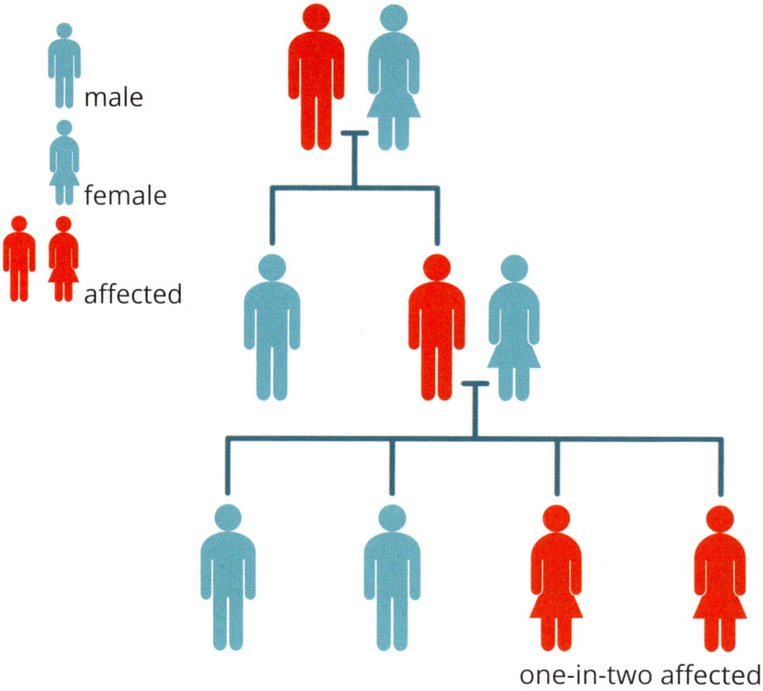

Dominant gene inheritance pattern

To recap, the major difference between dominant and recessive gene inheritance is as follows:

Recessive	For the child to inherit the condition they must inherit **both** variant (affected) chromosomes from **both** parents. The child has a 1:4 chance of inheriting the condition, a 1:2 chance of becoming a healthy carrier and a 1:4 chance of not inheriting the affected chromosome.
Dominant	One parent is affected; the other parent is healthy. At conception, if the variant chromosome of the affected parent is transferred, the child will inherit the condition. It does not matter if the other parent's chromosome is healthy. Thus the child has a 1:2 chance of inheriting the condition.

CHECK YOUR LEARNING

These can be tricky concepts to grasp. Imagine explaining chromosomes and their inheritance pattern at conception to a friend. Then write down your explanation.

Then imagine moving on to explain recessive and dominant inheritance. Make a summary of that too (instead of writing it you could use images like eye and hair colour).

CHROMOSOMAL CONDITIONS

We are now going to look at **chromosomal** disorders that occur at the moment of conception. To clarify:

* A genetically inherited condition (which we've just looked at) occurs when you inherit certain genes from your parent(s).
* Chromosomal disorders are also 'genetic' conditions, but they are *not* the same as 'genes' inherited from a parent(s). At the moment of conception, when the 23 chromosomes from each parent come together, they don't form in a typical way and this results in a chromosomal disorder.

Gene-linked disorders (e.g. cystic fibrosis, PKU and Huntington's disease) are different from chromosomal conditions such as Down syndrome.

Both occur at conception, but while gene-linked conditions are inherited, chromosomal conditions generally occur as a result of the presence of an extra chromosome that occurs at conception.

Each cell has 23 pairs of chromosomes. In Down syndrome, an extra copy of chromosome 21 is present, as seen in the below image.

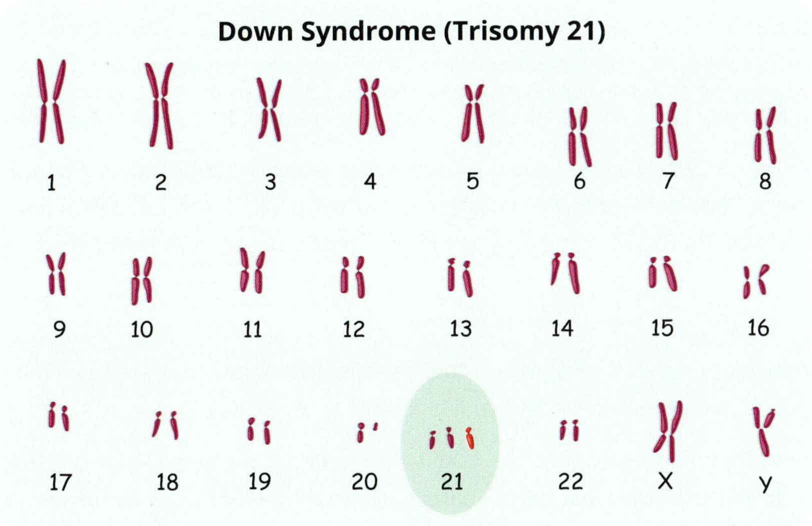

Other chromosomal syndromes include Patau syndrome (trisomy 13) and Edwards syndrome (trisomy 18). Sex-linked chromosome abnormalities can also occur (e.g. Fragile X syndrome).

DOWN SYNDROME

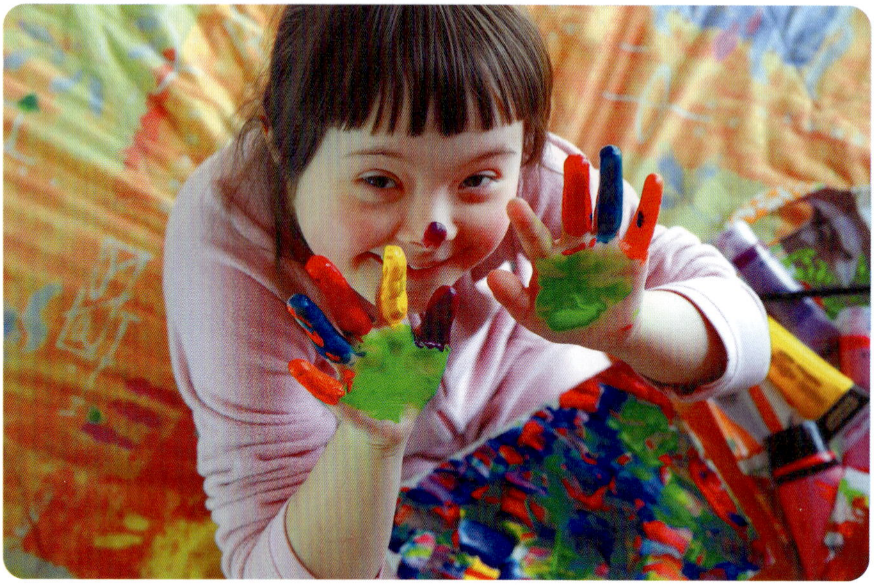

Child with Down syndrome

Down syndrome is sometimes referred to as **trisomy 21**, the 'tri-' referring to the three chromosomes that are present instead of two.

It is the most common of the chromosomal disorders. In Ireland, one baby in 600 is estimated to be born with Down syndrome. Physical characteristics associated with Down syndrome include a downward-sloping skinfold at the inner eye corners, flat appearance of the face, protruding tongue and low muscle tone (for babies who have Down syndrome their head and neck will need extra support). Down syndrome is accompanied by developmental delay; IQ can range from low to severe learning disability.

Share the journey is the motto of Down Syndrome Ireland. Its mission statement states:

> *People experience many great things and also face many challenges throughout their lives. People with Down syndrome are no different, but may need a little extra help and support along the way. Down Syndrome Ireland's goal is to help people with Down syndrome make their own futures as bright and independent as possible by providing them with education, support and friendship every step of the way.*

It is generally argued that it's important that people with disabilities are seen as individuals first, who happen to have a disability.

Down Syndrome Ireland says that 'the quality of life of people with Down syndrome has improved immensely in the last thirty years. Just like the rest of us, they now enjoy longer life expectancy and can live happy, fulfilling and active lives as part of the community.'

LINK

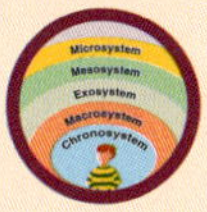

What do you think would have been the experience of a child born with Down syndrome in the 1940s? Do you think their experience would be different from a child with Down syndrome born in Ireland today? Recall Bronfenbrenner's bio-ecological theory and specifically the chronosystem in Chapter 2. Go back and see how you might use the experiences of people with Down syndrome as an example of the chronosystem.

Let's look at some evidence that highlights how different eras can affect people's development and life outcomes.

Louis Clifford: Survey of Learning Disability (1943)

The following is an extract from Griffin and Shevlin's *Responding to Special Educational Needs: An Irish Perspective* (2007). It highlights the attitudes and experience of those born with a disability in the 1940s:

Having a disabled child, according to Clifford, was widely seen by parents of the time as a disgrace and a reflection on the family. The more affluent and socially superior the family, the more the condition was resented and abhorred. Families from lower socioeconomic backgrounds were usually more philosophical about their misfortune. In his account, Dr Clifford records that disabled children were sometimes hidden away in top rooms and seldom taken out except at night (p.39).

From this perspective, it's hard to have imagined that 25 years later children and adults would be participating in an event such as the Special Olympics (the global Special Olympics began in 1968) yet change does occur.

Does a child born today with Down syndrome face a different experience from that same child born in the 1940s?

If your answer is Yes, this represents the *chronosystem* as conceptualised by Bronfenbrenner's bio-ecological theory: the life experience of a generation differs from that of another due to social changes. It also demonstrates the power and influence that social change can produce. This is particularly important in areas where people experience prejudice, such as those with disabilities, as it demonstrates the power of social change and the difference it can make to the lives of individuals, their development and their outcomes.

LINK

Revisit Chapter 1, page 17. What relevance does the preceding piece have to the nature versus nurture argument?

PRENATAL DEVELOPMENT

The prenatal stage is the time from conception until birth, usually 40 weeks unless the baby is born prematurely. During this period lots of growth and development takes place.

STAGES OF PRENATAL DEVELOPMENT

Prenatal development consists of three stages:

STAGE	PERIOD	WHAT HAPPENS
Germinal stage	Approximately the first 2 weeks of development	When a woman's egg (ovum) is fertilised by a man's sperm, the fertilised egg is called a **zygote** Once fertilised, a process of continual cell division begins Approximately 10–14 days after conception the zygote, which now contains a mass of cells, attaches itself to the mother's uterus
Embryonic stage	End of 2nd week to the 8th week	The cell mass is now called an **embryo** The placenta and umbilical cord begin developing during this stage and the bodily organs and systems begin to form By week 8 the heart is beating and the brain is forming Facial features such as eyes become discernible
Foetal stage	From 9th week until birth	The embryo is now a **foetus** At 24 weeks the eyes open At 28 weeks the foetus attains the age of viability, meaning that it is likely to survive outside the womb if born prematurely

Source: Hetherington & Parke (1999)

The following diagram is a useful illustration of the changes as they occur over the prenatal period. Keep it in mind for the next section where we look at hazards that can occur during the prenatal period and their impact on the developing foetus.

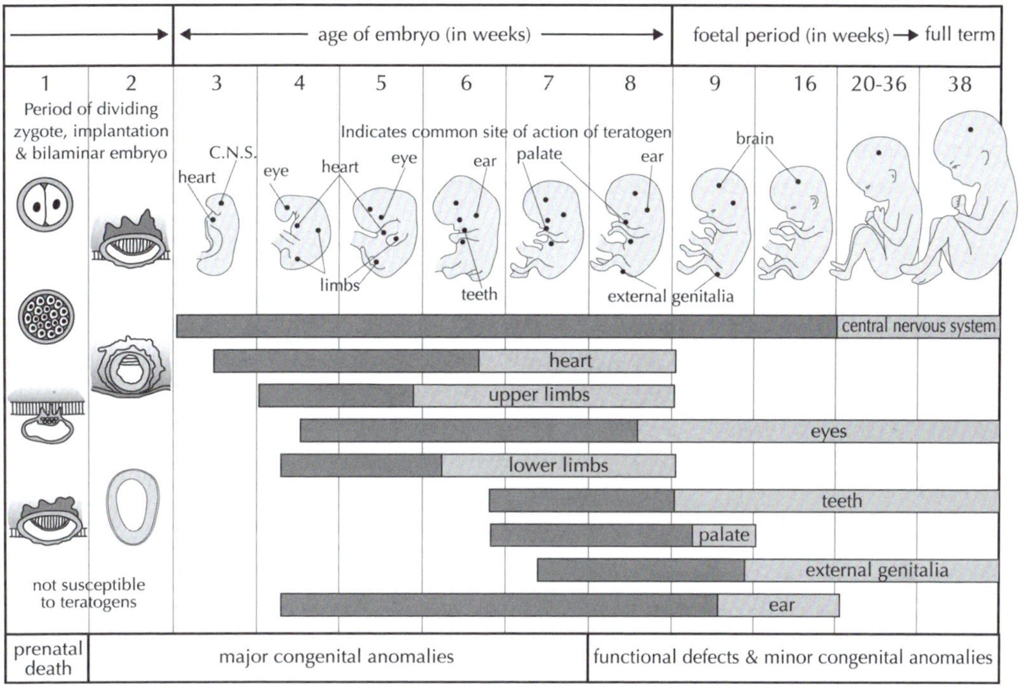

Critical periods in human development

HAZARDS DURING THE PRENATAL PERIOD

As we saw earlier, chromosomal and genetic disorders affect the foetus at the moment of conception.

Other external factors can affect and influence the foetus's development in the womb.

> **LINK**
>
> Look back to Chapter 1 to refresh your knowledge of what factors are and their role in development.

Influences on prenatal development include:

* Diet and nutrition. If a pregnant mother is not getting the required calories, the foetus is more likely to have a low birthweight compared to women who gain 26 lb (11.7 kg) or more during their pregnancy.
* Age
* Emotional stress
* Illnesses.

A protective factor is engaging with medical staff and supports during the pregnancy to reduce any of these potential risks.

HIV/AIDS

Approximately a quarter of infants born to HIV-infected mothers become infected. The virus crosses the placenta and enters the foetus's bloodstream, or it can be transferred in the birth canal during birth. Research has found that HIV-positive mothers who take the drug AZT have a decreased chance of passing the disease to their children.

RUBELLA

Rubella or German measles is most dangerous if contracted in the first weeks of pregnancy. It can cause hearing impairments, cataracts and heart defects.

DIABETES

For women who suffer with Type 1 or Type 2 diabetes or those who develop gestational diabetes this condition carries potential health risks for the developing foetus. These can include an increased risk of birth defects, stillbirths and preterm birth.

TERATOGENS

While maternal illness is one factor that can have an impact during the prenatal period, other factors also have the potential to negatively impact on the development of the foetus.

Teratogens are agents or substances that can adversely affect the foetus, causing physical or functional abnormalities or damage. Teratogens include drugs, alcohol, chemicals and infections.

LINK

Look back at critical versus sensitive periods in Chapter 1. Then see how the following information on teratogens might support the position of critical periods of development.

The timing of exposure and dose of a teratogen can make a difference to the outcome. Take the example of thalidomide. This was a drug used to ease morning sickness and was often recommended to pregnant women in the late 1950s. It became apparent as the pregnant women who had taken the drug began to give birth that their babies had been affected.

The infants were born with missing arms and legs or shortened limbs. If you look back at the diagram on page 71, you will notice that there are some periods when different parts of the body are more vulnerable to teratogenic exposure. These women were taking the medication for morning sickness which can occur early in the pregnancy, and as you will see from that table, limbs are especially vulnerable early in the pregnancy.

You can find out more about the thalidomide scandal and watch a video from a survivor explaining what it is like to live with the effects at: www.sciencemuseum.org.uk/objects-and-stories/medicine/thalidomide

As we examine different teratogens, bear in mind that the timing, dose and duration of exposure all interact together in determining outcomes.

Thalidomide Child

Teratogens and their effects

Smoking during pregnancy	Increases the risk of miscarriage, premature birth and low birthweight
Marijuana and heroin	'The infants of twice-weekly marijuana smokers suffer from tremors and sleep problems. They seem to have little interest in their surroundings for up to 2 weeks after birth ... both heroin and methadone ... can cause miscarriage, premature labour, and early death' (Boyd & Bee 2005, p.67) 60–80% of babies born to heroin- or methadone-addicted mothers are addicted themselves, suffering withdrawal symptoms exhibiting as high-pitched cries and convulsions
Alcohol	Can cause physical malformations and learning and behavioural challenges.

IN FOCUS: STRESS AND THE DEVELOPING BRAIN

While it's clear that drugs and toxins can affect the developing baby, other factors can also play a part. Music (2011, p.17) confirms that 'there is consistent evidence that high stress levels in pregnancy increases the likelihood of both birth complication and low birthweight. The stress hormone cortisol can cross the placental wall, affecting the foetus. The effect of maternal stress on foetal development has been shown to hold up even when other factors such as social class, diet, or smoking are screened out.' Once the baby is born its brain continues to develop thus remaining vulnerable to external influences. The concept of **stress** is well known to many of us but it might be a surprise that the effects of stress can impact the developing foetus. »

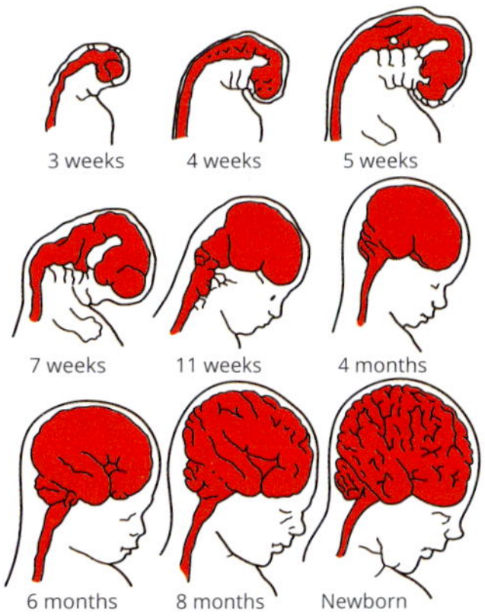

Brain development in foetus

Stress is 'a real or interpreted threat to the physiological or psychological integrity of an individual that results in physiological and/or behavioral responses' (Levine 2005, p.940).

Stress can affect the developing brain in utero, and increasingly attention is being paid to how stress can impact the developing brain once the child is born. We're going to look at how early experiences can affect later development

LINK

Read the following piece and jot down your thoughts. Do you believe this information supports some of the key debates examined in Chapter 1, for example the nature versus nurture debate and the idea that early experiences affect later development? Before you come to your conclusion, consider how some people appear unaffected by early experiences in the same way as others with similar experiences. What could account for this?

'Recent research has produced increasing evidence that early life stress (ELS), an experience of severe stress due for example to parental loss, abuse or neglect during the childhood years, may have profound long-term effects on the individual's physiology and psychology ... animal models have demonstrated that consequences of ELS may lead to physiological changes in the central nervous system that may be permanent' (Pesonen & Räikkönen (2012, p.722)).

So early life stress can alter the body and brain in such a way that it can leave the child at a higher risk of psychopathology (depression, addiction, etc.). How does this process occur?

According to Margot Sunderland, early relationships can have long-lasting effects on the brain. One can think of a child's brain as an ice sculpture which is 'shaped' through relational interactions, for better or worse.

Sunderland comments: 'the developing brain in those crucial first years of life is highly vulnerable to stress. It is so sensitive that the stress of many common parenting techniques can lay delicate "emotion chemical" balances and stress response systems in the infant's brain and body, and sometimes cause actual cell death in certain brain structures' (2006, p.27). She says that if children do not receive responsive and attuned relationships in early life that teach them to manage what she calls the 'big feelings', then the 'flight or fight' response that we experience when we are stressed becomes literally ingrained in the brain; it shapes and sculpts the brain, making the person unequipped to deal with stressful feelings in later life and in a state of permanent alert.

This has devastating effects in later life, for example:

- Depression
- Persistent states of anxiety
- Phobias and obsessions
- Physical symptoms/illness
- Being cut off emotionally
- Lethargy and lack of get-up-and-go
- Lack of desire and excitement
- Lack of spontaneity (p.32)

What Sunderland describes is often referred to as **toxic stress**.

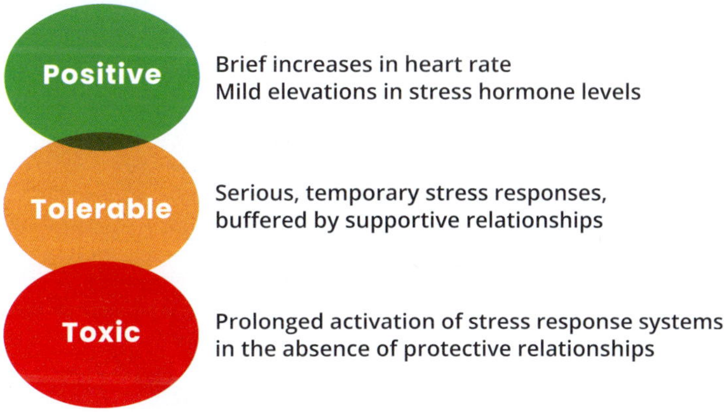

Toxic stress

The topic of toxic stress in childhood and its impact on children's development, including brain development, is contentious but lies at the heart of many discussions of supporting children and their development.

Check out the work of Harvard's Center on the Developing Child for some additional reading including studies on adverse childhood experiences (ACEs): https://developingchild.harvard.edu/resources/aces-and-toxic-stress-frequently-asked-questions

BIRTH

The beginning of labour is caused by a hormonal response encouraging contractions to start. Contractions cause the cervix to dilate (open) and allow the baby to move down the birth canal (vagina) and be born. The mucus plug is expelled and the waters break (sometimes this is done at the hospital if labour is progressing slowly).

THE STAGES OF LABOUR

The process of labour consists of three stages:

Stage 1:
The cervix relaxes causing it to dilate and thin out.

Stage 2:
Uterine contractions increase in strength and the infant is delivered.

Stage 3:
The placenta is expelled.

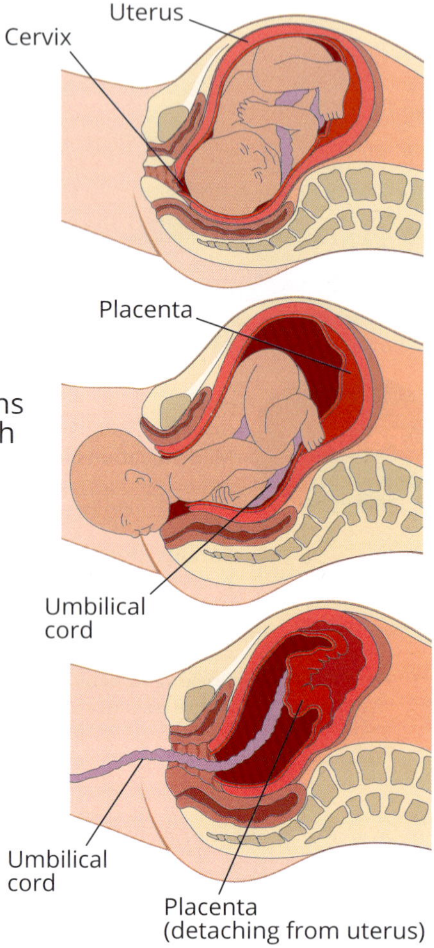

- **Stage 1:** Consists of contractions which can be 15 or so minutes apart. The purpose of these contractions is to open the cervix, which is at the neck of the womb. A typical pattern is to experience one contraction of about 40 to 50 seconds every ten minutes at the beginning of stage one, and one contraction lasting more than a minute and coming every 30 seconds or so at the end. By the end of the first stage of labour the cervix will be fully dilated at 10 centimetres.
- **Stage 2:** Begins when the baby's head starts to move down the birth canal. The mother actively pushes the baby down the birth canal. If you're having your 1st baby, this pushing stage should last no longer than 3 hours. If you've had a baby before, it should take no more than 2 hours.
- **Stage 3:** Delivery of the afterbirth – the placenta, umbilical cord and other membranes. This is the shortest stage of labour.

Immediately after the baby's birth, its health is assessed using the Apgar scale.

ASSESSMENT AND SCREENING OF NEWBORN BABIES

APGAR SCALE

The Apgar scale is used in the first minutes of a baby's life. It is a quick and simple method of evaluating the infant's health. It is administered within the first minute after delivery and then repeated five minutes later. The newborn is assessed on the following indicators.

Apgar scoring system

INDICATOR		0 POINTS	1 POINT	2 POINTS
A	Activity (muscle tone)	Absent	Flexed arms and legs	Active
P	Pulse	Absent	Below 100 bpm	Over 100 bpm
G	Grimace (reflex irritability)	Floppy	Minimal response to stimulation	Prompt response to stimulation
A	Appearance (skin colour)	Blue; pale	Pink body, blue extremities	Pink
R	Respiration	Absent	Slow and irregular	Vigorous cry

Each of these factors is given a score between zero and two and then added up. Most infants score between 7 and 10, with 10 being a perfect score.

Apgar scores

8–10	Excellent condition
5–7	Fair condition The baby might need some help with breathing
Under 5	The baby requires treatment A paediatrician may be called to assess the baby

It should be borne in mind that the Apgar scale is only intended to measure the health of the baby after delivery; it is not necessarily a predictor of long-term health.

There is good reason why the health of a baby is initially assessed after delivery. Checking for underlying conditions such as chromosomal disorders is one aspect. However, the birth process itself is not without some potential complications, one being anoxia.

Anoxia is when the foetus experiences a deprivation of oxygen either during the labour and/or in the delivery.

Depending on how long the foetus is starved of oxygen, anoxia can result in varying degrees of brain damage and, potentially, death. Births are usually closely monitored for signs of distress in the foetus. If there are problems, a caesarean section may be performed. This involves making an incision in the abdomen for the baby to be delivered. While some caesarean sections are emergency ones, increasingly they have become elective or pre-planned as an alternative to a traditional vaginal birth.

NEWBORN SCREENING IN IRELAND

Ireland was one of the first countries in the world to introduce screening of newborns for conditions that could affect their health and development. The aim of screening is to determine whether interventions are required to support newborns affected by certain conditions. You might recognise this as the **heel prick test**.

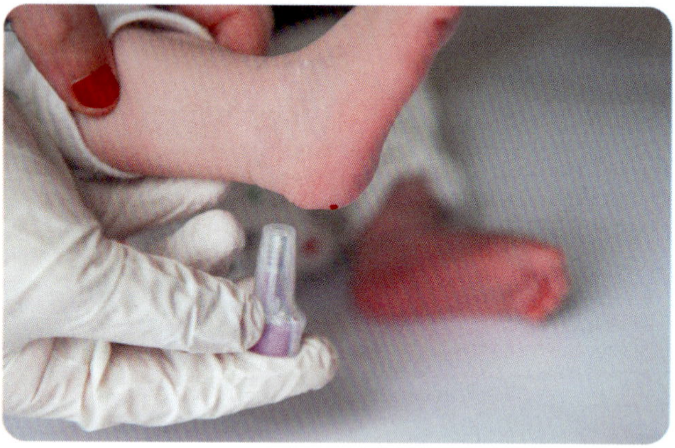

Heel prick test

PKU

In the section on conception we encountered a genetically inherited condition called phenylketonuria (PKU). This is a condition that causes a build-up in the body of an amino acid called phenylalanine, leading to brain damage. If it is diagnosed it can be treated with a specifically modified diet that excludes the specific amino acid, thus preventing it from accumulating in the child's system. Within the first few days of life blood is extracted via a pin prick on the infant's heel and analysed. According to the *National PKU News* (Fall 2001), since testing began in Ireland there has been an incidence rate of 1 in 4,500, far greater than the incidence rate of 1 in 12,000 seen in the USA.

The National Newborn Screening Programme was first established in Ireland in 1966 to screen all infants for PKU. Since then it has expanded its services and now tests for eight disorders that, if not caught and treated early, have the potential to cause brain damage:

* Cystic fibrosis (CF)
* Phenylketonuria (PKU)
* Classical galactosaemia (C Gal)
* Maple syrup urine disease (MSUD)
* Medium-chain acyl-CoA dehydrogenase deficiency (MCADD)
* Glutaric aciduria type 1 (GA1)
* Homocystinuria (HCU)
* Congenital hypothyroidism (CHT)

BIRTH STATISTICS AND TRENDS

Birthweight and premature birth can affect babies' development.

Low birthweight babies

Low weight	less than 5½ pounds (2,500 grams) at birth
Very low weight	less than 3 pounds (1,360 grams) at birth
Extremely low weight	under 2 pounds (907 grams) at birth

Preterm babies are babies who are born before 38 weeks' gestation, and most preterm babies are low-weight.

Cigarette smoking by the mother is the leading cause of low birthweight in infants (Unicef 2004). Adolescents who give birth when their bodies have not fully developed are also at risk of having low birthweight (LBW) babies.

Birthweight in Ireland

	2008	2019
Average birth weight	3,464 g or 7.6 pounds	3,437.5 grams
Low birth weight babies (weighing less than 2,500g or 5.5 pounds)	5.3%	Increasing to 6%
Preterm (Less than 37 weeks gestation) has increased from 5.5% in 1999	to 6.2% in 2008	To 7% of total births in 2019
Average age of mothers giving birth has increased from 30.1 years in 1999	to 31.1 years in 2008	To 32.5 years
First births to women aged 35 years or older rose from 8.6% in 1999	To 14.2%	To 27%
Delivery by Caesarean section (CS): In 2010, 27% of total live births were delivered by Caesarean section	CS accounted for 26.7% of all live births	35% of total live births were delivered by CS, with 34% of singleton and 71% of multiple live births delivered by this method.

Source: Irish National Perinatal Reporting System (2021)

Think about it

What do these trends over the last 20 years suggest? What might be some of the factors that are causing these changes?

LINK

Revisit Chapter 1 where we examined factors to refresh your learning.

IN FOCUS: LOW BIRTHWEIGHT AND SOCIAL INEQUALITY

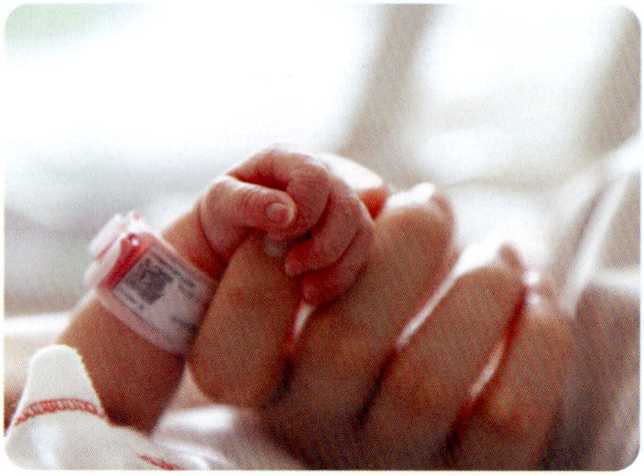

Low birthweight (LBW) as a factor affecting the developmental outcomes of children has long been recognised. LBW can be an important predictor of newborn health, growth and developmental outcomes (Mishra *et al.* 2021). Also well-established is the link between LBW and social inequality (which includes poverty, marginalisation and disadvantage).

In a report entitled *Unequal at Birth*, McAvoy *et al.* (2006) observe an increased risk of LBW where social inequalities exist. They identify particular groups of women who are more vulnerable to social exclusions and poverty and who are, therefore, at more risk of experiencing health inequalities in relation to their pregnancy and their babies. These include:

- teenage mothers
- lone parents
- disabled women
- Travellers
- refugees and asylum seekers
- other ethnic minority women
- women prisoners
- homeless women (McAvoy *et al.* 2006, p.28).

Let's take a look at one group from this list.

Teenage pregnancy is more prevalent in lower socioeconomic groupings and teen mothers are more likely to have premature and LBW babies (Connolly *et al.* 1998).

Almost 90% of attendees at a Dublin adolescent antenatal booking clinic were recorded as being in the lowest socioeconomic group. Most had poor educational attainment and 87% had left school. 'It is also well recognised that pregnant schoolgirls are more likely to live in areas with poor housing, overcrowding and high unemployment rates' (Connolly *et al.* 1998, p.23).

Think about it

Given that teen mothers are likely to leave school early, what might be the implications? For example: could they be at higher risk of unemployment, or of being in a low-paying job if employed, or of remaining in poverty?

LINK

When we explore factors we should also think about how they might relate to other factors, for example how they might improve or reduce life outcomes and affect developmental outcomes in children. A factor such as poor education might link to other factors such as unemployment and poverty.

Think about it

From the list of women identified as being vulnerable to experiencing inequalities in their pregnancy, pick two and make notes as to why you think they are part of this list. What are the possible influences and factors?

Evidence from more recent research continues to support the relationship between LBW and social inequality. McGovern (2011, p.21) confirms that there is a strong relationship between social factors and birthweight and also between birthweight and later outcomes. Factors involved in birthweight included:

- Household type
- Smoking behaviour
- Absence of a mother's family
- Maternal health
- Maternal employment.

Using data from *Growing Up in Ireland*, Madden (2012, p.2) examined the relationship between LBW and socioeconomic status (SES) and found that children who are LBW have poorer outcomes including 'foetal and infant mortality, as well as with short and long-term morbidity. In addition, there is fairly extensive evidence that LBW is also regarded as a risk factor for a number of health and non-health outcomes in later life.' In the table below, Madden analyses birthweight by social class, with 'no class' signifying that the person has never worked. Intrauterine growth restriction (IUGR) (poor growth of the baby while in the womb) was also included along with preterm and LBW babies.

Birthweight by social class

	PROFESSIONAL, MANAGERIAL	NON-MANUAL, SKILLED MANUAL	SEMI-SKILLED, UNSKILLED	NO CLASS
LBW (%)	5.18	5.49	6.89	9.35
Preterm (%)	5.72	6.68	8.18	8.71
IUGR (%)	1.87	2.01	2.01	3.94

»

As you can see from the table, these conditions are more prevalent in those groups with lower SES. Regarding IUGR, Madden points out that there is relatively little difference between the first three social class groupings but there is a substantial jump for those who have never worked ('no class'). Overall, those in the 'lowest' SES are at higher risk of having a baby born with LBW or IUGR. All this research shows the impact that social factors can have, and not just in the short term; they literally have the potential to affect a child across their lifespan.

IMPACT OF THE COVID PANDEMIC ON PREGNANT WOMEN

The effects of inequality were clear during the Covid pandemic.

Research carried out by Stanford University found that the rate of depression in pregnant women doubled during the pandemic. Those most vulnerable to the effects of depression were 'those who were already experiencing challenges due to socioeconomic inequality, such as persons of colour and immigrants, as well as women with pre-existing poor physical health and histories of mental disorders' (Hadhazy 2021).

LINK

It doesn't just end with the mother; this is where you can see what Bronfenbrenner's bio-ecological theory captures – how factors and people around the developing child can impact on the child's development.

One of the lead authors of the research observes, 'Because depression in pregnancy may affect the developing foetus as well as the relationship between the mother and the infant after birth, these effects are unlikely to cease when the pandemic ends.'

So we can see that the relationship between caregivers and the infant is crucial to the child's development. One theory which explores this relationship is attachment theory, which we will explore in depth in the next chapter. The effects of the pandemic on a range of many different areas and topics will unfold in the coming years, and psychologists are already trying to capture and understand its effects.

LINK

How might this research support your understanding of protective and risk factors (see Chapter 2)? Identify the possible risk factors mentioned above. Then see if you can place these factors within Bronfenbrenner's bio-ecological model (use the template on page 58).

CHECK YOUR LEARNING GOALS!

You should be able to:

1. Explain what a zygote is.
2. Describe the process of fertilisation.
3. Define a chromosome and a gene, explain how they differ, and say how many pairs of chromosomes humans have.
4. Explain the difference between a genotype and a phenotype.
5. Describe what dominant and recessive genetic inheritance means. Is cystic fibrosis a result of dominant or recessive inheritance?
6. Explain the genetic inheritance pattern of someone who has blond hair.
7. Define the term 'trisomy' and give an example of a trisomic condition.
8. Apply Bronfenbrenner's chronosystem to the lived experiences of people with Down syndrome.
9. Describe the three stages of prenatal development.
10. Name two hazards in prenatal development and outline some of the effects of these hazards on the developing foetus.
11. Define a teratogen, using examples.
12. Explain what thalidomide was and why it affected the limbs of the foetus.
13. Define toxic stress.
14. List some of the ways stress can affect the developing brain.
15. Outline the three stages of labour.
16. Describe the Apgar scale and detail the five aspects it assesses in newborns.
17. Name the eight conditions screened for at birth in Ireland.
18. Name the test used to assess the eight conditions.
19. Describe the difference between a low birthweight baby and a premature baby.
20. Identify four groups of women at risk of health inequalities in pregnancy.
21. Discuss what is meant by social inequality and how it relates to low birthweight.

4

Infancy and the First Two Years of Life

In this chapter we will discover:

- The newborn
  - Reflexes
  - The five senses
  - Maternal bonding theory
  - How to promote infants' development
- Developmental milestones
- Physical development
  - Periods and patterns of growth
  - The infant brain
  - Sensation
- Cognitive development
  - Perception
  - Piaget's sensorimotor stage
  - Imitation
  - Language development
- Socio-emotional development
  - Freud's oral stage
  - Erikson's psychosocial stages
  - Attachment
  - In Focus: The implications of disorganised attachment for psychopathology

We begin this chapter by looking at the newborn and some developmental aspects that are present at birth. Of all the species on the planet, human offspring remain the most dependent for the longest period. Newborns are highly dependent on others for their care; this is not surprising, given that we are born with only 25% of our total adult brain size at birth – I think we can understand there is good reason why our heads at not any bigger at birth! That means that newborns have limited developmental capacity, but, on the flipside, in their first two years of life they achieve remarkable levels of growth and development.

THE NEWBORN

In the first few days, a newborn will lose between 5% and 7% of their total body weight. This is normal and reflects their new adjustment to feeding outside the womb.

The brain is approximately 25% of its eventual size, growing to 75% by the age of two.

One of the most obvious features of the newborn is their primitive reflexes.

REFLEXES

Infants are born with a number of instinctual responses to stimuli, for example touch and bright light. These responses are called **primitive reflexes**. These reflexes develop while the infant is in the womb and are present at birth.

We are born with these reflexes because a newborn has no control over voluntary movements of the body. They gradually diminish as higher-functioning parts of the brain develop, enabling the brain to take control, as motor (movement) development increases. However, we do retain some of these reflexes, including our gag and blink reflex. The reflexes we shall examine here are those that disappear in the first year of life.

Primitive reflexes

Swallowing and sucking reflex	When something is placed in the mouth the baby will automatically suck and swallow. These reflexes, which are common to all mammals, ensure that the baby is primed and ready for feeding. The sucking and swallowing reflexes disappear after approximately four months.
Rooting reflex	If you touch a baby's cheek the baby will turn in the direction of the touch and the mouth purses, searching for the nipple. This behaviour assists feeding.
Walking or stepping reflex 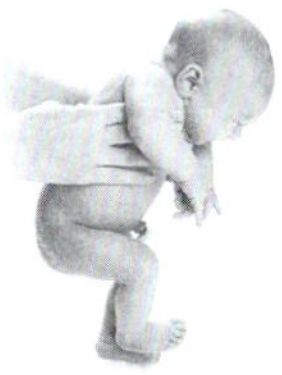	If a baby is held upright with their feet on a firm surface and tilted slightly forward, they will attempt to make stepping movements.
Palmar grasp reflex	The infant closes its fingers tightly when pressure is applied to the palm of the hand either by a finger or an object. When an object is placed in the palm of the baby's hand it will grasp it. This grasp is incredibly strong. This reflex continues for approximately five or six months after birth.
Moro or startle reflex 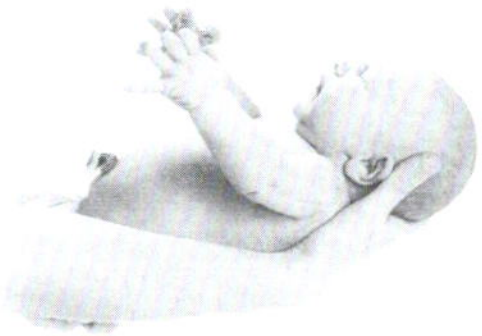	If a baby thinks they're about to fall they will throw their arms out, their palms open, and make a grabbing movement by bringing their arms back into their chest, almost as if they're trying to catch hold of something. (Imagine if you were falling – you would probably throw your arms out and try to grasp something to stop yourself.) This reflex generally disappears at between three and four months of age.

Reflexes are an important indicator of the health of the baby as reflexes are governed by the central nervous system. If a reflex is absent or impaired it indicates that further investigation is warranted.

THE FIVE SENSES

From birth, newborns rely heavily on sensation – their senses – to take in information from the environment around them. Similar to reflexes, in the beginning their senses are not as developed as they will eventually become.

Smell 	Neonates can differentiate odours and recognise their mother's odour at two days (MacFarlane 1975).
Hearing 	DeCasper and Spence (1986) found that infants display a preference for familiar sounds transmitted through the womb in the final months of pregnancy. This finding further contributed to the growing evidence of prenatal learning.
Sight 	Neonates can distinguish their mother from another female at five days old (Bushnell *et al.* 1989).
Touch 	Touch is one of the first senses to develop. During this stage touch helps calm babies resulting in them crying less and helping them sleep better.
Taste 	During their first three months, babies can distinguish between sweet and bitter tastes. They prefer sweet flavours, like the taste of breast milk.

Sensation and perception are linked, as we saw in Chapter 1. Sensation is how we take information in from the world; perception is how we make sense of it. Later in this chapter we will explore these concepts further.

MATERNAL BONDING THEORY

A link between infants' senses and mothers' response, which was conceptualised in the 1970s, is known as maternal bonding theory.

LINK

Look back at the critical versus sensitive periods debate in Chapter 1.

Maternal bonding theory suggests that there is a critical period in the first few hours after birth when bonding must take place.

At the heart of this theory is the argument that the mother needed to engage in bonding with her baby through tactile (touch), visual and olfactory (smell) stimulation. It was suggested that if this bonding is interrupted (if, for example, the baby is removed to intensive care) that it could have long-term negative effects on the mother–child relationship. (Herbert 2006)

Studies have found no evidence that disruption of 'close contact' between mother and child has any impact on their relationship or the women's ability to mother the child.

While this theory was influential in the 1970s thankfully this very stark belief has lost favour but the idea of maternal bonding itself still holds interest.

Think about it

Why do you think this theory was called 'maternal' rather than 'paternal' or even 'parental'?

When we examine ideas in psychology, we must be aware of the era they come from and how values and attitudes have changed.

Are there other theories or ideas you have come across that reflect attitudes and values different from those of today?

This also reminds us of Bronfenbrenner's bio-ecological theory, particularly the chronosystem and exosystem. Both capture the passing of time and value and belief systems respectively.

What can newborns do?

Newborns can:

* Focus on objects less than one metre away
* Show a marked preference for human faces
* Recognise their mother's voice
* Use their senses to explore their new environment (seeing, hearing, smelling, tasting and touching)
* Make eye contact and cry to indicate need
* Often imitate adults, e.g. copying an adult sticking out their tongue.

LINK

Consider again the nature versus nurture debate: has what you have learned about newborns changed your opinion as to whether nature or nurture is more important?

HOW TO PROMOTE INFANTS' DEVELOPMENT

* Provide lots of physical contact and maintain eye contact
* Talk lovingly to babies and give them the opportunity to respond
* Pick babies up and talk face to face with them
* Use bright, contrasting colours in furnishing
* Feed babies on demand; expect no set routine within the first few weeks
* Encourage babies to lie on the floor and kick and experiment safely with movement. (Meggitt 2006, p.11)

Think about it

What kind of environment do you believe represents the best for a baby? Write down your ideas and see if they change or if you find information to support them as you continue to gather knowledge.

This brief introduction to the newborn opens the door for us to consider their journey through infancy to two years old. Many have argued that the first two years of a child's life are especially important in setting the foundation blocks for future development.

LINK

Does this argument remind you of a debate in psychology? Look back to Chapter 1 and the sections on early experience shaping later development.

Think about it

As you are introduced to different concepts and arguments, make a note of any information you feel contributes to the debate that early experiences shape later development.

WHAT IS A DEVELOPMENTAL MILESTONE?

Before we begin to explore how children change across the different areas of development, it's important to highlight that there are milestones we expect *typically* developing children to achieve, and within a certain time frame.

Developmental milestones include physical, language, cognitive and socio-emotional development and behaviour. If these are not present or delayed past the expected range, it is recommended to assess the child to ascertain the causes of the delay.

The table shows some of the milestones we would expect to see between birth and two years old. As you move through the chapter see how the theories and information might link in with these milestones.

Developmental milestones (approximate ages)

AGE IN MONTHS	MOST CHILDREN WILL BE ABLE TO:
12	Begin to develop bowel control
14	Begin to feed themselves messily with a spoon Begin to take clothes off easily
16	Begin to build with blocks
17	Be dry in the day (between now and 3 years)
18	Enjoy scribbling with crayons Say between six and 20 recognisable words singly; can understand more
19	Learn to kick and throw a ball
20	Point to parts of the body Put at least two words together

PHYSICAL DEVELOPMENT

The first two years of life are a time of remarkable development and growth. This is very obvious to see in physical development; within a year, an infant will generally be able to crawl, stand and begin to walk.

Development includes changes in weight, height, muscle growth, length of bones, laying down of fat, and the growth of internal organs such as the heart, lungs, brain and nervous system. In the first year of life, a baby will generally grow 25–30 cm in length and triple their body weight.

From a lifespan perspective it is argued that these years are particularly significant for future functioning in later life.

As we saw in Chapter 1, psychologists use categories as a way of organising and making sense of information. So, as we will see here and in the following chapters, development is broken up into different domains or areas: physical, cognitive (thinking) and socio-emotional. As well as the different 'domains', the lifespan is broken up into distinct periods of time – this will be reflected in the chapters covering different age stages.

PERIODS OF GROWTH

Here we shall look at **periods** of development in a slightly different way and specific to physical development.

* **Synchronous** periods of development: development follows a steady, stable and predictable course. It is seen in childhood from two years until the start of puberty.
* **Asynchronous** periods of development: development is rapid and uneven and varies from individual to individual. It is witnessed in children aged 0–2 years and in adolescence.

So what does this mean? Asynchronous growth can be unpredictable. In teenagers, we see some who start to change physically much quicker than others. Sometimes those who are late developers suddenly 'shoot up' and change very quickly. Not all teenagers physically experience physical changes at the same pace. This is the same with infant and toddlers in the first two years of life.

PATTERNS OF GROWTH

Psychologists have observed patterns of growth common in childhood.

The **cephalocaudal** pattern of growth refers to growth developing from the head down to the toes. At birth a baby's head is disproportionately bigger than the remainder of the body. This is because the baby's head grows rapidly just before birth. After birth the rest of the body catches up.

The **proximodistal** pattern of growth refers to growth from the torso (main body) to the extremities. ('Proximo' relates to proximity and 'distal' refers to distance.)

An example of the **cephalocaudal** pattern can be seen in the motor development of the child. Within the first few months, if laid on their stomach (in the prone position), a baby will attempt to raise themselves up; this reflects the growth and increased strength in shoulders and arms. As growth continues down the body in accordance with the cephalocaudal principle, the baby will begin to crawl as strength and growth in the lower half of the body now develops.

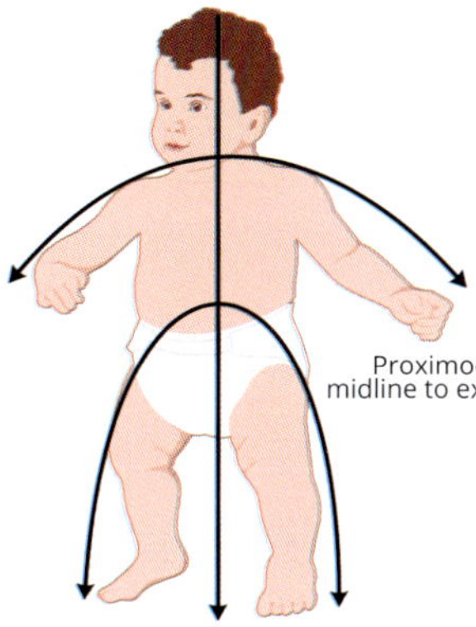

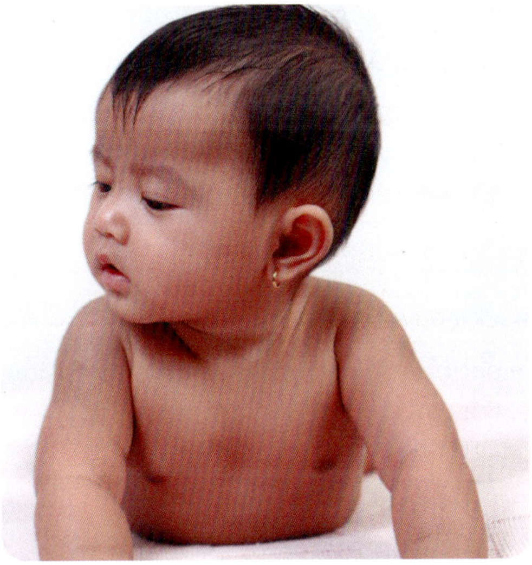

Cephalocaudal pattern

Proximodistal pattern

The **proximodistal** pattern is most easily recognised in infants as they acquire skills involved with grasping and manipulating objects.

Think of a young infant attempting to hold a cup. Initially they will grasp the cup with both hands, locking the palms of their hands around the object. As they develop they will gain more control of their fingers until they are finally able to pick up the cup with their fingers. It's similar to learning to hold a pencil: young children will grasp the pencil in the palm of their hand but as they develop, in line with the proximodistal principle, the continued development in their fingers will enable them to hold the pencil between their fingers and thumb with greater control.

As these patterns of development emerge, we start to observe changes in the child's physical development, including their increasing range of motor (movement) skills.

Motor skills are fundamental movement patterns performed with increasing accuracy, precision and control.

There are two types of motor skills to be aware of:

Gross motor skills involve the use of large muscles to perform a movement task, for example crawling, walking and jumping. In line with the proximodistal principle, large muscles usually develop before smaller or 'fine' motor skills.

AGE (IN MONTHS)	GROSS MOTOR SKILL
1–2	Holds head up and steady
2–3	Holds up head and chest with arms during tummy time Sits with support
3–4	Rolls from tummy to back
6–7	Rolls from back to tummy
6–8	Sits without support
8–9	Pulls towards standing position
9	Crawls
9–10	Walks with support (holding hands)
11–12	Stands without support
12–13	Walks without support

Fine motor skills involve using small muscles to perform a movement task with precision. These include the manipulation of small objects, the pincer grasp (seen in young children when they grasp items between their thumb and forefinger), writing and typing.

AGE (IN MONTHS)	FINE MOTOR SKILL
0	Reflexes such as grasping
1–3	Reaching (ineffective)
3	Grasping
4–5	Reach and grasp
6–7	Control of reach and grasp
9	Pincer grasp
10	Clasps hands
12–14	Releases objects crudely
18	Controlled release

How de we move? Our limbs and muscles need to grow, but it is the **central nervous system** – the brain, the spinal cord and the nervous system – that sends information to and from the brain. A healthy nervous system improves co-ordination of the limbs and movement.

THE INFANT BRAIN

The role of the brain, as we discussed in Chapter 1, is of increasing interest in psychology. Its involvement in every aspect of our development, including sense of self and personality, is recognised more and more.

The brain at birth is 25% of its eventual adult weight. By the child's second birthday the brain will have increased to 75% of its adult weight.

This gives us some insight into the rapid changes that occur in the brain during the first two years of life. In the previous chapter we looked at the reflexes that an infant is born with and how these diminish as the brain develops and takes over from these reflexes. The brain is involved in all aspects of development: motor (movement), sensory, cognitive, social and emotional.

Before we look at the changes experienced in the brain we need to learn a little more about the structures of the brain.

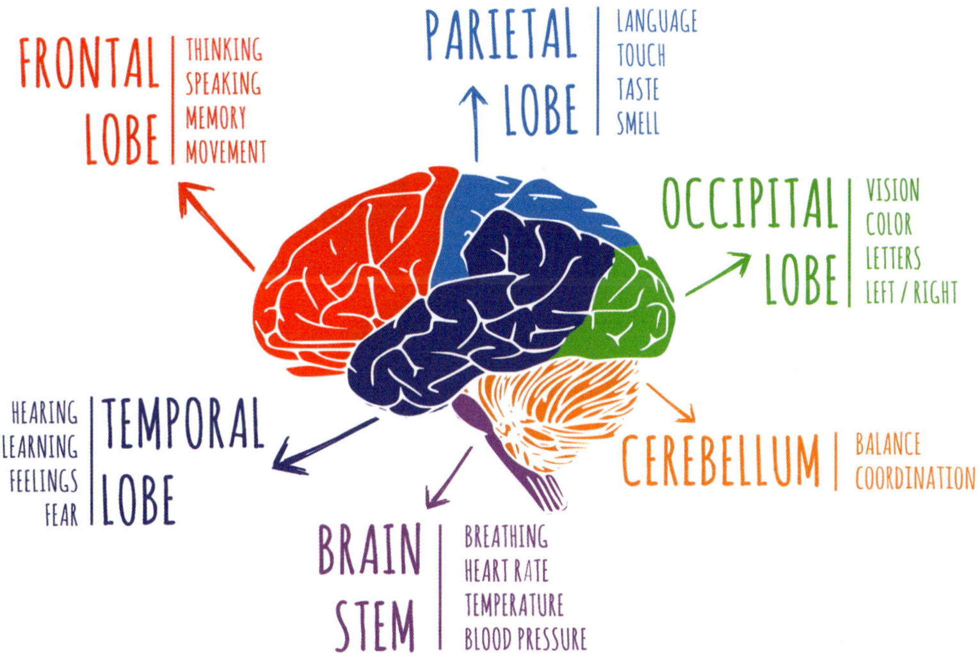

Brain anatomy and function

In addition to the brain stem and cerebellum ('little brain'), you can see the four main **lobes** in the brain. Each has a different function:

NAME	LOCATION	MAIN FUNCTIONS
Frontal lobe	Behind the forehead; the 'front' of the brain	Higher forms of thinking (e.g. reasoning) and voluntary movements. Not fully developed until adolescence
Parietal lobe	Behind the frontal lobe, at the top of the head	Processing information about physical sensations
Occipital lobe	At the back of the brain	Vision
Temporal lobe	At the side of the brain	Hearing

The brain is not one huge mass; rather, it is divided into two halves or **hemispheres**, which are connected by a bundle of nerves called the **corpus callosum** that allows each half to communicate with the other and work in unison.

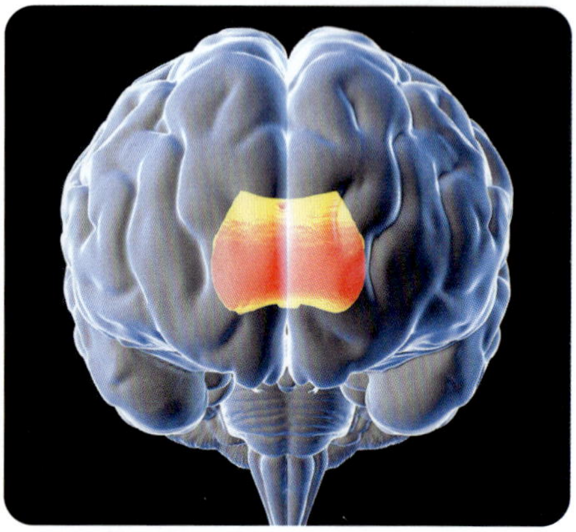

Brain hemispheres with highlighted corpus callosum

Lateralisation refers to the specialisation of function in one or the other hemisphere. For example, while one hemisphere can have a particular function – for example, in most people the left side of the brain is generally responsible for language – this does not mean that the right side has no role at all in that function; it has a role, but not the dominant role. It is generally accepted that lateralisation occurs between the ages of two and twelve.

An infant is born with all the brain cells they need; in fact, they are born with more than they need. As the brain develops it will cut back or 'prune' cells and pathways it does not need or use.

Think about it

Imagine a city that has hundreds of little roads. It comes to the mayor's attention that some of these roads are not very efficient or not being used and that an overhaul is needed. So she orders the removal of inefficient or superfluous roads that aren't contributing to the smooth running of traffic. When this is done the traffic moves more smoothly and quickly and it is easier to get from one point to another. Although there are fewer roads, the roads that are left are the ones that work best and ensure that traffic flows quickly and efficiently.

This is similar to how the brain operates in pruning away underutilised or unnecessary neural pathways and cells – it is ensuring that the brain works more efficiently.

Can you think why some 'roads' might not be used or might prove to be inefficient?

Remember looking at stress and the developing brain – could that be one reason? Certainly, the saying 'use it or lose it' applies to the brain. If a young child is not accessing a stimulating environment where they are engaged with and their potential supported, in some cases, these potential brain pathways that aren't used are 'pruned'.

LINK

What is increasingly apparent is that the interaction of the child with its environment influences the development of the brain. How might you use some of the information in this chapter to argue the nature versus nurture debate?

SENSATION

According to William James (1890), 'the world of the newborn is a buzzing, blooming confusion, where the infant is seized by eyes, ears, nose and entrails all at once.'

Over one hundred years on and a lot of research later we now know that babies are more competent than first imagined and better equipped to make sense of their new world. It is not quite the 'buzzing confusion' first thought of by James. As we saw in Chapter 1, **sensation** consists of the sense organs (vision, hearing, taste, touch and smell). Sensation refers to the awareness of conditions or feelings inside and outside the body.

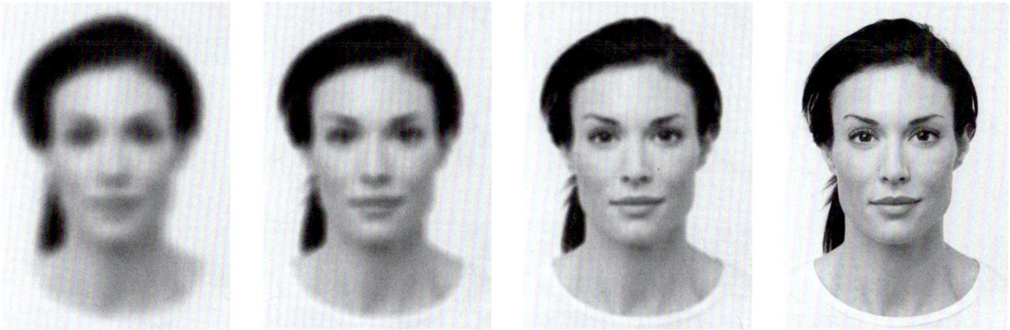

1 month 2 months 3 months 1 year

Baby vision

Changes in the first two years

Vision	In the newborn this is one of the least developed systems, but within a few days they can see objects about a foot away. Infants also display visual preferences (see Fantz's experiment on the next page).
Hearing	According to Aslin (1987) babies show a preference for high-pitched voices more typical of a female voice and will turn their head in the direction of the sound. A baby can distinguish their mother's voice from that of another female (DeCasper & Spence 1986).
Taste	Babies show a preference for sweet-flavoured substances and will grimace if they taste bitter or sour flavours. Explanations offered for this preference refer to the fact that breast milk is sweet, suggesting that the infants are primed to prefer sweetness. Generally, toxic or poisonous substances have a bitter taste, so it is arguable that infants have an innate aversion to these dangerous substances.
Smell	Week-old infants have been shown to indicate an odour preference for the mother's breast milk when presented with pads of milk from other mothers (MacFarlane 1975).
Touch	Newborns respond to touch and to changes in body temperature.

The child's ability to take in information from their environment through the five senses increases significantly as they grow. But taking in the information is just one step. They also have to use 'perception', which means interpreting this information and giving it meaning.

COGNITIVE DEVELOPMENT

PERCEPTION

One of the most famous experiments that demonstrated children's perceptual ability was Eleanor Gibson's **depth perception experiment**.

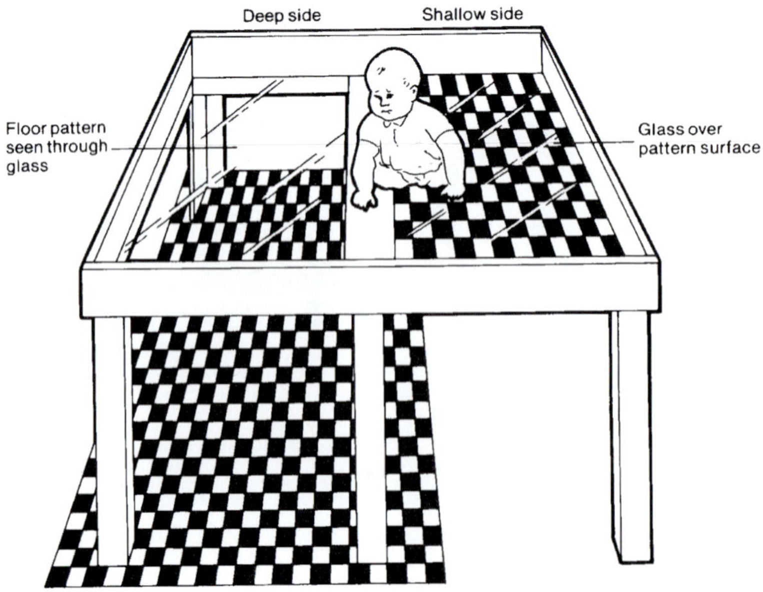

Gibson depth perception experiment

Gibson, an eminent psychologist, spent her long career investigating perceptual development and is well known for her investigation of depth perception using the visual cliff experiment (Gibson & Walk 1960). As you can see from the image, Gibson simulated a cliff or drop using a table with a glass top. Most infants refuse to crawl beyond the apparent cliff edge despite the coaxing of their mothers. This has also been seen in young animals. Gibson took an ecological approach to her theory of perception and saw children as active participants in their environment. She also believed that the human species has evolved adaptive ways in how we perceive our environment.

Gibson coined the word 'affordances' to describe the opportunities an environment holds for learning and adaptation. An example of this would be a hill which a baby has to try to climb and negotiate. The hill (or environment) offers an opportunity or 'affordance' for the baby to learn something new. Gibson was interested in how infants, in such an information-laden world, decide what pieces of information to ignore and which to take on board. Children have been described as the 'hunters and gatherers' of the information world. Gibson argued that when children interact with their environment it enables them to adapt to it. She focused on the question: How do we learn to perceive our environment? Her response was that children become increasingly selective as they develop and learn to detect information that identifies events and objects that they can use for their daily activities.

Another experiment which shows us how children take in information and make sense of it is **Robert Fantz's face perception experiment**.

Fantz's face perception experiment

Fantz (1961) devised an experiment to test whether infants show a preference for human faces. He showed infants ranging in age from four days old to five months sets of faces: a discernible face, a scrambled-up face and a blank face. Fantz used a technique called 'preferential looking', which involved measuring the length of gaze of the infant to determine which image was of most interest or was most familiar to them. He found a definite preference for the 'realistic' face. Fantz's research suggests that the ability to recognise faces is either innate or learned very quickly after birth. Thus not only does Frantz's research shed light on infants' face perception, it also adds to the debate of whether perception is innate or learned.

LINK

Consider Fantz's and Gibson's findings: do infants have some innate abilities such as not crawling off a cliff or the ability to perceive a human face, or do they learn these after birth?

In Chapters 1 and 2 we discussed what is meant by cognitive development and theories related to it. Here we are going to look at theories of cognitive development at specific age periods or stages.

PIAGET'S SENSORIMOTOR STAGE (0–2 YEARS)

Features of this stage include:

* Object permanence
* Causality
* Representational ability
* Imitation.

We saw in Chapter 2 that the sensorimotor stage is the first stage of Piaget's cognitive theory. The name of this stage gives us a clue as to how learning is accumulated during this period. In this stage we witness the use of the senses and movement by the infant to learn about their world and to construct knowledge of it.

As they develop, infants realise that they can make things happen; they bang spoons and throw objects from their highchair. This also highlights that the infant sees themselves as separate from their environment and that they are developing a sense of agency over their actions; in other words, they realise that they are the agent or initiator of their actions. Another aspect to this is **causality**, when the child begins to recognise causal relationships; for example, if I shake this rattle it will make a noise.

Another interesting aspect of this stage, which reflects causality in a different way, is **animism**. This is when the child attributes consciousness to an inanimate object, for example a favourite teddy or doll which they name and treat as if it has consciousness. Another feature that is vital to the child's increasing cognitive abilities is **object permanence**. Its acquisition towards the end of this stage is considered an important milestone in cognitive development (see page 43).

Object permanence is the understanding that objects continue to exist even when we can no longer see them.

A simple test for object permanence is to show a child a toy and then place the toy under a blanket. If the child seeks the toy out it is an indication that they understand that the toy continues to exist even when they can no longer see it.

Related to object permanence is **representational ability**. This involves the ability to make a 'mental representation' of an object; that is, to be able to represent it mentally or within your mind. This enables the child to manipulate the object, which can lead to the further acquisition of problem-solving skills. A good way to understand 'representational ability' or 'mental representation' is to imagine you're driving to college/work and you get stuck in a traffic jam. If you know the area you can mentally map it out and start working out a new way to get to your destination. You map out your new route in your mind before you commit to it. The ability to map the area in your mind is representational ability. Piaget believed it develops between the ages of 18 and 24 months.

Piaget suggested that **imitation** is achieved at roughly nine months of age and that deferred imitation occurs after the acquisition of mental representation.

Imitation is the reproduction of an expression or behaviour.

Meltzoff and Moore (1977) found that within a few weeks of life babies could imitate or reproduce a facial expression made by an adult, such as sticking out their tongue. Some have argued that this is merely a reflex, but Meltzoff and Moore believed it reflects a biologically based capacity to imitate. Meltzoff (1988) also found evidence of what he believed to be a nine-month-old's capacity for deferred imitation. This means that the infant reproduces a gesture after a certain amount of time has elapsed, for example the following day.

Think about it

From either personal or professional experience, recollect children's behaviour where they have imitated another person. Can young children's use of imitation have potentially less desirable outcomes; for example, copying a parent's smoking. Could this be a possible factor in the development of adverse behaviours? Can a child 'imitate' from wider circles of influence: siblings, peers, community and the media?

How can the concept of imitation be used and applied to interventions or supports that promote positive outcomes in children?

CHALLENGING PIAGET'S IDEAS

Piaget did not believe that children acquire object permanence until the end of the second year. In order to have object permanence the child must be able to make a mental representation of the object; that is, they must be able to represent it mentally in order to know that the object continues to exist even though they can no longer see it. Yet in order to imitate a facial expression, these very young infants must already possess these abilities to some degree. Not only does Meltzoff and Moore's research demonstrate that imitation is acquired earlier than Piaget proposed, their research would suggest that infants acquire concepts such as object permanence and mental representation earlier than proposed by Piaget.

CHECK YOUR LEARNING

Write a summary explaining why Meltzoff and Moore's research is important in challenging Piaget's ideas. How does their research support criticisms of Piaget's theory?

LANGUAGE DEVELOPMENT

LINK

Look back to Chapter 2, where we discussed Vygotsky's theory that language is learned through our interactions with others. Do you think he is right? Or do you agree with Piaget that it is more biologically based and that language emerges as our brain and cognitive abilities develop?

Language and speech development

AGE	LANGUAGE AND SPEECH
3 months	Coos and laughs Responds to sounds Plays with speech sounds
6 months	Will make babbling sounds Attempts to match what they hear
9 months	Begins to understand words, e.g. 'no' and baby's name
12 months	Says first words Understands function of naming things
18 months	Says first sentence consisting of two words Refers to themselves by name Echoes the last part of what others say (echolalia)
24 months	Exhibits an expanding vocabulary No longer babbles, wants to talk

Language helps us convey ideas and express our needs to those around us. During the first two years the building blocks of our relationships are formed, and how we come to know ourselves is often through others.

SOCIO-EMOTIONAL DEVELOPMENT

We begin this section by revisiting Freud and Erikson and exploring in depth the relationship of the brain to attachment theory. The debate around early experiences and later development can be seen when we look at the long-term effects of a disorganised (type D) attachment pattern. Finally we will examine the emergence of a sense of self and how our temperament is with us from birth.

FREUD'S ORAL STAGE (0–2 YEARS)

The mouth is the primary source of pleasure and Freud believed that feeding and more particularly the weaning period should be handled with care. He advised against weaning a baby too early or indulging the infant and weaning too late; either could result in the infant becoming 'fixated' at the oral stage. This would have negative consequences in later life that might include swearing, smoking, biting one's nails and overeating. All these behaviours are related to the area of the mouth. Freud advised that through oral satisfaction, the baby develops trust and an optimistic personality. If the child experiences oral dissatisfaction the personality may become pessimistic, aggressive and distrusting.

ERIKSON'S PSYCHOSOCIAL STAGES

Erikson's lifespan stage theory includes two stages in the first two years of life.

STAGE	AGE	CHARACTERISTICS	APPLICATION
Trust vs. Mistrust	0–1 year	In the first year of life the infant is completely dependent on its caregivers. How well the infant's needs are met and how sensitive the parenting is determines whether the infant develops trust or mistrust of the world.	Hold babies close and have warm physical contact with them when they are being fed. Also responding to them immediately when they are distressed or crying can promote a sense of trust. (Gahart Mooney 2000, p.41)
Autonomy vs. Shame and Doubt	1–2 years	Children begin to walk and assert their independence. As the term 'autonomy' suggests, children can come to believe in themselves and their abilities through the encouragement and support of their caregivers. If the child's efforts are ridiculed, the child will develop feelings of shame and doubt. Toilet training is seen as one of the key events which can influence the outcome of this stage.	To support the child's drive for autonomy, give children simple choices to reduce the likelihood of the child feeling confused. Setting clear boundaries and limits will aid the child to develop inner control. (Gahart Mooney 2000, p.47)

Think about it

Do you think Erikson's first stage of 'Trust vs. Mistrust' is reminiscent of John Bowlby's concepts relating to attachment, particularly the importance of a critical stage where bonding and trust is built?

Both Erikson and John Bowlby were originally followers of Freud's ideas that early experiences are taken into the unconscious and also how important early experiences are.

ATTACHMENT

In Chapter 2 we examined one of the most important theories in psychology – attachment theory. Here we examine how attachment evolves in the first two years and how a failure to achieve successful attachment can lead to difficulties later in life.

LINK

What debate in psychology does attachment theory reflect? Revisit the early experiences/later development debate in Chapter 1.

Attachment simply refers to the long-enduring and meaningful tie we have to another.

Attachment develops over the first two years of life, following a pattern of stages.

Stages of Attachment

Pre-attachment: Birth to 6 weeks
Baby shows no particular attachment to specific caregiver

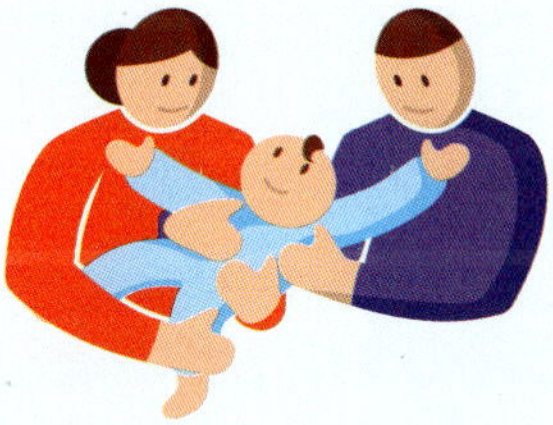

Indiscriminate: 6 weeks to 7 months
Infant begins to show preference for primary and secondary caregivers

Discriminate: 7+ months
Infant shows strong attachment to one specific caregiver

Multiple: 10+ months
Infant shows growing bonds with other caregivers

How would we observe attachment behaviours? Herbert (2006, p.69) suggests we should observe whether the parent does the following:

* Initiates positive interactions with the infant
* Responds to the infant's vocalisations
* Changes voice tone when talking to the infant
* Shows interest in face-to-face contact with the infant
* Shows the ability to console or comfort the infant
* Enjoys close physical contact with the infant
* Responds to the infant's indications of distress
* Responds promptly to the infant's needs
* Responds consistently
* Interacts smoothly and sensitively with the infant.

Think about it

Conduct your own research into parenting practices in different cultures.

Are some practices more likely to be assessed as atypical from an attachment theory perspective?

From your own experiences, consider the development of relationships within different cultural and ethnic groups. How are they similar? How do they differ? How would you respond to parenting approaches other than the one you are used to? Write down your observations as a reflection piece, remembering that the attitudes we hold can affect our interactions with others.

BEHAVIOURS THAT PROMOTE ATTACHMENT

Bowlby believed 'parental sensitivity' is important for the development of attachment. Ainsworth *et al.* (1978, p.152) found that four scales are strongly linked to secure attachment:

* Sensitivity
* Acceptance
* Co-operation
* Accessibility.

Interestingly, De Wolff and van Ijzendoorn (1997) found that 'playing' is an important factor in promoting attachment.

Just as certain behaviours can promote attachment, others can damage it or are more likely to elicit an insecure attachment pattern. Radke-Yarrow *et al.* (1985) examined patterns of attachment in two- and three-year-old children of depressed and 'normal' mothers. They found that the children of mothers with major depression are more likely to have an insecure attachment pattern (types A and C).

Having supportive interactions and consistent caregiving are recognised as important for the development of secure attachment. Our first relationships are so important, creating a template (internal working model) from which we make sense of future relationships.

These 'schemas' or templates have a cognitive aspect; they involve our thinking capacities as we make sense of these experience and store them in our memory (conscious and unconscious). We have seen the role of the brain too in the developing child. Increasingly research is uncovering the relationship between the brain and attachment.

THE BRAIN AND ATTACHMENT

Bruce Perry (2008, p.85), a leading expert on toxic stress (see Chapter 1), describes how these 'templates' develop through parenting and brain development:

> *If you are one of the majority of infants born to a loving home, a consistent, nurturing caregiver – say a mother or father – will be present and repeatedly meet your needs. Time and again, one or both parents will come when you cry and soothe you when you are hungry, cold or scared. As your brain develops these loving caregivers provide the template that you use for human relationships. Attachment, then, is a memory template for human-to-human bonds. This template serves as your primary 'world view' on human relationships. It is profoundly influenced by whether you experience kind, attuned parenting or whether you receive inconsistent, frequently disrupted, abusive or neglected 'care'.*

According to Shaver (2010, p.167), there is no one brain system solely responsible for the 'attachment behavioural system'. Rather, 'brain circuitry used for a range of purposes, such as social perception and memory, emotion, and emotion regulation, underlies attachment-related emotions and behavior as well.' So several different parts and functions of the brain are involved in attachment.

Shaver says that evolution has shaped the human brain to reflect our reliance on relationships with others. Therefore, our brain's default setting is to depend on 'social regulation'. When an individual is forced to survive without this social co-regulation, the brain develops and functions in a less than optimal way. What does that mean?

LINK

Does what you have learned support the argument that early experiences affect a person's later development? Write down your observations using what you have read to support your views on this key debate. See if this next piece strengthens your opinion.

We need the interaction and positive support of others to reach our optimum potential in terms of attachment and related behaviours. When we don't receive such interaction and support (secure attachment) we are negatively affected in terms of our developmental outcomes and in our behaviour.

Research focusing on the effects of attachment disruption and of insecure attachment suggest that this early relationship impacts on our later development.

What might that look like? Let's take a look at the possible relationship between attachment pattern Type D and mental health challenges in later life.

IN FOCUS: THE IMPLICATIONS OF DISORGANISED ATTACHMENT FOR PSYCHOPATHOLOGY

While a secure attachment pattern (Type B) is associated with healthy parenting and positive outcomes for the child, research has considered the long-term impact of insecure attachment and found that a disorganised attachment pattern is highly predictive of difficulties later in life. (As we've seen, the category of **disorganised attachment** was added for children who didn't fit into Ainsworth's original three classifications.) According to Music:

> *These were children who had been subjected to unpredictable and traumatising parenting, and had failed to develop a coherent and consistent strategy to deal with these frightening experiences ... The parent, who should provide solace or comfort when [the child is] distressed, was for these children often the person causing the distress, such as by being violent, and so these children could not find a way of getting their attachment needs met ... Not all insecurely attached children have a bad prognosis, but disorganised attachment, that most worrying kind, is a good predictor of psychopathology at 17 years old. (Music 2011, p.62)*

Think about it

What kind of parenting behaviours do you think might have a negative impact on the development of a healthy, secure attachment pattern? Compare some of your ideas with the theories and research on parenting (see Chapter 6).

What does disorganised attachment look like in a child? The disorganised child is likely to:

- Suffer from high stress levels
- Be hyperalert
- Display hostile behaviours

- Have difficulties coping
- Be hyperactive
- Experience difficulties in school
- Have a deficit in cognitive capacities.

These difficulties may continue into adulthood, where they may display:

- Controlling behaviours
- Difficulties maintaining and/or managing relationships
- Continued challenges regulating their emotions.

Smith *et al.* (2003, p.105) observe that many fail at school, and advance along worrying trajectories, such as into the criminal justice system, psychiatric or other services. 'Given the prior links to parental maltreatment and abuse, it may be that the disorganised attachment pattern will be found to be the most relevant aspect of attachment in understanding severely maladaptive or antisocial behaviour in later life.'

LINK

We looked at factors in Chapter 1. Disorganised attachment often occurs alongside other risk factors, such as poverty, single parenthood, violence, drug and alcohol use, and poor neighbourhoods.

Think about it

Why, do you think, might the other factors identified above be more likely to be seen in families where there is disorganised attachment present? How might the concept of 'double jeopardy' (see page 14) apply here?

THE DEVELOPMENT OF 'SELF'

Our sense of self is very much informed by the people close to us, and our experiences in our emerging years shape us. However, all children seem to follow similar processes in the development of self:

- At 18 months old children learn to recognise themselves.
- At two years old children begin to express their emotional states. Then they must make the distinction between self and other.

The mirror test for self-awareness

Psychologists devised a test to see when children first show signs of self-awareness. As adults, we take it for granted that we've always being self-aware and able to recognise ourselves. But that's not the case; as with all other areas of our development, self-awareness emerges and grows.

In this experiment, devised in the 1970s, a dot of red lipstick was placed on the nose of the baby, who was then placed in front of a mirror. The psychologists then observed how the children responded:

6–12 months	They appeared to view their reflection as being another baby. They smiled and approached this baby in a friendly and inquisitive manner.
12–20 months	These babies appeared more hesitant when they were placed in front of the mirror. Researchers were not clear if this hesitancy was nervousness about seeing 'another baby' or if they did in fact recognise themselves but were unsure.
20–24 months	These toddlers clearly recognised themselves. They would touch the dot of lipstick on their own nose rather than touching the mirror.

The table below charts this growing awareness of self and the ways we can support it.

Awareness of self

AGE	BEHAVIOURS	STRATEGIES TO SUPPORT THE CHILD
0–9 months	▪ Demonstrates interest in faces and voices of others ▪ Explores their hands and feet ▪ Recognises own name	▪ Use the child's name during interactions ▪ Provide mirrors for the child to look at self ▪ Read books together ▪ Acknowledge the child's efforts to initiate and engage
6–18 months	▪ Engages in joint attention with those close to them ▪ Responds with vocalisations or gestures when name is said ▪ Demonstrates interest in looking in mirror ▪ Uses gestures and some words to express feelings, e.g. 'no' ▪ Points to and identifies body parts on themselves	▪ Use names when referring to important people in the child's life ▪ Use 'attunement' to match the feelings of the child, e.g. use facial expressions and body language to express the same emotions the child is vocalising ▪ Allow child to express wants and desires ▪ Provide choices in order to allow the child some control
16–24 months	▪ Able to express their name ▪ Refers to self with gestures and language ▪ Demonstrates understanding and use of concepts through words such as 'mine', 'me' and 'you' ▪ Points to self in images	▪ Provide words to the emotion the child is expressing ▪ Acknowledge the child's feelings ▪ Engage often in conversations with the child ▪ Provide opportunities for the child to talk about themselves

TEMPERAMENT

Temperament is a biologically based propensity for individuals to react emotionally and behaviourally to events in a certain way.

What kind of temperament did you have as a baby? Were you a happy or easy-going baby or did you frequently throw tantrums?

Temperament is believed to contribute towards the development of personality. What do we mean by this? 'Temperament' is generally understood to be present from birth and have a genetic or inherited aspect. Personality, on the other hand, evolves over time and is more influenced by the external environment.

Thomas and Chess (1977, 1986) asked parents to fill out reports of their babies' behaviour and devised a classification of three types of temperament:

* **Easy babies** (40% of sample): These babies were reported to have regular feeding and sleeping patterns and were not fussy eaters. They were playful and reacted well to new situations.
* **Difficult babies** (10% of sample): These babies had fussy eating habits, and irregular sleeping and eating patterns. They were irritable, threw tantrums when frustrated and cried more.
* **Slow-to-warm-up babies** (15% of sample): These babies had mildly negative reactions to new situations. Unlike the difficult babies, whose tantrums might include spitting out food, these babies showed more of a passive resistance, for example they would let the food drool out rather than spit it out.

Think about it

Can you see any difficulties with this study? Before reading on, make a note of what you think might be the issue with this research.

The issue is that it's based solely on parental reports of the infant's behaviour and as such might lack objectivity. As you come across different experiments and research, try to approach them with a critical eye and see if you can recognise any potential issues with the research design. Designing and conducting research is an important part of psychology; so, too, is being able to look at it with a critical eye.

Yet the idea of infant temperament is an important one and researchers have continued to develop ways of measuring it. Newer approaches include observing the infant directly and asking not just the parents but other adults to rate the child's behaviour.

With regard to infancy, theorists have tended to focus on whether an infant's temperament impacts on parent–child interactions. Another area of interest is whether temperament is stable across a person's lifespan and if childhood temperament predicts adult outcomes.

Temperament has been found to be not that stable in infancy, meaning it can change as the child grows older (Buss & Plomin 1984). Yet others have found stability in some aspects of temperament.

Shyness is part of a more general temperament style called **behavioural inhibition.** Researchers examined infants with inhibited behaviours (infants who were quiet, shy and would withdraw from unfamiliar people and objects) and uninhibited behaviours (more sociable, spontaneous and open to new experiences). They found that extremely inhibited or uninhibited temperament was predictive of childhood shyness or sociability. For example, a highly uninhibited infant became a sociable and talkative seven-year-old, while an extremely inhibited infant developed into a shy and quiet child (Kagan *et al.* 1988). Kagan's work suggests that there is some evidence of long-term stability in certain aspects of temperament.

This is just an introduction to the remarkable world of infants as they move through the toddler phase. Can you see how much change is occurring and how many factors are involved, from the child's immediate environment to more distant factors? This period also offers a window into further understanding some of the key debates in psychology we first met in Chapter 1. Hopefully your opinions on these are growing and deepening as you encounter new information.

CHECK YOUR LEARNING GOALS!

You should be able to:

1. List and explain three reflexes present at birth.
2. Explain two senses, using examples to illustrate a newborn's capacity.
3. Describe how we can promote development in newborn babies.
4. Define an 'asynchronous' period.
5. Explain the cephalocaudal and proximodistal patterns of development.
6. Explain the size of the brain at birth in relation to its final size.
7. Describe, in your own words, Gibson's perception experiment.
8. Recall the face preference that infants in Fantz's experiment showed and suggest what this preference implies.
9. Explain the sensorimotor stage of cognitive development and name the theorist who proposed it.
10. Describe object permanence and explain why it is important.
11. Describe imitation.
12. Explain how Meltzoff and Moore's research offers a criticism of Piaget's work.
13. Describe the first stage of Freud's psychosexual theory.
14. List the behaviours we might see if an individual is 'fixated' at the oral stage.
15. Name the first two stages of Erikson's psychosocial theory, with the age ranges.
16. Define 'autonomy'.
17. Define 'attachment'.
18. Explain what is meant by the concept of the 'internal working model'.
19. Explain the relationship between the brain and attachment.
20. Name the attachment pattern associated with the most negative outcomes in later life.
21. Describe the mirror test experiment and say at what age a child can recognise themselves.
22. Define temperament and explain how it is different from personality.
23. Outline the three types of temperament identified by Thomas and Chess.

5

Early Childhood (2–5 Years)

In this chapter we will discover:

* Physical development
  - Physical changes
  - The brain
  - Motor skills
* Cognitive development
  - Piaget's preoperational stage
  - Language development: Is it uniquely human?
  - Theory of mind
  - In Focus: Autism
* Socio-emotional development
  - Freud's psychosexual theory
  - Erikson's initiative vs. guilt
  - Socialisation
  - Development of gender and sex role differences
  - Play
  - In Focus: Parent–child play and its implications

As we have seen, the early years are a time of particular importance for children's development. As you read this chapter you will see how the information supports (or not) some of the key debates in psychology such as early experiences and later development.

Think about it

Continue to make notes on this chapter to chart how your opinion is changing as you encounter more information.

In this chapter we shall look at the developmental milestones we would expect to see in a typically developing child from the age of two years to five years.

Think about it

Consider how these milestones tie in with the information in this chapter. For example, in the piece on autism, identify which developmental milestones are affected.

PHYSICAL DEVELOPMENT

PHYSICAL CHANGES

The child has now moved to a period of **synchronous growth** which begins at two years and ends at puberty. This period, in comparison to the period from birth to two years, is characterised by a slow, steady pattern of development. During this period the child is still growing in height and weight.

- Height gain: 6.5 cm (2.5 inches) per year
- Weight gain: 2.25–3 kg (5–7 lb) per year

It's important to remember **individual variation**. Children develop at different rates: for example, some children start walking early, before 12 months; others a little later at 16 months.

Think about it

When observing (and assessing) children's developmental milestones we must allow for individual variation. That's why we allow for a range of ages we expect to see typically developing children achieve developmental milestones. If a child falls outside this typical range, then we might consider assessing the child for developmental delays.

During this period, children benefit from opportunities to move and be active to help them develop their physical capacities such as motor skills and balance. We can see the importance of movement and being active in policies and interventions that encourage physical activity. The *Physical Activity Strategy for the WHO European Region 2016–2025* from the World Health Organization (WHO) has designated improving children's level of physical movement as a priority.

Think about it

Why, do you think, the WHO physical activity strategy is focused on Europe and not other parts of the world?

Do you think access to television, the internet, games and social media has had an impact on children's physical and motor development? Increasingly, research suggests younger and younger children are becoming less active.

Can you think of ways you might try to reverse this or suggestions to encourage children and families to be more active?

In the next chapter we will examine the growing rates of obesity in children.

Other physical changes are witnessed in this period and sex differences start to become more apparent.

Sex differences

* Girls are generally lighter, smaller and have more fatty tissue.
* Boys have more muscle tissue.
* Growth between 2–6 years is less rapid with gains of approximately 5–8 cm a year in height and about 2.5 kg in weight annually.

THE BRAIN

We saw that in the first two years of life the brain grows from 25% to 75% of its full size. During this period the brain continues to grow but at a more steady rate. Some changes include the following:

* The number and size of nerve endings increase
* The process of myelinisation continues, with a resulting increase in the speed of information transmission between cells
* There is rapid growth in the frontal lobes.

MOTOR SKILLS

As the physical body develops and the brain continues to increase in size and complexity, we see the effect in children's improving gross and fine motor skills.

Key Forms of Play in Early Childhood

Exploratory play	Using physical skills and sensations to learn about materials and their properties, what they feel like and what can be done with them.
Constructive play	The manipulation of objects and materials to build or create something using natural or manufactured materials such as blocks, playdough, junk and collage materials, sand and water. Involves creating, recognising and solving problems.
Creative play	Using open-ended materials such as art materials and natural materials in ways that encourage fluency, flexibility originality, imagination, embellishment and making novel connections.
Pretend, fantasy and socio-dramatic play	Includes: role play, pretending with objects, pretend actions and situations, persistence with the imaginary play frame to create a play episode or event. When it involves interaction and verbal communication with one or more play partners regarding the play event it is termed socio-dramatic play (Monighan Nourot 2006).
Physical locomotor play	Activities that include all kinds of physical movement for their own sake and enjoyment. In this type of play a range of fine or gross motor skills are practiced and mastered.
Language or word play	Unrehearsed and spontaneous manipulation of sounds and words, often with rhythmic and repetitive elements. As children get older, this type of play often incorporates rhyme, word play and humour.

Source: Kernan (2007: 35)

GROSS MOTOR DEVELOPMENT		FINE MOTOR DEVELOPMENT	
Age	**Skills**	**Age**	**Skills**
2–3 years	Stand on one foot Walk up steps with alternating feet Kick a large ball Hop two to three times	2–3 years	Pick up blocks Turn pages of a book Hold cup in one hand
4 years	Throw a ball overarm Run with ease Pedal a bike with stabilisers Skip and hop	4–5 years	Hold a pencil with pincer grip Copy a square accurately Colour within the lines
5 years	Walk in a straight line Walk down steps with alternating feet Catch a bounced ball		

COGNITIVE DEVELOPMENT

The changes in the brain also have an impact on cognition. Children's capacities for thinking and reasoning continue to emerge and grow in sophistication. Let's start with a recap of the two main theorists in cognitive development.

PIAGET'S PREOPERATIONAL STAGE (2–7 YEARS)

One of the most notable features of this stage is that the child is **egocentric**. They think that everyone else sees the world through their eyes. They do not understand that other people might see or think about things differently and this is reflected in their thinking.

The **Three Mountains task** was devised to assess egocentricity in the child and progression on from that stage. As you can see in the image, the child is being tested to see if they can take the perspective of another person (the doll) into account. The child is asked to describe what the doll is seeing (the doll's perspective). Children who are egocentric will describe their own view (perspective) as they are unable to recognise that the other (the doll) has a different angle and viewpoint.

Three Mountains task

As we have seen, language is linked to cognitive ability. Piaget said this relationship can be seen in **symbolic thinking**. As the child begins to acquire language (made up of symbols) they can use this newly developed ability to enhance their thinking.

The child can now use words and images (symbols) to represent objects. For example, when a toddler sees a dog they might exclaim 'woof woof'. Here the child is using that noise to represent a dog.

What we can see from the Three Mountains task is that children think differently from adults and their thinking changes as they grow. According to Daniel *et al.* (2010, p.180), 'if children's thought processes seem bizarre or unusual it may be helpful to try and see the world from their own viewpoint and work out what their logic is.' Daniel suggests making things more 'concrete' or real for them, using dolls or drawings.

In relation to reasoning and planning, children under the age of seven work directly from what they have actually experienced and through their senses. They remain tied to 'concrete experiences' at this stage.

CASE STUDY

Liam is five years old and has to go into hospital for an operation. You have been asked to discuss this upcoming event with Liam, who is worried and scared about it.

Keeping in mind what you have learned from Piaget's theory, how would you approach this? What would you need to bear in mind about Liam's ability to understand?

Perhaps consider that if Liam has had no direct experience of hospital, it is hard for him to make sense of it; the same goes for an operation. Liam might be relating an action on his part (being bold) to a belief about why people go to hospital or have operations (as a punishment).

In supporting Liam, you need to make the ideas as 'real' as possible; if you can't take him to the hospital beforehand to have a look around, then a book with pictures would be helpful. Use play for Liam to work through this new experience or help him to create a storybook around this topic. Ask Liam about his beliefs about hospital and operations and why he is having one, to gauge his thinking and see the world from his perspective.

Vygotsky, another cognitive theorist, also emphasised the importance of play. According to Vygotsky, play allows for language to be used in the interaction between peers, through negotiation of rules for games and discussions around role-playing. Vygotsky emphasised that language and development build on each other.

Think about it

Can you think of games you played when you were young that involved the use of language? Write them down.

Now try to think how you would have played these games without using language. How would you have interacted and communicated with your friends or about the rules of the game? Children's growing language skills enable more than just interacting with friends. They enable information to be communicated, for rules to be developed and problems solved. Think of how the games you played became more sophisticated as you got older and your language abilities improved.

We shall look more closely at play later in the chapter.

LANGUAGE DEVELOPMENT: IS IT UNIQUELY HUMAN?

The acquisition of language is undoubtedly one of humans' greatest cognitive feats. Noam Chomsky and others such as Philip Lieberman have argued that humans possess an inherited biological readiness to recognise and produce the structure and sounds of whatever language they are exposed to, unlike any other species, including non-human primates.

Yet research in the field of primates and language acquisition continues to grow and provide interesting results that fuel the debate as to whether animals really can acquire language.

Research involving Washoe, a chimpanzee who was 'cross-fostered', meaning he was raised in a home and treated like a human child, were at the forefront of this debate. In 1966 Allen and Beatrice Gardner taught American sign language to the ten-month-old chimp. By the age of five Washoe had acquired 160 signs and was also able to combine signs. The Gardners replicated their research with four other chimpanzees with the same result. It was also noted that the chimps had started to sign to one another.

In light of this development Herbert Terrace also attempted to teach a chimpanzee sign language in the hope of facilitating communication between apes and humans in the future. He found the results disappointing and concluded that the chimp, named Nim Chimpsky, was not displaying language and was unable even to create a sentence. Terrace concluded that all that had been witnessed was the **imitation** of language. He did not believe that the primates were able to generate real language.

Think about it

We have seen how the concept of imitation is used to explain how we learn. How do you think we develop our language abilities: through imitation, or is it more biologically based, developing as we evolved as a species, and as a baby's brain develops?

What might this research involving the chimps suggest about language in humans and whether it is nature or nurture that is more influential?

We've seen arguments as to how important language is in facilitating communication with one another. Another aspect of this is the ability to understand that others 'think' differently from us. This is called 'theory of mind'.

THEORY OF MIND

Theory of mind is the understanding that others see and understand things differently from you.

The term 'theory of mind' refers to the ability to understand what another person might be thinking. This ability is vital in the arena of social relationships, it enables us to predict others' reactions and give us insight into their behaviours and actions. Piaget suggested that children do not develop this ability until the age of six or seven; however, research has demonstrated that children typically acquire theory of mind earlier than that.

The **Sally–Anne test** can be used to assess if theory of mind is present.

Imagine a young child is watching a puppet show with two dolls, Sally and Anne. Sally decides to go for a walk but before she leaves she places her marble in her basket. After Sally leaves Anne removes the marble from the basket and places it in her box.

Think about it

When Sally returns, where will she look for her marble?

What did you say? More than likely you surmised that Sally will look in the basket – where she left it.

Write down why you gave this answer: this is your own explanation of theory of mind.

If the child replies that Sally will look for the marble in Anne's box (where Anne put it), the child doesn't yet possess theory of mind. After all, how can Sally know the marble was moved there? That knowledge is known only to the child who witnessed it. To demonstrate theory of mind, the child has to be able to appreciate that Sally has her own beliefs about the world, which may be different from the child's own.

Theory of mind is important in the social sphere of our lives, where the ability to understand other people's state of mind is essential.

A deficit in theory of mind has been implicated in autism.

IN FOCUS: AUTISM

Autism is a developmental condition that becomes apparent by the age of two. Its characteristics can include communicative and social deficits. Autism spectrum disorders (ASDs) are part of the spectrum of pervasive development disorders.

Autism is a qualitative impairment in reciprocal social interaction, in verbal and non-verbal communication and in imaginative activity. Individuals with autism can have mild to severe symptoms.

Autism was first described by Hans Asperger and Leo Kanner, independently of one another, in the 1940s. They used the term 'autistic' to reflect one of the main characteristics often witnessed in autism – a withdrawal from others. (*Autos* denotes 'self' in Greek.) Frith (1989, p.7) comments that 'this narrowing could be described as a withdrawal from the fabric of social life into the self'.

Rates of ASDs have increased In the last twenty years. Recent information from the Centers for Disease Control and Prevention (CDC) in the USA (April 2018) reported the prevalence of ASDs in America 'as 1.68% in the surveillance year 2014 but ASDs have been reported to be as high as 2.6% in South Korea and as low as 0.39% in China' (DoH 2018, p.4).

Think about it

What factors do you think might account for the differences in rates across countries? What factors might cause a higher rate of ASDs in one country and a lower rate in another?

Could it be cultural? There can be stigma attached to disabilities in some countries so perhaps parents are less willing to have their child assessed. This would be a sociocultural factor.

Another answer might lie in how ASDs are measured and assessed. In the West, the *Diagnostic and Statistical Manual of Mental Disorders* (DSM) is used to assess ASDs. It outlines the signs and symptoms that should be present for a mental health condition to be diagnosed.

Some of the characteristics associated with ASDs include the following:

- It predominantly affects males (the male:female ratio is 3:1 or 4:1)
- Individuals with autism appear to face challenges in their capacity for reciprocal social interaction
- Language and communication abilities can be affected
- Individuals with autism also display repetitive behaviours and activities of play (Carr 2003).

In the past there were several categories under the umbrella term 'autism', ranging from classic autism to high-function autism, which is often termed Asperger's syndrome. Recently there have been changes in how autism is classified. In the latest DSM, the separate labels for autistic disorders have been replaced with an umbrella term: autism spectrum disorder (ASD). ASDs are now assessed in terms of severity (level 1 (mild) up to level 3) across several areas, including:

- challenges with communication
- restricted levels of interest
- amount of support needed
- repetitive behaviours.

ASDs may coexist with intellectual disability or other disorders of development and can occur with other physical or psychological disorders. It is estimated that 40–60% of those diagnosed with ASD have intellectual disability. »

WHAT CAUSES ASDS?

There is no one clear cause of ASDs, but it's generally acknowledged that it has a genetic aspect – ASDs often appear to run in families.

Initially, the possibility of a genetic factor in autism was disregarded, as early studies suggested that the likelihood of having more than one autistic child in a family was relatively low at 2%. However, more recent studies have calculated the incidence rate at four per 10,000 of the general population, which is considered quite high. Subsequent twin studies confirm a very strong genetic component, and it is now accepted that the inheritance of autism exceeds 90% (Rutter *et al.* 1997).

Biological accounts suggest a neurodevelopmental aspect. The autistic artist Jose described in Oliver Sacks's book *The Man Who Mistook his Wife for a Hat* had developed caused swelling to the brain that led to irreparable damage. Jose displayed many autistic characteristics and this could suggest that in some cases neurological damage can be held accountable.

Recent developments and research in neurology claim to have found that some autistic people have shorter brain stems than individuals with normal development.

Another possible explanation comes from the cognitive field of psychology – the theory of mind. Research conducted with children of typical development, those with autism and those with Down syndrome found that both groups of children *without* autism did well on the Sally–Anne test, which tests the existence of theory of mind, while the children with autism performed poorly.

Think about it

An example of this was a story related by Margaret Dewey (Frith, p.182) of an autistic boy who was sent to the kitchen to get himself a drink of milk. His father came in to find the child pouring the carton of milk down the drain. The father started shouting at his son to stop, which the child did and began crying but made no attempt to explain why he had done it.

It later transpired that the child believed the milk had gone off and was doing what he had witnessed his parents do with bad milk – pour it down the drain.

Why do you think the child did not explain why he was pouring the milk down the drain?

The child did not defend his actions when told to stop, which is exactly what one would expect from a child who does not realise that someone else does not necessarily have the same knowledge as himself. Thus being shouted out was a shocking turn of events that made no sense to him at all.

TREATMENTS

While there is no cure for autism (Cohen & Volkmar 1997), there are treatments. These tend to take a behavioural modification approach; for example, the Lovaas method is popular, particularly for targeting challenging behaviours.

The TEACCH approach emphasises an intensive structured educative programme that aims to make the world intelligible to the autistic person by acknowledging deficits and building on the strengths of the child. The provision of a structured environment seems to be desirable, according to the findings of Rutter and Bartak (1973).

CASE STUDY

Stephen (not his real name) has been referred as the school he attends has reported increasing behavioural issues. Stephen struggles to sit still for more than two minutes and starts moving around and fidgeting. This is now affecting his ability to complete his work. Recently his behaviour and frustration have been escalating, with incidents of physical harm towards both the staff and other children, including biting.

Stephen possesses good language skills and a typical IQ, but he is struggling to interact socially with the other children and is often isolated. His interactions range from being overly boisterous when talking to pushing and shoving them. He struggles to take turns in games and tries to dominate conversations. Staff are concerned at his increasing isolation, which is causing Stephen distress.

After being assessed, including observation both at home and at school, it was agreed that Stephen is exhibiting **sensory-seeking** behaviours.

Most people with autism have some issues with sensory processing. This can include sensory-seeking behaviours – intentionally seeking out sensory input through smell, touch, taste, sight or sound.

Additional reading

Research some intervention strategies for sensation-seeking (you can also include autism in your research) and summarise some strategies that might be helpful for a child like Stephen. Here's one website to get you started: www.hse.ie/eng/services/list/1/lho/corknorthlee/therapy/paediatric-occupational-therapy/sensory-processing.pdf

SOCIO-EMOTIONAL DEVELOPMENT

The ages of 2–5 years is a time of significant growth as children continue to navigate their social world, making sense of relationships around them. It is also marked by a growing sense of 'self' – their emerging and separate identity. Let's start with a quick recap of what the major theorists suggest is happening.

FREUD'S PSYCHOSEXUAL THEORY

ANAL STAGE (2–3 YEARS)

The focus of pleasure shifts to the anus, helping the child become aware of their bowels and how to control them. By taking control of their own bowel movements, the child takes an important step towards independence, developing confidence and a sense of when to 'give things up'. However, over-strictness about forcing a child to 'go' or about timing or cleanliness can cause personality problems, for example anal fixation – forcing a child to 'go' may cause reluctance about giving away *anything*. The person may become a hoarder or miser. Conversely, over-concern about 'going regularly' may cause obsessive time-keeping or always being late.

PHALLIC STAGE (3–6 YEARS)

Children become aware of their genitals and sexual differences. This stage is where the paths of males and females begin to diverge as they realise their differences.

Oedipus complex

Each boy unconsciously goes through a sequence of stages beginning with the development of a strong desire for his mother, noticing the bond between his parents (i.e. sleeping together), becoming jealous of his father and hating him, then becoming afraid of his father lest he discover his son's true feelings which results in the final substage of fearing punishment – castration.

Think about it

Why do you think many psychologists, including Erikson, have criticised Freud's theory? Why do some see it as sexist, especially the Oedipus complex?

LINK

In Chapter 1 we saw how sociocultural factors can have a significant impact on our development. What do you think were the beliefs about women in Freud's time? Were they seen as equal to men? Perhaps we see the values of that time in his theory – beliefs we no longer share. What do you think?

ERIKSON'S INITIATIVE VS. GUILT (3–5 YEARS)

As the child becomes older they exhibit increasing curiosity and interest, they initiate play and question more. The main aim of this stage is to acquire a sense of purpose. If this is discouraged or they are held back they will not develop self-initiative and instead will hold back in later life.

Practical applications:

* Encourage children to be as independent as possible
* Focus on gains as children practise new skills, not on the mistakes they make. (Garhart Mooney 2000, p.53)

What is clear is that our social and emotional development is shaped by the culture we are part of and the relationships around us.

SOCIALISATION

Socialisation refers to how we all learn the values and beliefs of the culture we are part of.

'**Socialisation** is the process by which children acquire the values, standards, practices and knowledge of the society into which they are born. It is through this process that children typically come to share many of the aspects of the behaviour, cognition and emotion of members of their society.' (Bennett 2005, p.383)

At the beginning of this book I posed the question, 'Why are we the way we are?' This very question is central to the study of socialisation. Sociology focuses on societal influences, of course, and psychology encompasses many disciplines, among them genetics, biology, anthropology and sociology. Psychology approaches the study of 'socialisation' in a domain-/area-specific way, looking at particular topics such as gender or moral socialisation.

Traditionally children were thought of as 'vessels' or blank slates to be filled by their elders. We have moved away from this reasoning, recognising the 'active child' who is not a passive agent but an active participant shaping and influencing their environment and also their own socialisation.

LINK

Does this remind you of the principle of 'bi-directionality' in bio-ecological theory? Refresh your memory and check out page 56.

One area where we have seen significant societal change is how we think about gender itself. Some question the existence of a binary categorisation of male and female. Increasing numbers of people now identify as non-binary or transgender. In this chapter, we are looking at what psychology has theorised historically about the development of gender and sex role differences in young children.

DEVELOPMENT OF GENDER AND SEX ROLE DIFFERENCES

From two years of age children appear to show sex differences in relation to their choice of toys. Boys tend to choose trucks, cars and blocks. They also engage more in play involving gross motor activity such as kicking and throwing a ball.

Girls, on the other hand, tend to show a preference for dolls, dressing up and domestic play. In school, both opt for same-sex partners when playing, boys preferring outdoor play or sport-related activities while girls opt for indoor, sedentary activities.

Kuhn *et al.* (1978) found that by two and a half years of age children had beliefs about sex role stereotypes (a belief that certain activities are suitable for girls and vice versa). Children reported that girls liked to play dolls and to help their mother whereas boys liked helping their father.

Think about it

Do you think that as values and beliefs around gender continue to change, perception of the findings of older research may change too?

If your answer is yes, does this demonstrate the role of culture and society in our development?

DEVELOPMENT OF GENDER IDENTITY IN YOUNG CHILDREN

'Are you a boy or a girl?' This question will stump or confuse most two-year-olds, but if you show them a stereotypical picture of a girl and a boy, 76% will correctly identify the gender. By 30 months this figure rises to 83% and by 36 months to 90%.

By three years of age, most children can correctly label their own and others' sex, or gender. This marks the acquisition of 'gender identity'.

Gender stability	Approximately 4 years old	Most children understand that the gender of a person remains the same or stable. If asked, a girl will answer that she'll be a mummy when she grows up.
Gender constancy	By 7 years of age	Awareness that being male or female (the biological sex of a person) does not change, for example if a boy grows his hair long, he is still a boy.

Source: Smith *et al.* (2003)

As gender identity develops children also acquire **sex role stereotypes** – beliefs about what are considered appropriate characteristics and behaviour for boys and girls. This process of learning is called **sex-typing**. As might be apparent, sex-typing is learned through a process of **socialisation.**

GENDER SOCIALISATION

Many explanations have been proposed as to how we are socialised. Let's look briefly at two:

* Child effects
* Systems theory (Sameroff).

Child effects

Child effects are the innate individual differences children have and that can impact on their parents' treatment of them.

Bennett (2005) notes that children's gender, physical attractiveness and, most important, temperament have all been found to have marked influences on parental behaviour.

So, from birth, 'child effects' can be seen in how parents treat girls and boys in systematically different ways, both consciously and unconsciously.

Systems theory

Key to this approach is that the child is conceived as embedded in a variety of mutually influencing relationships and social structures.

A systems theory of socialisation was developed by Sameroff (1983). It is not just the immediate family that socialises the child; that family is part of a wider system incorporating school, peers, parental employment, etc. Arguably the most important force in the socialisation process is the media: television, the internet, as well as computer games, etc. All play a central role in our lives and thus a central part of the socialisation process. (In Chapter 7 we shall look at research exploring the role of the media in eating disorders.) Gender identity is also powerfully shaped by the process of socialisation.

Think about it

Compare and contrast the cultural or social expectations regarding appropriate behaviour for a girl today compared with a girl born fifty years ago. Do you think attitudes and expectations have changed? How about females in the West compared to those in other parts of the world? Do differences still exist?

Can you see how this reflects both the exosystem and the chronosystem parts of Bronfenbrenner's bio-ecological theory?

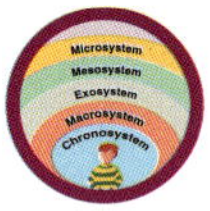

PLAY

'Children's play is freely chosen, personally directed behaviour, motivated from within by needs, wants and desires. Play can be fun or serious. Through play children explore social, material and imaginary worlds and their relationship with them, elaborating all the while a flexible range of responses to the challenges they encounter. By playing, children learn and develop as individuals and as members of the community.' (Kernan 2007, p.10)

WHY IS PLAY SO IMPORTANT?

From a psychological perspective, according to Valentino:

> *Play is an essential activity of early childhood as it contributes to the cognitive, social, emotional and motivational development of children. Through play, children are able to create and explore a world they can master. Moreover, within the context of play children learn, develop and practise innovative behaviours and social competencies. During the first few years of life, parents have a critical role in influencing children's play and developing social and communicative behaviours. (Valentino et al. 2011, p.1280)*

The benefits of play include:

* Promoting children's development, learning, creativity and independence
* Keeping children healthy and active
* Allowing children to find out about themselves, their abilities and their interests
* Giving children the chance to let off steam and have fun
* Having a therapeutic effect by helping children to deal with difficult or painful circumstances, such as emotional stress or medical treatment. (DCYA 2004, p.12)

PLAY DEPRIVATION AND ITS EFFECTS

As there are benefits to play, so too there can be negative consequences to a lack of play, especially in the early years of children's development. The notion of **play deprivation** has been gaining currency in recent years. Initially focus concentrated on the negative impact on children's physical development from a lack of play. According to Kernan, 'chronic play deprivation particularly during the period between birth and seven years has been linked to impaired brain development, lack of social skills, depression and aggression' (2007, pp.11–12). We shall considering the implications of parent–child play interactions in more depth in the In Focus piece on page 132.

KEY FORMS OF PLAY IN EARLY CHILDHOOD

We have defined play and seen the impact, both positive and negative, that play brings to a child's development. So what are the different types of play?

Exploratory play	Using physical skills and sensations to learn about materials and their properties, what they feel like and what can be done with them.
Constructive play	The manipulation of objects and materials to build or create something using natural or manufactured materials such as blocks, playdough, junk and collage materials, sand and water. Involves creating, recognising and solving problems.
Creative play	Using open-ended materials such as art materials and natural materials in ways that encourage fluency, flexibility, originality, imagination, embellishment and making novel connections.
Pretend, fantasy and socio-dramatic play	Includes: role-play, pretending with objects, pretend actions and situations, persistence with the imaginary play frame to create a play episode or event. When it involves interaction and verbal communication with one or more play partners regarding the play event it is termed socio-dramatic play.
Physical locomotor play	Activities that include all kinds of physical movements for their own sake and enjoyment. In this type of play a range of fine or gross motor skills are practised and mastered.
Language or word play	Unrehearsed and spontaneous manipulation of sounds and words, often with rhythmic and repetitive elements. As children get older, this type of play often incorporates rhyme, word play and humour.

Source: Kernan (2007, p.35)

While the table above gives an overview of the different types of play that exist, this is just one perspective.

THEORETICAL APPROACHES TO PLAY

There are many perspectives on play, reflecting its centrality in children's development. As we saw in Chapter 2, both Piaget and Vygotsky recognised the pivotal role of play in development.

Piaget

Piaget linked the development of play to intellectual growth and moral development. He surmised that the two main activities of play are:

* **Play** – a product of assimilation
* **Imitation** – a product of accommodation.

Pretend play is another feature of this stage – a stick is transformed into a sword, for example. Piaget believed that play and imitation are important activities for the developing child. While he saw play's primary function for children as one of enjoyment, he felt that imitation reflects the child's attempt to master or copy some new movement or action from another. Piaget proposed that while play involves a process of assimilation by the child, imitation is a product of accommodation in their construction of knowledge.

Piaget conceived that the development of play is broken into three parts:

* **Mastery stage** – sensorimotor stage
* **Play stage** – preoperational stage
* **Game stage** – concrete operational stage.

According to Piaget, the **play stage** – the second stage – is witnessed during the preoperational period between the ages of three and six years. This stage is dominated by the child's egocentrism, so the child engages in mainly solitary play as they are generally too egocentric to play co-operatively with others. Parallel play does occur. In the preoperational stage symbolic thinking is emerging and this is reflected in the child's play through the symbolic use of objects and actions during their pretend play. Thus a cardboard box becomes a boat, for example.

Piaget believed that symbolic representation is tied to social perspective-taking skills. In other words, play enables genuine interaction and the creation of shared meaning between individuals, which is a fundamental social skill milestone.

Vygotsky

Vygotsky maintained the central position of play: 'Play creates a Zone of Proximal Development (ZPD) on the child ... in play a child always behaves beyond his average age' (Barnes 2002, p.241). Vygotsky believed that the appearance of imagination can be viewed as the psychological basis that later becomes the origin of play.

George Herbert Mead

Mead (1863–1931) was a psychologist and sociologist and was instrumental in the development of the **symbolic interactionist perspective**. This approach emphasises the importance of language and social interaction in the development of the self.

Mead maintained that the child acquires a sense of who they are through play and that **role-play** and **pretence** are particularly important in achieving this goal. He suggested that children do not develop a mature sense of self until they learn to take on the role of the other.

Many other theorists have posited accounts of the role of play in development; below is a brief summary of some of the most important contributors.

Theorists on the role of play

Friedrich Froebel	Play exemplifies development from within the child, but can be nurtured.
Karl Groos	Play provides exercise and elaboration of skills needed for survival.
Maria Montessori	Like Froebel, she saw the value of self-initiated activity. She placed an emphasis on learning about real life.
Susan Isaacs	Play is essential to both the emotional and cognitive growth of young children.
Jerome Bruner	Play serves both as practice for mastery of skills and as an opportunity for trying out new combinations of behaviour in a safe context.

Parents occupy a pivotal role in the developing world of the young child and this can be witnessed in parent–child play interactions. Research has shone a light on its importance and the impact it can have on children's developmental outcomes.

IN FOCUS: PARENT–CHILD PLAY AND ITS IMPLICATIONS

It's clear that parents play a central role in children's lives. The younger the child the more dependent they are on their parents to care for them, support and nurture their development. The following research highlights not just the central role of parents in a child's life but also the importance of play in supporting cognitive, social and emotional development and reaching those developmental milestones.

In a study of the impact in the first two years of life of an abusive or 'maltreating' family environment, Valentino *et al.* examined mother–child play interactions comparing children from non-maltreating and maltreating family homes. Looking at maltreated children's social play with peers, they found that by ages four and five, maltreated children:

- Engaged in less overall play
- Had lower-level cognitive play compared to their non-maltreated peers
- Showed differences in their pretend play, such that their play is more imitative of everyday routines and less fantasy-based
- Socially, were found to be more aggressive and less competent with their peers
- Demonstrated poorer skills in initiating peer interactions
- Found maintaining self-control more difficult (Valentino *et al.* 2011).

Valentino *et al.* describe how 'mother–child interactions among abusing and neglecting families tend to include less verbal interaction, limited playful exchanges, and less harmony compared to non-maltreating families' (2011, p.1282). They report that physically abusive parents demonstrate fewer physical and positive behaviours during mother–child interactions, such as handing objects to the child or praising the child. These maladaptive parent–child interactional patterns are likely to have adverse effects on maltreated children's play and social development.

INITIATING PLAY

The study places particular emphasis on the ability of a child to initiate actions and, especially, social interactions. This is an **important developmental milestone** as:

> *[I]nfant behaviour shifts from reacting to the environment to initiating actions. The latter of these behaviours is more cognitively and socially complex as it requires infants to formulate social goals and signal their requests without structure from their interactive partner.*
>
> *Children's increased capacity for initiating or directing social exchanges and their ability to respond to parental requests are two critical aspects of social competence during the second year. Reduced social initiation hampers a child's ability to form successful relationships with peers and increases the likelihood of problem behaviours in the future.*

So what was the impact on toddlers?

Toddlers from abusing families demonstrated significantly less child-initiated behaviour during play than did toddlers from neglecting and non-maltreating families. The authors argue that this shows that while basic cognitive processes appear unaffected, 'maltreatment does adversely affect early social and emotional development' (Valentino *et al.* 2011, p.1290).

The significant difference in outcome was that the group of children from abusive backgrounds had poorer outcomes than those from neglectful homes or homes where there was no maltreatment.

It may appear odd at first that the children from neglectful homes were not as adversely affected as those from abusive homes. The authors offer some explanation for this: in an abusive home, the children may have learned early on not to initiate interactions with a parent who is volatile, unpredictable and potentially violent. Thus avoidance of interaction would be adaptive in this scenario and thus 'reduced child-initiated play may be experience-dependent and observed among young children from abusing families as an attempt to avoid further abuse experiences.'

IN SUMMARY

Overall, these finding suggest that by the preschool years, maltreated children already demonstrate delays in 'play maturity and social competence'. These findings demonstrate the importance of play in children's early development, especially in terms of social and cognitive development. Play is more than just children having fun; it provides fundamental building blocks of development which sow the seeds of their future ability to form successful relationships.

Hopefully you are beginning to see how different factors and influences shape our development. Identifying factors enables prevention, intervention and support initiatives and programmes, reminding us of the vital role we all play in children's developmental outcomes.

CHECK YOUR LEARNING GOALS!

You should be able to:

1. Differentiate between synchronous and asynchronous periods of development and say which category this age group falls into.
2. Explain 'individual variation'.
3. Explain which lobe of the brain rapid growth is seen in.
4. Outline some gross motor skills seen during this period.
5. Outline some fine motor skills seen during this period.
6. Explain the Three Mountains task and what it tells us abut children's thinking.
7. Explain symbolic thinking, using an example.
8. Describe Vygotsky's view of the relationship between play and language.
9. Explain how language is acquired, according to Noam Chomsky.
10. Define 'theory of mind'.
11. Describe the Sally–Anne test and explain its purpose.
12. Describe Freud's anal stage and explain what is meant by the tern 'anal fixation'.
13. Explain the 'phallic' stage.
14. Explain which of Erikson's psychosocial stages can be seen at this age, and outline its practical applications.
15. Summarise 'socialisation'.
16. Describe a systems theory of socialisation.
17. Chart the development of gender identity.
18. Define the age at which children achieve gender constancy.
19. List the key forms of play.
20. Outline the benefits of play.
21. Describe Piaget's theory of play.

6

Middle Childhood (6–11 Years)

In this chapter we will discover:

* Physical development
  - Growth patterns
  - Motor skills development
  - In Focus: Childhood obesity – a growing issue
* Cognitive development
  - Piaget's concrete operational stage
  - Vygotsky – school and the ZPD
  - Gardner's theory of multiple intelligences
* Socio-emotional development
  - Freud's latency stage
  - Erikson's industry vs. inferiority
  - Friendship formation
  - In Focus: Children's understanding of wellbeing
  - In Focus: Parenting

For most children, this period in their lives is marked by some important milestones. They will enter a whole new environment when they start school, marking another step towards independence. Peer relationships and learning in a new environment are challenges for the child to meet. School can have quite an influence on the development of a child. Some children will experience bullying, but for most it is a positive time. By the end of this stage they will be on the cusp of puberty, the transition from childhood towards adulthood.

PHYSICAL DEVELOPMENT

GROWTH PATTERNS

This period exhibits a **synchronous** pattern of growth – slow, steady and consistent development:

* 'Baby fat' declines
* Muscle mass and strength improve
* Children gain 2.25–3 kg (5–7 lb) in weight
* Children grow approximately 5–7.6 cm (2–3 inches) in height.

Physical development during this time is sometimes seen as the calm before the storm of puberty with the dramatic physical changes that come in its wake.

MOTOR SKILLS DEVELOPMENT

Gross and fine motor skills from six to eleven years

AGE (YEARS)	GROSS MOTOR SKILLS	FINE MOTOR SKILLS
6–7	▪ Can catch and throw a ball ▪ Can hop easily ▪ Can skip in time to music	▪ Can build a tower of blocks that is straight ▪ Can hold a pencil in a similar way to an adult
8–9	▪ Increased body strength ▪ Faster reaction time ▪ Can ride a two-wheeled bike easily	▪ Greater control over small muscles and thus can draw and write with improved skill ▪ Beginning to join letters together in handwriting
10–11	▪ Boys and girls differ in physical maturity: girls experience puberty two years ahead of boys	▪ Greater ability for detailed tasks, e.g. needlework ▪ Uses joined-up letters

The increasing myelination of the central nervous system (brain and spinal cord) contributes to improved motor skills and co-ordination.

Generally speaking there is a tendency for girls to be better co-ordinated in their movements, while boys have greater speed and strength.

The topic of obesity, which can have damaging psychological as well as physical outcomes, reflects the interdependent spheres of physical, social and emotional development.

IN FOCUS: CHILDHOOD OBESITY – A GROWING ISSUE

The rates of overweight and obesity are increasing with alarming speed over the last three decades, resulting in the World Health Organization (WHO) describing it as a 'global epidemic'.

In the USA, based on current projections, it is expected that half the population will be obese by 2025. This staggering increase in overweight/obesity is reflected in Ireland; six in 10 adults are classified as overweight or obese.

Worryingly, children are reflecting the trends among adults. One in four children are now classed as being overweight, and it is suggested that the number of children who are significantly overweight has trebled over the last decade. Childhood obesity has long-term consequences, physically and psychologically, for children as they move through their life.

The latest figures from Growing up in Ireland (GUI) 2018 (the national longitudinal study by the ESRI and Trinity College Dublin) show significant levels of overweight and obesity in nine-year-olds. Children's height and weight measurements were recorded to calculate their body mass index (BMI), which is widely used to determine if children have a healthy body weight. GUI (2018) found that:

- More than one in five nine-year-olds were overweight or obese.
- At age nine (as at age five), girls were more likely than boys to be overweight/obese (23% and 21% respectively).
- There were substantial inequalities in being overweight/obese, with a rate of 32% in the lowest income group compared to 14% in the highest income group.
- Physical activity is considered essential to the health and wellbeing of children with a recommendation of 60 minutes' vigorous physical activity each day. Only one-quarter of nine-year-olds met the recommended level of physical activity.

»

Screen time and social media usage amongst nine-year-olds was also researched as part of the GUI report:

- Over 90% of nine-year-olds spent at least some time watching TV/DVDs both at the weekend and on weekdays.
- Fifteen per cent of them spent two or more hours watching TV/DVDs on a weekday.
- Nine per cent spent over two hours on other types of screen-based activities (such as on a computer) on a weekday.
- Twenty-three per cent had an online profile, 26% of boys and 21% of girls. Boys' profiles were largely related to computer gaming and girls' more often related to social media.

Recent research by the Childhood Obesity Surveillance Initiative (COSI) (Mitchell *et al.* 2020) supports many of these findings and highlights the continuing and significant difference in the prevalence of overweight/obesity between children in schools designated as 'disadvantaged' compared to peers in other schools.

Think about it

Can you think of possible reasons why there are higher levels of obesity in children from lower socioeconomic backgrounds? Use the information in this chapter to help guide your answer.

The authors note:

> *The findings of this COSI report indicate that we still have a significant way to go to create environments in our homes, schools and communities that support every child to grow and develop healthily from birth through to adulthood, particularly for those who experience socioeconomic disadvantage. Lifestyles and health are intrinsically linked and are heavily influenced by the prevailing environment.*

Think about it

What are the main factors you can identify from these findings that might be involved in childhood obesity? Make a note of them.

LINK

Is there a theoretical framework that captures factors from those in the immediate child's environment to wider ones? Go back to Chapter 2 and refresh your understanding of Bronfenbrenner's bio-ecological theory. We'll now use the framework of that theory to better picture all the factors identified in child obesity and gain more insight into this issue.

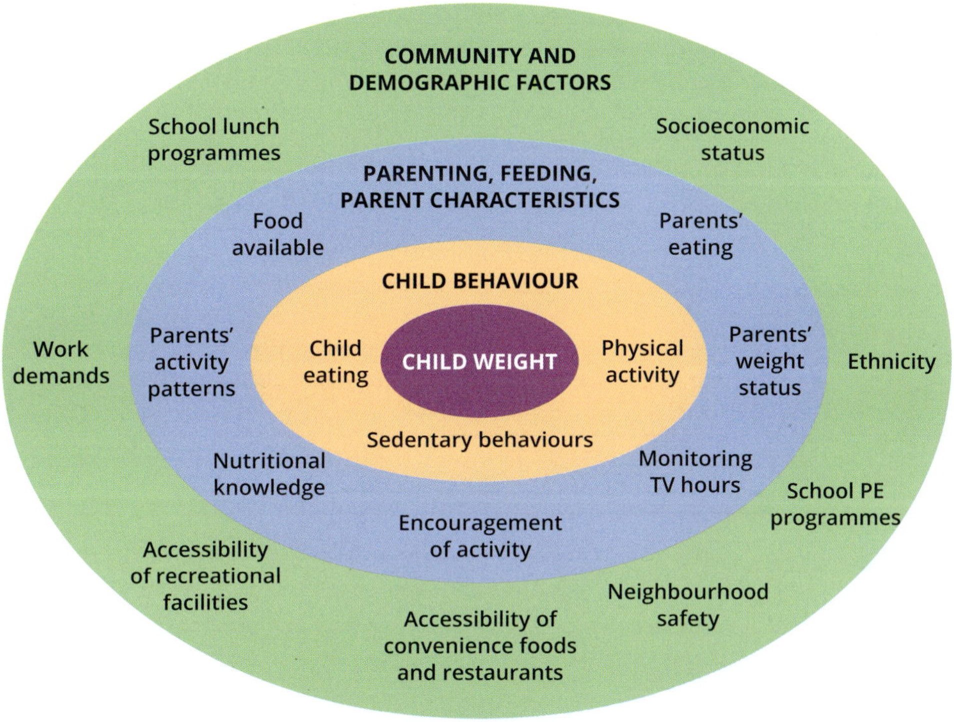

Ecological obesity

The Six Cs developmental ecological model of contributors to childhood obesity (Harrison *et al.* 2011) highlights the different levels and areas of influence that affect childhood obesity.

There are six factors or spheres mentioned by Harrison, the first he refers to as 'Cell' and relates to underlining biological and genetic characteristics that may be involved with the individual's body composition etc. We'll look at the remaining five spheres using an example for each of them. As you read the examples, try to place each in the different systems in the bio-ecological model. »

SPHERE	FACTORS
Child	Media use and exposure are a particular risk factor in childhood obesity, from the amount of time spent watching television or playing computer games to the role of food advertising in encouraging greater caloric intake and appetite priming (encouraging eating) among children.
Family	Harrison *et al.* (2011, p.52) explain that the family 'is the central socialisation context for most young children'. Thus it makes sense that parents play a primary role in children's eating habits. As Puder and Munsch (2010, p. 38) say, 'Children learn via observation and imitation, as well as by modelling the behaviours of their parents.'
Community	There are many factors in this sphere of influence. It can be found early in childcare settings if nutritional and healthy meals are not provided. In schools, vending machines can contribute to a culture of eating unhealthy/ fast food eating. Another level of influence is peer reaction and attitudes to obesity. According to Harrison, obese children and adolescents are more likely to be socially marginalised, bullied and depressed than non-obese children.
National	Emerging evidence suggests that economic issues such as a pandemic or recession can contribute to child obesity rates by prompting parents to favour low-cost, low-micronutrient, high-calorie foods such as convenience foods and fast foods. Government policy, from health promotion to how healthy food is made more affordable (through pricing and taxation), influences an individual's eating habits and consequently their weight.
Culture	Different cultures have different values regarding body shape; in some cultures being slim is considered unattractive and unhealthy.

Before we leave this topic, let's revisit the research on screen time and social media. (We shall look at this issue in more depth in the next chapter.) Social media, e.g. YouTube, Snapchat, Facebook, Instagram, can be seen as a platform that transmits attitudes regarding body size, obesity and thin idealisation. Age restrictions are placed on many social media platforms such as Facebook (age 13). Ofcom (2017) reports that half of 11- and 12-year-olds have a social media profile.

Social media forums such as Twitter and Facebook contain significant amounts of weight-related derogatory comments, including instances of bullying (De Brún *et al.* 2014). Such bullying includes verbal aggression. Jeon *et al.* (2018) report that these comments are often derogatory, contributing to obesity-related stigmatisation. Media portrayal of stereotypical images increases implicit bias in the general public (Hinman *et al.* 2015). Children who have viewed high levels of mass media report greater dislike of peers with overweight and obesity (Latner *et al.* 2007).

Can you recognise the many layers of influence in which the child is nested, from the immediate, such as family, to more distant factors such as media?

Childhood obesity can have long-term, lifelong consequences in terms of physical development; more than 60% of people who are overweight as children will remain overweight as adults. Obesity brings health risks including high blood pressure, heart disease and diabetes. Psychologically, being overweight can contribute to low self-esteem and depression. It has even been linked with under-achieving academically in school. Therefore, it is essential that this epidemic is tackled early in life to support the best outcomes for children as they move through their lives. Prevention is always better than cure.

COGNITIVE DEVELOPMENT

During middle childhood we continue to see children's increasing ability and sophistication emerge in their thinking and reasoning capacities.

PIAGET'S CONCRETE OPERATIONAL STAGE (7–11 YEARS)

This is the third stage in Piaget's theory of cognitive development. The main features of this stage are:

* **Reversibility:** The understanding that numbers or objects can be altered and then returned to their original state
* **Conservation:** The understanding that quantity, volume and length remain the same even though the appearance of something may change
* **Decentring:** Children become less egocentric.

Children learn through their interaction with concrete or 'real' objects; further, they can apply the learning strategies they have developed to real and immediate situations.

The process of decentring, when they become less **egocentric**, enables them to become more flexible in their thinking as they are now able to factor in other ways of looking or thinking about a situation.

REVERSIBILITY

This is an important feature of this stage. It is the understanding that some actions can be completely reversed or can be reversed to an earlier action. For example, a child rolls out a ball of playdough and understands that it can be returned to its original state.

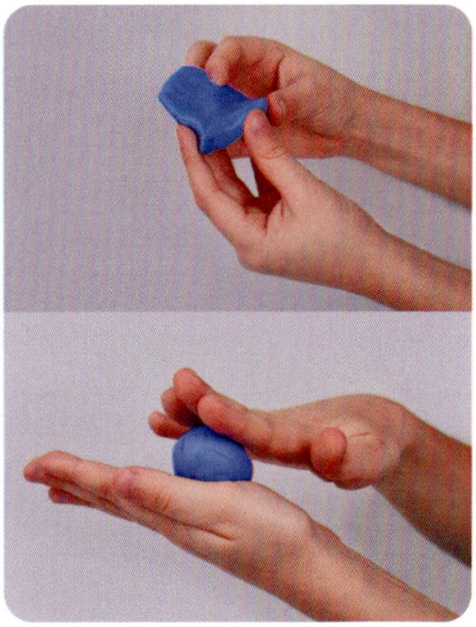

Reversibility is needed for more complex maths problems. It is also necessary for the acquisition of conservation.

CONSERVATION

When given the choice between a biscuit or half a biscuit, which would you choose? The whole biscuit is the obvious choice! However, for a child who has not yet acquired **conservation** it's not quite that straightforward. If I was offered two halves of a biscuit or one whole one I would know them to be the same amount. Not so for a young child who would reason they were getting two biscuits instead of one. During the concrete operational stage children begin to acquire this ability. Piaget believed that the acquisition of **conservation** is an important developmental milestone.

As you will see from the diagram below, there are several forms of conservation.

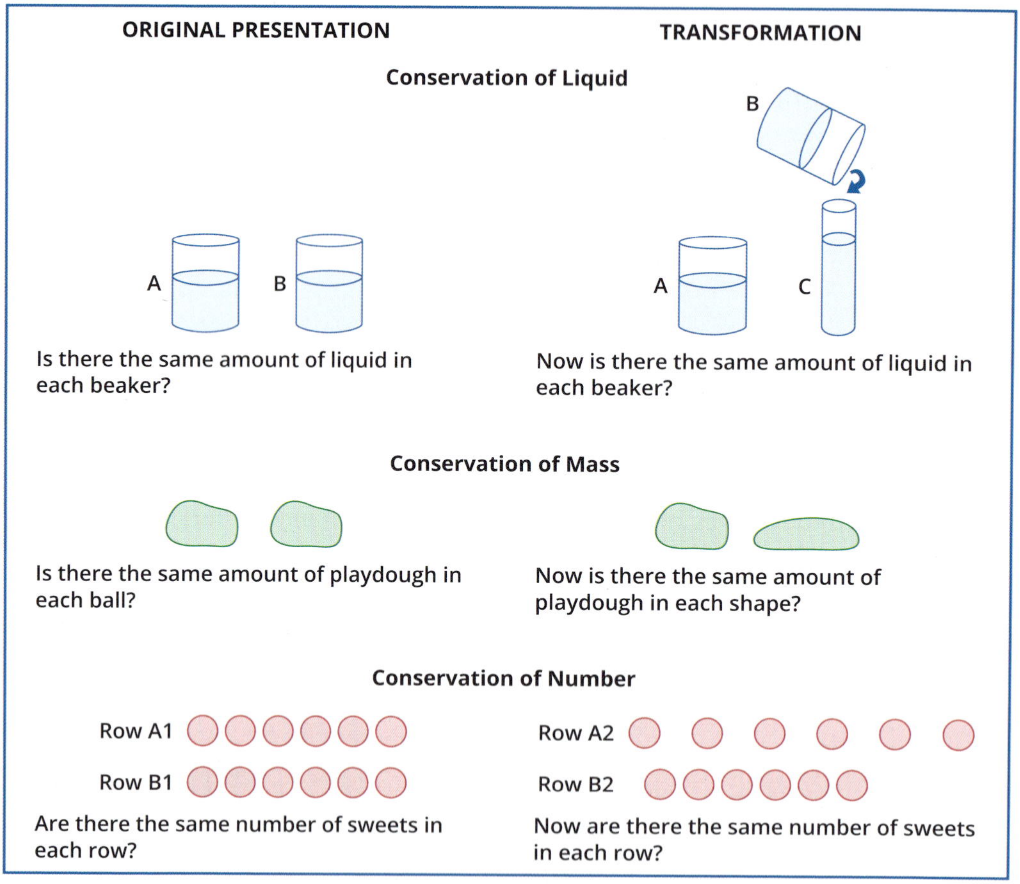

Piaget's conservation studies

According to Smith *et al.* (2003), conservation is achieved at the following ages:

- Conservation of **number**: At about five to six years of age
- Conservation of **weight**: At seven or eight years of age
- Conservation of **volume**: Between ten and eleven years of age

DECENTRING

An important aspect of this stage is that children become less egocentric.

Egocentrism is the belief that everyone else sees the world as you do; children do not understand that other people might see or think about things differently, and this is reflected in their thinking. Piaget suggested that egocentric thinking is based on the child's view that the world is 'centred' on them. An example of this is when a child, when asked how the moon moves, says it 'follows' them.

Children who are egocentric struggle to **decentre**, as can be seen in the following dialogue (Smith *et al.* 2003, p.399):

> *Adult: Have you any brothers or sisters?*
>
> *John: Yes, a brother.*
>
> *Adult: What is his name?*
>
> *John: Sammy.*
>
> *Adult: Does Sammy have a brother?*
>
> *John: No.*

Think about it

Decentring means that children can take on board the perspective of another person: see things through their eyes, so to speak. What practical implications might this have?

Imagine explaining to a child of ten that their mum is unwell and needs help to get better, so the child needs to go and stay with a family member. Will the child be better able to process that information and understand why their mum needs support if decentring has occurred?

VYGOTSKY – SCHOOL AND THE ZPD

School marks an important milestone in the life of most children and it is here that you can see some of Vygotsky's concepts of how children learn in action.

The **zone of proximal development** (ZPD) is the distance between what a child can do or learn alone and what they can achieve with the help of others.

For Vygotsky, teachers and more experienced peers act as a support to help the child bridge the gap between what they could learn alone and the further learning they could achieve with these supports. Vygotsky used the term 'scaffolding' to refer to the role played by teachers who act as a bridge or scaffold, enabling the child towards further learning, learning they could not as easily achieve on their own. Vygotsky believed that social interaction is essential to learning.

Practical suggestions

* Pair children together so they can learn from each other.
* Plan activities that are within the child's ZPD but stretch them developmentally.
* Encourage conversations. (Garhart Mooney 2000)

While Piaget believed children learn through their own personal experiences, Vygotsky advocated that they learn through their interactions with others.

Both Piaget and Vygotsky have been at the forefront of cognitive theories and how we develop our reasoning and thinking skills. We are going to look at a theory that might give insight into the **individual variation** we can see in how we learn.

GARDNER'S THEORY OF MULTIPLE INTELLIGENCES

'An **intelligence** is the ability to solve problems, or to create products, that are valued within one or more cultural settings.' (Gardner 1983)

In his book *Frames of Mind* (1983), Howard Gardner suggested that there are seven types of intelligence. He would later consider adding a further two types, however he decided upon excluding existential intelligence as it did not meet his criteria for inclusion, settling on eight types. Gardner suggested that intelligence is not necessarily one unitary concept; rather, it is several different types of intelligence that exist independently of one another but interact with each other on a daily basis. Each of us has different strengths and these represent our unique mix of different types of intelligence.

Gardner's multiple intelligences

Linguistic	Reading, writing, talking, listening
Logical–mathematical	Numbers, scientific thinking
Bodily–kinaesthetic	Use of one's body; sport and dance
Musical	Singing, playing and composing
Interpersonal	Ability to understand and relate to others
Intrapersonal	Self-understanding
Spatial	Used in navigation
Naturalistic	The ability to recognise and categorise objects in nature (plants and animals)

Gardner's theory has been criticised on the grounds that it lacks scientific rigour and that some of his intelligences aren't within the cognitive area. Gardner countered that criticism of his multiple intelligence approach represents a fear of moving away from measuring intelligence through the use of traditional standardised tests towards his less quantifiable approach in conceptualising intelligence.

SOCIO-EMOTIONAL DEVELOPMENT

FREUD'S LATENCY STAGE (6–11 YEARS)

During this stage sexual urges remain repressed and there are no significant developmental events. Freud believed that the most significant thing about children's social behaviour during this period is their preference for playing and interacting with same-sex peers.

ERIKSON'S INDUSTRY VS. INFERIORITY (6–12 YEARS)

This stage is very much influenced by the child's experiences in school. During this time the child begins to attend school and they interact more with their peers. If praised for their efforts they develop a sense of industry and feel good about what they have achieved, which encourages the feeling that they can fulfil their goals. If they repeatedly fail or are not praised when they try, a sense of inferiority may develop.

THEORIES OF MORAL DEVELOPMENT

We have come across 'socialisation' several times so far and here we meet it again, this time implicated in a child's moral development.

> '[T]he end product of **socialisation** is an individual who can distinguish right from wrong and is prepared to act accordingly ... such an individual can be said to have acquired a sense of morality, that is he or she will behave in ways that uphold the social order and will do so through inner conviction and not because of a fear of punishment.' (Shaffer 1996, p.290)

Moral development can be seen as the understanding of 'right' and 'wrong'. The first thing that should be apparent to us is that different cultures/societies, even families, can have very different ideas about what 'right' and 'wrong' are.

Socialisation, as we saw in the previous chapter, is the process by which a person acquires the beliefs and values of the culture or society they live in. Sociologists argues that we learn it from:

- Primary agents of socialisation, e.g. parents
- Secondary agents of socialisation, e.g. school, religious affiliation, society.

Freud believed that children develop a moral conscience from their parents.

Think about it

How do you think you 'learned' your morality? Was it from your family? What about other sources? Do you share the same sense of what is 'right and wrong' or is it different? If it is different, does that suggest that parents/family aren't that pivotal? What do you think?

PIAGET'S THEORY OF MORAL DEVELOPMENT

Piaget suggested that peer interaction at this age occurs around rule-based games. He developed a two-stage theory of moral development through his observations of young children playing and their use of rules when they play. Piaget noticed that younger children had less of a grasp of the rules than older children. Piaget questioned children of different ages about the rules of the games and formulated the following theory.

* **Pre-moral:** Before the age of five, children do not consider what is right or wrong.
* **Moral realism** is witnessed in middle childhood: children's understanding of rules is governed by the influence of authority figures. They believe that rules can't be changed, that they are inflexible.
* **Moral relativism** is present from roughly eight years onwards and reflects the child's growing sophistication in thinking. Children now understand that the rules can be modified through agreements with others. Rather than fixating on the rules being followed to the letter, children can modify the rules to meet their particular needs. They understand that this doesn't change the nature of the game. The important aspect is that all those participating are in agreement and following the same rules.

According to Piaget, moral development is completed at approximately 12–13 years of age. By this age children operate on rules from a place of 'mutual respect', where rules are negotiated rather than them being imposed from outside.

Older children understand that rules are not absolute but are devices used by humans to get along co-operatively and therefore can be modified with the agreement of others.

> *When, for example, the young child hears about one boy who broke 15 cups trying to help his mother and another boy who broke only one cup trying to steal cookies, the young child thinks that the first boy did worse. The child primarily considers the amount of damage – the consequences – whereas the older child is more likely to judge wrongness in terms of the motives underlying the act. (Piaget 1932, p.137, cited in Crain 1985, p.118)*

The fact that Piaget developed a theory of moral development tells us that he believed that cognitive processes are at the heart of understanding right from wrong.

We have encountered Piaget as a cognitive theorist, someone interested in how children think and learn to think. Yet reasoning is a cognitive skill and so it's not such a jump to see Piaget interested in how children reason on a moral level. Piaget believed the ability to 'decentre' is fundamental as it allows the child to see things from another person's point of view.

One criticism of Piaget's conceptualisation of moral development is his idea that we complete this development at 12 or 13 years of age. It is recognised nowadays that development can change constantly across the lifespan, and moral development is no exception.

As we age and gain new life experiences or interactions with others, our attitudes change to reflect this. Thus one might anticipate that our ideas of 'right' and 'wrong' will change.

Another criticism is culturally based. In the West, we are more individualistic, valuing the rights of the individual. In more collectivist societies the individual is seen as part of a group and that group has a higher value than the needs of one particular individual. This can have a bearing on the 'moral' reasoning behind individuals' decisions.

To summarise, Piaget proposed a two-stage theory: before the age of ten children believe that rules are fixed; after this age they progress to believing rules are flexible and can be modified with the agreement of others.

Piaget influenced the work of Lawrence Kohlberg, who expanded his theory to a six-stage conceptualisation of moral development.

KOHLBERG'S THEORY OF MORAL DEVELOPMENT

In devising his six-stage approach, Kohlberg interviewed children and adolescents about moral reasoning. He composed 'moral dilemmas' to assess the children, and their answers were used to develop his theory.

The Heinz dilemma

A woman was near death from cancer. There was one drug that her doctor thought might save her. The pharmacist in her town had recently discovered this drug and was charging ten times what the drug cost him to make. He paid €400 for the core ingredient and charged €4,000 for a small dose of the drug. The sick woman's husband, Heinz, went to everyone he knew to borrow the money and tried every financial means available to him, but he could only get together about €2,000, half of what it cost. He explained to the pharmacist that his wife was dying, and asked him to sell it cheaper or let him pay later. But the pharmacist said, 'No, I discovered the drug and I'm going to make money from if.' So, Heinz gets desperate and breaks into the man's store to steal the drug for his wife. Should he have done it?

Think about it

What would your response be, and why? Put this question to children and adolescents of different ages and see what their responses are and their reasoning behind their answers.

Using this dilemma, Kohlberg posed questions including whether it was right or wrong to steal the drug. He wasn't particularly interested in the 'yes' or 'no' answer but in the reasoning behind the answer.

Kohlberg's six-stage theory of moral development

As a follow-up to Kohlberg's theory, Colby, Kohlberg *et al.* (1983) undertook a 20-year longitudinal study of moral judgement. Findings included as follows:

* The use of stages 1 and 2 decreased over time.
* Stage 4, which did not appear at all in the moral reasoning of ten-year-olds, was reflected in 62% of 36-year-olds.
* Stage 5 did not appear until age 20–22 and never characterised more than 10% of the individuals.

The research suggests that Kohlberg's moral stages appeared somewhat later than he initially suggested. Further, the higher stages, in particular stage 6, was very elusive.

Gilligan's criticism of Kohlberg's work

A former student of Kohlberg, Carol Gilligan, has been a major critic of his work. Gilligan claims that Kohlberg's theory is flawed as his research was based on male responses, and as such it represents a male perspective of moral development and reasoning.

Gilligan through her work with women proposes that women apply an ethic of care in their judgements rather than an ethic of justice, which, she claims, is a male approach to moral judgements. An ethic of care means that the person considers other people and their welfare in their judgement-making process. Gilligan states that Kohlberg's work excludes and devalues how women approach moral reasoning. Yet it is interesting that Gilligan falls foul of the precise accusation she levels at Kohlberg: her research has been with women only, thus excluding and marginalising the male perspective.

FRIENDSHIP FORMATION

An important part of childhood is the ability to make friends. Forming friendships is a pivotal developmental task that does not end in childhood; being able to form friendships continues to be necessary across the lifespan. Robert Selman proposes the following theory of friendship development.

Selman's stages of friendship development

Stage 1 (6 and under)	▪ Friendship is based on physical or geographic factors ▪ Children are self-centred ▪ They possess no understanding of the perspectives of others
Stage 2 (7–9)	▪ Friendship begins to be based on reciprocity ▪ Awareness of other people's feelings emerges ▪ It begins to be based on social actions and evaluation by others
Stage 3 (9–12)	▪ Friendship is based on genuine give-and-take ▪ Friends are seen as people who help each other ▪ Mutual evaluation of actions occurs ▪ The concept of trust appears
Stage 4 (11–12 and older)	▪ Friendship is seen as stable and continuing ▪ It is seen as a relationship based on trust ▪ Children can observe the relationship from a third-party perspective

Friends are becoming increasingly important as the child grow older, not just in terms of social relationships and their ability to form them but also how they inform their emotional development and how they feel about themselves. As we will see in the following piece of research, children identify friends as being important to their sense of wellbeing.

IN FOCUS: CHILDREN'S UNDERSTANDING OF WELLBEING

Wellbeing is 'healthy and successful individual functioning (involving physiological, psychological and behavioural levels of organisation), positive social relationships (with family members, peers, adult caregivers, and community and societal institutions, for instance school and faith and civic organisations), and a social ecology that provides safety (e.g. freedom from interpersonal violence, war and crime), human and civil rights, social justice and participation in civil society' (Andrews *et al.* 2002, p.103).

»

We are going to look at very innovative research carried out by Nic Gabhainn and Sixsmith (2005), whose aim was to explore Irish children's understanding of wellbeing. The research was innovative because of the method used by the researchers: they distributed disposable cameras to children of primary- and secondary-school age, from rural and urban backgrounds. The children were asked to take pictures of things that represented wellbeing to them. The pictures were developed and another set of children sorted them into themes. Finally, older children were gathered to discuss the themes that had been agreed on. Several findings emerged from the study regarding children's understanding of wellbeing.

Themes such as family, friends, school, music and sport emerged, which was in line with other research, but interestingly, pets were identified in this Irish research as being important to children's wellbeing. The authors state:

> *A number of specifically interesting factors emerged during both the categorisation and schema development phases. The centrality of interpersonal relationships with family and friends (including school friends) emerges strongly, as does the value of activities or things to do.*
>
> *During all phases, children discussed how aspects of the various categories made them feel; how relationships (with people and animals) and the activities within the context of those relationships gave them a sense of belonging, being safe, loved, valued and being cared for.*
>
> *While many of the categories identified may have been predicted from reviewing previous work and so validate these aspects, the categories of* ***pets/ animals*** *and* ***environment/places*** *are relatively unexpected ... These categories illustrate the extent to which children interact with the natural world around them, as well as the interpersonal environment in which they are located. These factors certainly deserve further attention from researchers, policymakers and practitioners. (Nic Gabhainn & Sixsmith 2005, p.64)*

Think about it

Research should inform policy, which should inform practice. This research illustrates the interesting methods that can be used to obtain information but also the importance of gathering research to gain further understanding of children's lives.

Based on these research findings, how do you think the Covid pandemic may have impacted on children?

IN FOCUS: PARENTING

As we have seen in previous chapters, parenting is intrinsically central to attachment and the development of relationships in later life and has a vital role, positive and negative, in play and child development. Given its fundamental role in understanding children's early experiences (and their impact on later development) we are going to take a deeper look at parenting, beginning with some theories of parenting. Areas of research interest in parenting will be considered. Finally, the findings of recent Irish research on parenting styles and effective parenting will be outlined.

Before we go further it is important to acknowledge that, according to Sroufe (2005, p 354), 'When one grasps the critical importance of contexts, the pointlessness of blaming parents is immediately obvious.' Sroufe is suggesting that it is our context or environment that is more influential over all elements of development.

LINK

How does Sroufe's statement link to the work of Bronfenbrenner and his central tenet of the importance of contexts?

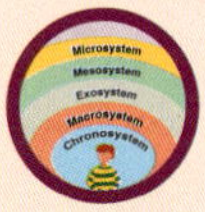

In order to understand human development, one has to look at the person in their environment, which is made up of immediate and more distal influences. Sroufe's point is that it is too simplistic to 'blame' parents; we must look at the bigger picture when unravelling the processes of development.

EARLY THEORIES OF PARENTING

Freud is, arguably, one of the greatest influences on developmental theories of parenting and families. As you will recall from Chapter 2, Freud believed that **early experiences affect later development**. So it is no surprise that he emphasised the importance of parent–child relationships and their role, positive and negative, in the child's present and later identity and life. While psychoanalysis fell from favour, learning theories become more popular in the twentieth century and offered another window into parenting, focusing on the observation of parenting interactions and parents as role models. Nowadays there is no one unified theory, rather a collection of perspectives and approaches. According to Lewis (2005), there are five strands of research relating to parenting:

1. Parenting styles
2. Social learning theory
3. Attachment theory
4. Ecological approach
5. Behavioural genetics.

We have explored attachment and Bronfenbrenner's bio-ecological theory in previous chapters.

»

SOCIAL LEARNING THEORY

'Learning is a process by which experience produces a relatively enduring change in an organism's behaviour or capabilities' (Passer 2007, p.192). The 'social' element highlights that we live in social groups and are shaped by our interactions with and observations of others. Within this framework that 'modelling' of behaviours by parents is considered crucial in understanding children's behaviour and outcomes. Bandura, a leading exponent of social learning, undertook research into aggressive children and found they were influenced by parental modelling of aggression – to put it simply, 'monkey see, monkey do.'

BEHAVIOURAL GENETICS

This is similar to the nature/nurture debate, as it looks at the role of genetics in a child's behaviour and their interaction with the environment.

PARENTING STYLES

Parenting style is a combination of parental control and parental responsiveness.

Psychological research has focused heavily on 'parenting styles' to study the effects of parenting on child developmental outcomes. The following table captures this approach. We shall examine Diane Baumrind's theory, which fed into this conceptualisation of parenting styles.

A two-dimensional classification of parenting styles

		PARENTAL ACCEPTANCE	
		Accepting, responsive	Rejecting, unresponsive
PARENTAL CONTROL	Demanding, controlling	**Authoritative**	**Authoritarian**
	Undemanding, low in control	**Permissive–indulgent**	**Permissive–neglectful**

Source: Maccoby and Martin (1983)

Attachment is an important aspect in the study of the relationships between parent and child. Another area of research that has developed is parenting style and the differences that appear to exist (e.g. some parents advocating a strict approach while others do not). Diana Baumrind, in her paper 'Effects of authoritative parental control on child behavior' (1966), suggested the following three styles of parenting:

Permissive	▪ Parent tends to be relaxed about discipline, avoids exercise of control ▪ Parent makes few demands upon the child regarding household chores or orderly behaviour ▪ Parent sees themselves not as an active agent shaping the child but as a resource for the child to use ▪ Parent does not encourage the child to obey externally defined standards
Authoritarian	▪ Parent values obedience, child in its place ▪ When disagreement exists between parent and child, parent favours a punitive approach ▪ Parent believes that the child should accept the word of the parent, does not believe in verbal give and take or discussions
Authoritative	▪ Parent encourages verbal give and take ▪ Parent willing to share reasoning behind their decision-making with the child and is open to adapting ▪ Parent sets standards for future behaviour ▪ Parent praises and affirms the child's qualities

At the heart of this and other research on parenting styles is that different parenting styles can lead to different outcomes for the child.

For example, Dekovic and Janssens (1992) found that children of authoritative parents tended to be more popular, while children of authoritarian parents were less so.

Not everyone is convinced that 'parenting styles' offers the most convincing explanation of parenting. Belsky (1984) argues that it is more complex and proposes what he calls 'the determinants of parenting'.

BELSKY'S DETERMINANTS OF PARENTING

Belsky (1984) challenged the 'parenting styles' approach typified by Baumrind. He argues that an important factor – why parents parent as they do – was being ignored. He states:

> *[B]y tradition, students of socialisation have directed their primary energies toward understanding processes whereby parents' childrearing strategies and behaviours shape and influence their offspring's development. It is of interest to learn that, while great effort has been expended studying the characteristics and consequences of parenting, much less attention has been devoted to studying why parents parent the way they do – beyond, of course, social-class and cross-cultural comparisons and investigations examining the effect of the child on parenting behaviour. (Belsky 1984, p.83)*

»

Belsky suggests we need to take a broader view of many influences if we truly want to understand why parents parent as they do.

Belsky identifies three main influences on parental functions. These are:

1. Parent's own psychological functioning
2. Child characteristics
3. Context-based stressors and supports

This diagram captures the central aspects of Belsky's approach.

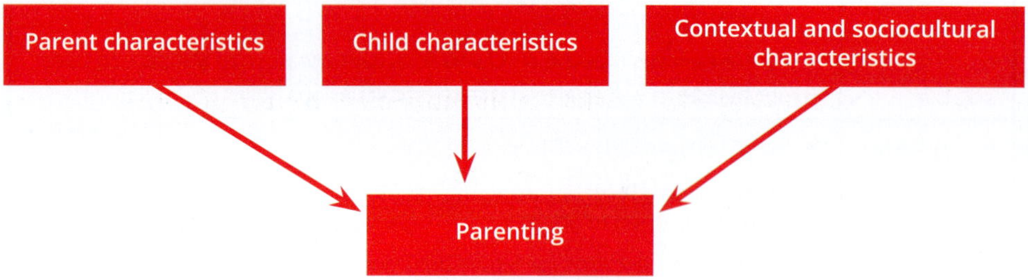

Belsky's determinants of parenting

Determinants of parenting

DETERMINANT	DESCRIPTION	EXAMPLE
Parent characteristics/ psychological function	Parent's own developmental background, which has an influence on aspects of personality, then influences parenting. Parents were once children themselves and were as shaped by their early experiences as they now have the potential to shape their own children's.	One example is depressed mothers who, Belsky relates, 'offered a disruptive, hostile, rejecting home environment to their children, which, not surprisingly, undermined child functioning' (1984, p.85).
Child characteristics	Most of the relevant research has looked at the influence of the child's temperament in making them easier or harder to parent. (We discussed the different temperaments a baby can be born with in Chapter 4.)	A baby with a difficult temperament can be more challenging to parent and place greater stress on parents. This is one example of a child characteristic impacting on the parenting dynamic.
Context-based stressors and supports	These represent the ecological context within which parenting takes place, e.g. marital relationship, social supports, un/ employment. Belsky maintained that the most important factor within this sphere was the quality of the marital relationship 'with inherent potential for exerting the most positive or negative effect on parental functioning.'	A very recent example is the Covid pandemic which saw parents and children in lockdown and having to navigate working and schooling from home. This was recognised as a significant stressor for parents and their offspring

Belsky attempted to capture the complex interaction of different variables (**factors**) involved in parenting. It is interesting to note that 'child characteristics' impact parenting. This a shift away from the traditional approach whereby influence was one-way (from parent to child). There is now greater recognition that influence is often **bi-directional**, certainly within parenting, so children (their temperaments, illness, personality) can exert influence on how their parents parent and interact with them.

Think about it

What theory does this approach – bi-directionality and factoring in different contexts – remind you of? That's right – Bronfenbrenner's bio-ecological theory!

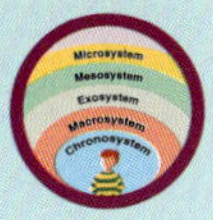

Think about how this theory could be used to understand Belsky's conceptualisation that different aspects need to be considered when looking at parenting.

Additional reading

Parenting is complex, and as we have seen there are many factors at play. Its crucial role in healthy social and emotional development is undeniable. Intervention programmes have been developed to strengthen parenting in the knowledge that this will strengthen families and outcomes.

Research some programmes and initiatives that support parents; summarise their approaches; and reflect on how they might link in with some of the theories and material covered in this book.

CHECK YOUR LEARNING GOALS!

You should be able to:

1. Say what period of development is present during middle childhood.
2. List motor skills you would expect to see in children during this stage.
3. Outline the three main features of Piaget's stage.
4. Explain why 'decentring' is considered an important capacity to gain.
5. Explain the three different types of 'conservation'.
6. Outline what Vygotsky meant by the term 'scaffolding'.
7. List Gardner's initial eight types of intelligence and the further two he later added.
8. Describe each of these intelligences in your own words.
9. Describe one criticism of his theory.
10. Describe the 'latency stage' theorised by Freud.
11. Identify and describe Erikson's stage associated with 6–12-year-olds.
12. Summarise the key theories of moral development.
13. Explain some of the criticisms of Kohlberg's theory of moral development.
14. Outline the four stages of Selman's theory of friendship formation.

7

Adolescence

In this chapter we will discover:

* What is adolescence
* Physical development
  - Growth patterns
  - The adolescent brain
  - Sexual maturation
  - Pubertal timing
  - In Focus: Eating disorders
* Cognitive development
  - Piaget's formal operational stage
  - Elkind's adolescent egocentrism theory
* Socio-emotional development
  - Erikson's identity vs. role confusion
  - Marcia's identity formation
  - Identity, self-concept and self-esteem
  - In Focus: Lesbian, gay, bisexual and transgender (LGBT) people
  - Gender
  - In Focus: Social media

Adolescence is a truly fascinating period of development. It involves significant biological changes to the body and brain. Accompanying these are questions of identity, which is recognised as a developmental milestone. Adolescence, more than most, is a period that highlights the role of sociocultural influences and how these can shape and inform the developing person. Adolescence is a very Western concept and one that continues to evolve; for example, the cut-off age for it is now argued to be 23 years rather than 18. In other cultures, 'adolescence' is understood differently. However, one thing remains constant and that is the physiological changes that occur as the individual transitions from being a child to an adult.

WHAT IS ADOLESCENCE?

Adolescence, from the Latin *adolescere* meaning 'to grow up', is seen as a unique transitionary period from childhood to adulthood encompassing not just physical but also social, emotional and cognitive changes. **Puberty** refers to the commencement and maturation of biological, physical and sexual characteristics and is generally seen in most countries to signify the change or transition from childhood to adulthood.

Adolescence encompasses behavioural, social and emotional aspects, which are influenced by physical and social/cultural factors. The WHO defines adolescence as the second decade of life, from ten to 20 years of age.

Yet adolescence is not merely chronological age, it is also socially constructed, which means that some societies have different ideas about what 'adolescence' means. In some cultures, puberty marks the child's coming of age and an ability to take on 'adult' roles. Girls may marry or begin childbearing far earlier than we would anticipate in the West.

PHYSICAL DEVELOPMENT

We start our journey through adolescence with the physical changes that can be so apparent, and some that are more hidden.

The process of physiological change is set in motion with the release of hormones by the pituitary gland in the brain. The increase in these hormones begins at approximately eight or nine years of age. It is also then that we start to see sex differences emerge as different hormones effect different changes.

GROWTH PATTERNS

In boys there is an increase in the hormone testosterone and in girls an increase in oestrogen. These hormones cause physical and sexual changes.

BOYS	GIRLS
Shoulders broaden	Hips widen
Legs lengthen	Gain fat
Gain more muscle	Become more 'curvy'

There is a difference in the age at which males and females start their growth spurt:

* Girls: approximately 10 years of age
* Boys: approximately 12 years of age.

So, as we can see, girls begin this stage of development about two years earlier than boys. It is worth noting that these ages merely indicate the beginning of the biological changes and not necessarily the associated secondary sexual characteristics associated with adolescence, which we will look at later.

In relation to motor skills, there's a tendency for girls to be better co-ordinated in their movements, while boys may have greater speed and strength.

Growth uses up fuel, so appetite and the need for sleep will vary to support growth. Levels of activity will also vary, because growing consumes energy. Fatigue from growth will also induce changes in mood such as irritability and lethargy. The response of parents and teachers at this stage is to encourage the consumption of a balanced diet with adequate calories for the body and brain, and to recognise the need for sleep and rest.

Think about it

Earlier in the book, we discussed individual variation. How might the information on the differing patterns of physical changes in individuals be used to support this concept?

Adolescence is a time of spectacular change in the human body. We encountered the proximodistal and cephalocaudal principles of growth in earlier chapters and we saw that in the growing foetus and baby, growth happens from head to toe (cephalocaudal) and from the trunk outwards to the extremities (proximodistal).

In adolescence there is a **reversal** of the proximodistal principle of growth. Instead of growth occurring from the trunk and spreading out to the extremities, change first begins in the extremities (hands and feet) and works back towards the trunk. Adolescents' hands and feet grow to their adult size first before changes occur to the remainder of the body. This is sometimes held accountable for the apparent clumsiness and physical awkwardness seen in young teens who, in theory, have a child's body but adult-sized feet and hands.

Another pattern of growth to note is that this is an **asynchronous** period, which means that changes are rapid and uneven. This is in contrast to the period preceding adolescence where the changes were slow and steady.

THE ADOLESCENT BRAIN

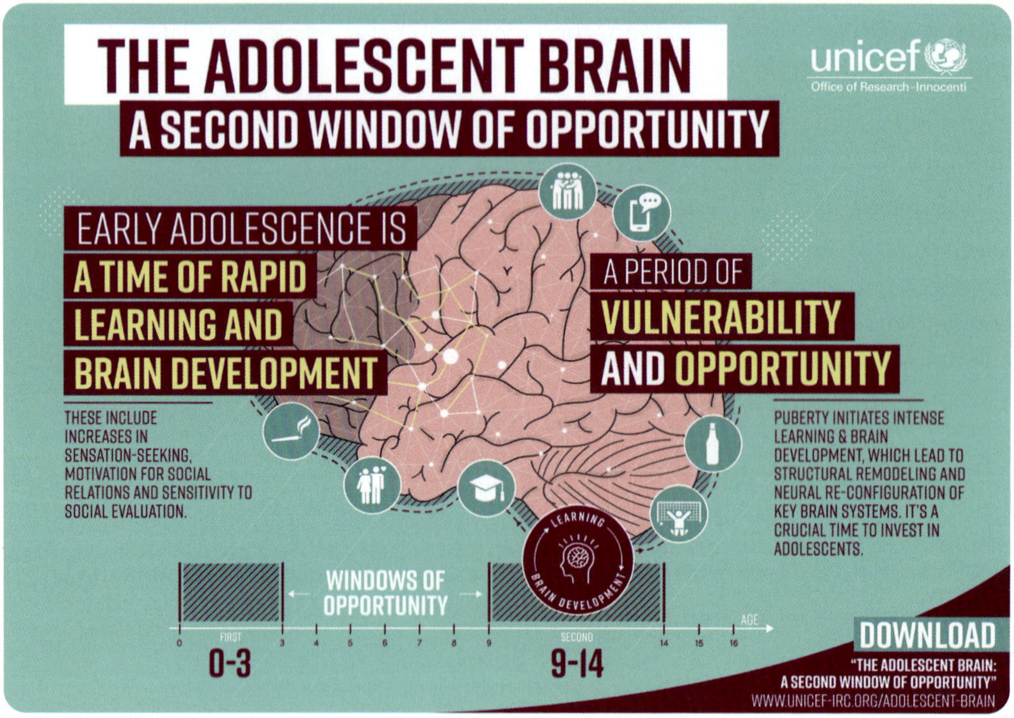

The brain undergoes a major growth spurt at the beginning of puberty, particularly in the frontal cortex.

CHANGES IN THE PREFRONTAL CORTEX

An infant has far more brain cells and synapses (cell connections) than it needs, so the brain 'prunes' the superfluous and inefficient cells and connections.

Jay Giedd has discovered that a second wave of synapse formation occurs just before puberty in the prefrontal cortex, whose functions include planning, memory and organisation.

A maturing prefrontal cortex increases the teen's ability to reason, to control their impulses and in general to make better judgements.

During adolescence 'pruning' occurs again, with the brain discarding cells that are not stimulated and used. It's similar to the idea of pruning a tree and cutting back the dead or weak branches. The principle 'use it or lose it' has been argued to be important in brain development. If a teen takes part in sport or plays a musical instrument, for example, it is these connections that become 'hardwired' in the brain because they have been reinforced. If, on the other hand, the teen watches television most of the day, those are the cells and connections that will be maintained. Further, an immature prefrontal cortex and its associated functions have been implicated in the risk-taking behaviours seen in some adolescents.

> *Now that MRI studies have cracked open a window on the developing brain, researchers are looking at how the newly detected physiological changes might account for the adolescent behaviors so familiar to parents: emotional outbursts, reckless risk taking and rule breaking, and the impassioned pursuit of sex, drugs and rock 'n' roll. Some experts believe the structural changes seen at adolescence may explain the timing of such major mental illnesses as schizophrenia and bipolar disorder. These diseases typically begin in adolescence and contribute to the high rate of teen suicide. Increasingly, the wild conduct once blamed on 'raging hormones' is being seen as the by-product of two factors: a surfeit [excessive amount] of hormones, yes, but also a paucity [lack] of the cognitive controls needed for mature behavior. (Giedd 2004)*

Indeed, it is suggested that the brain does not fully mature until 25 years of age. As the physical brain develops and matures, we would expect to see the cognitive (thinking) functions increase and mature as well.

SEXUAL MATURATION

Some of the most obvious characteristics associated with adolescence are related to the changing appearance of the teenager. **Pubertal timing** refers to the onset of puberty and its associated physical and sexual changes. Noticeable changes in girls are the development of breasts and in boys the appearance of facial hair. There is a difference between primary and secondary sexual characteristics.

Primary sexual characteristics are the changes and development that directly involve the sex organs:

* **Girls – menarche:** The start of menstruation (periods). The timing of menarche for Irish girls is 13.5 years with a range of 10.9 to 16.1 years of age (Malina *et al.* 2004, p.314). The average age for menarche in the USA is 12.8 years of age.
* **Boys – spermarche:** This term was coined to mark the sexual maturation of boys, when males become capable of reproduction. 'Spermarche' refers to the first time a boy ejaculates; as this is a private event it is difficult to surmise an age for this event or gather much research.
* **Maturation of reproductive organs:** In males this includes the growth of the penis and changes to the scrotum and testes. In females the development of vagina, ovaries and uterus would be classified as primary sexual characteristics.

Secondary sexual characteristics are visible evidence of changes occurring in the adolescent:

- Girls – development of breasts
- Boys – facial hair and voice change
- Both – underarm hair.

PUBERTAL TIMING

While puberty involves changes in both males and females, we're going to examine the onset of menarche (periods) specifically to better understand some of the factors involved in the timing of puberty.

Factors in the timing of puberty include hereditary and nutrition. A trend for earlier menarche has been identified, with societal influences being implicated. Over the last century girls have reached menarche at increasingly younger ages in the developed world. The age of menarche stabilised in the 1960s at 12.8 years in the USA and 13.2 years in the UK; in Ireland the mean age is 13.5 years. Factors implicated in the timing of menarche include weight, exercise and nutrition. Let's take nutrition, for example: if the body experiences a lack of food it perhaps hasn't the 'fuel' it needs to sustain the immense changes that occur in adolescence and in particular with menarche. Since this is the beginning of reproductive ability in females it would make sense, if resources are scarce, for the body to delay possible pregnancy, which would put further strain on the body's resources.

Garcia-Moro and Hernandez (1990) found among Spanish females in the 1920s an average age of 13.91 years for the start of menarche; this stabilised to 12.92 in the 1950s and has remained approximately the same since. This is representative of the levelling out of the mean age of menarche that has been witnessed in the West. One would imagine that there has to be a natural cut-off point where the body cannot begin sexual changes any earlier. Yet we need to remember that not every girl in Ireland begins her period at 13.5 years of age, that a range exists and that early and later maturations exist.

EFFECTS OF PUBERTAL TIMING

The effects of early and late pubertal maturation in females and males has been a popular source of research and the findings suggest different outcomes. Brooks-Gunn *et al.* (1985) suggested that adolescents who are 'off-time' (early or late maturation) with their peers experience more stress and are more susceptible to adjustment problems in adolescence. A second explanation is that early developers, especially girls, face more social pressure. If they mature earlier, they will face the attention of male sexual interest earlier; and since the physical development of their body does not match that of their brain and their cognitive development, they have less 'thinking' skills to handle the increased attention that their early maturation attracts. As the teens look older there can be a tendency for them to be viewed as more socially and cognitively developed than they actually are. It is also suggested that in developing earlier these adolescents miss the opportunity to complete the normal development tasks of middle childhood as they fast forward past this stage.

Maturation

TIME OF MATURATION	BOYS	GIRLS
Early	Appears to be associated with more positive outcomes, particularly in terms of social development; enjoy prestige	Face more problems, including greater likelihood of negative moods and behaviours. Negative body image (Brooks-Gunn *et al.* 1985) Higher vulnerability to engaging in risk-taking behaviours including smoking, drinking and sexual activity at an earlier age (Magnusson *et al.* 1985).
Late	Lower achievement (Dubas *et al.* 1991); lower self-esteem and happiness (Crockett & Petersen 1987)	Higher achievement (Dubas *et al.* 1991)

Think about it

Summarise how early and late physical maturation can impact on the social and emotional development of the teen. Do you think this highlights the interaction of nature versus nurture in developmental outcomes?

What we are seeing is that physical changes can have a relationship to others areas of development. Starting adolescence early is more likely to have a 'positive' effect on a boy and a negative effect on a girl. This reminds us of the importance of recognising that all aspects of development are inter-related and also of the role of societal and cultural influences. Eating disorders are a very clear illustration of this.

IN FOCUS: EATING DISORDERS

Eating disorders (EDs), while they manifest themselves in the physical domain (weight loss and disturbed eating patterns), are seen as a psychological disorder. Examining them offers us a bridge between the physical and psychological domains of functioning.

According to the HSE, 'Eating disorders have the highest mortality and morbidity of all the mental disorders' (2018, p.11).

The causes of EDs are a complex mixture of biological, psychological and social factors; 40–60% of the estimated causality of anorexia nervosa and bulimia nervosa is heritable or genetic.

»

Think about it

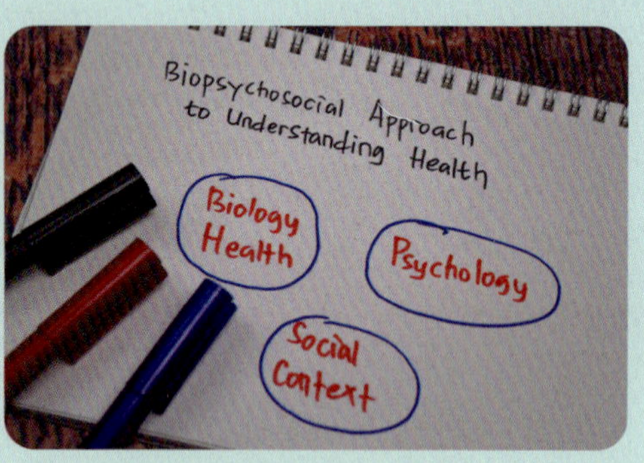

The biopsychosocial model (see page 2) remains dominant in psychology as a way of understanding the possible factors involved in human wellbeing. Bronfenbrenner's bio-ecological theory is similar to this approach. Note the different factors involved in EDs and decide whether they are biological, psychological or social. Can you use the 'biopsychosocial model' to understand other conditions?

Eating disorders are increasingly common, and serious, conditions which tend to peak in adolescence. The average age of onset of eating disorders is reducing (Favaro 2009). For anorexia nervosa, the peak incidence of onset is 14–18 years and for bulimia it is 14–22 years. Binge eating disorder (BED) is most commonly presents in the late teens or early 20s.

We are going to look at anorexia nervosa and bulimia.

ANOREXIA NERVOSA

Anorexia nervosa, from the Greek meaning 'loss of appetite', is an eating disorder whereby the individual inflicts self-starvation. In this disorder, adolescents gain control by limiting food intake. Anorexics often obsess about thinness, need attention, lack individuality and deny sexuality. Affecting females fifteen times more than males, it usually begins during adolescence or in early adulthood, but hardly ever occurs in women past the age of twenty-five.

BULIMIA

Bulimia comes from the Greek words meaning 'ox' and 'hunger' – the sufferer eats like a hungry ox. A bulimic eats in unrestrained sprees. One major characteristic of bulimia is binge eating, in which an individual can consume between 10,000 to 20,000 calories. These binge-eating episodes are usually followed by episodes of purging, accomplished by vomiting, laxatives, diuretics, enemas, compulsive exercising, weight-reducing drugs or intermittent periods of strict dieting.

The *Diagnostic and Statistical Manual of Mental Disorders* (DSM) is used to outline the characteristics of mental health disorders and to enable diagnosis. Below is a table highlighting the most recent classifications of three common EDs.

DSM-5 diagnostic criteria for eating disorders

Anorexia nervosa	**A.** Persistent restriction of energy intake, leading to significantly low body weight (in the context of what is minimally expected for age, sex, developmental trajectory and physical health). **B.** Intense fear of gaining weight or of becoming fat, or persistent behaviour that interferes with weight gain (even though at significantly low weight). **C.** Disturbance in the way one's body weight or shape is experienced, undue influence of body shape and weight on self-evaluation or persistent lack of recognition of the seriousness of the current low body weight. *Subtypes* **1.** Restricting type **2.** Binge/purging type (based on last three months)
Bulimia nervosa	**A.** Recurrent episodes of binge eating. An episode of binge eating is characterised by both of the following: **1.** Eating, in a discrete period of time (e.g. within any 2-hour period) an amount of food that is definitely larger than most people would eat during a similar period of time and under similar circumstances **2.** A sense of lack of control over eating during the episode (e.g. a feeling that one cannot stop eating or control what or how much one is eating). **B.** Recurrent inappropriate compensatory behaviour in order to prevent weight gain, such as self-induced vomiting, misuse of laxatives, diuretics or other medications, fasting or excessive exercise. **C.** The binge eating and inappropriate compensatory behaviours both occur, on average, at least once a week for three months. **D.** Self-evaluation is unduly influenced by body shape and weight. **E.** The disturbance does not occur exclusively during episodes of anorexia nervosa. »

Binge eating disorder	**A.** Recurrent episodes of binge eating. An episode of binge eating is characterised by both of the following: **1.** Eating, in a discrete period of time (e.g. within any 2-hour period), an amount of food that is definitely larger than most people would eat during a similar period of time and under similar circumstances and **2.** A sense of lack of control over eating during the episode (e.g. a feeling that one cannot stop eating or control what or how much one is eating) **B.** Associated with three or more of: • Eating much more rapidly than normal • Eating until uncomfortably full • Eating large amounts of food when not feeling physically hungry • Eating alone because of embarrassment over how much one is eating • Feeling disgusted with oneself, depressed or very guilty afterwards **C.** Marked distress regarding binge eating is present. **D.** Binge eating occurs, on average, at least once a week for three months. **E.** Binge eating is not associated with the recurrent use of inappropriate compensatory behaviours and is not occurring exclusively during the course of bulimia nervosa, anorexia nervosa or avoidant/restrictive food intake disorder (ARFID). Note: Binge eating disorder is less common but much more severe than overeating. It is associated with more subjective distress regarding the eating behaviour, and commonly coexists with other psychological problems.

Source: HSE (2018) Eating Disorder Services

PSYCHOLOGICAL CHARACTERISTICS ASSOCIATED WITH TEENAGERS SUFFERING FROM EDS

It is important for people to understand that adolescents suffering from eating disorders, both male and female, may not appear to be underweight. Weight is only a physical sign of an eating disorder; in fact the adolescent is likely suffering from a deeper emotional conflict that needs to be resolved. Eating disorders are addictions to a behaviour and the obsession with food is only a symptom of deeper problems such as low self-esteem, depression, poor self-image and self-hate.

Hilde Bruch, an eminent psychiatrist, described the relentless pursuit of thinness as an effort to mask underlying problems (Bruch *et al.* 1988.) The following are some of the mental characteristics of adolescent males and females suffering from eating disorders.

Mental characteristics of eating disorders

Perfectionism	Many adolescents suffering from eating disorders are perfectionists and high achievers. They strive to reach perfection, are eager to please and in the process lose their true selves. When they feel they've failed to reach perfection they often unrealistically blame themselves for their failure and attempt to punish themselves. Punishment often occurs in the form of starvation for anorexics and purging for bulimics.
Low self-esteem	Feelings of inadequacy are common among teens suffering from eating disorders. They have a poor self-image and perception of themselves. They irrationally believe they are fat regardless of how thin they become. They experience a sense of inner emptiness, uncertainty and helplessness, and a lack of self-confidence and self-trust (Bruch *et al* 1988.) They feel confident if they are losing weight but suffer from feelings of worthlessness and guilt if they are not (Pipher 1994). It is also common for them to believe they do not deserve good things or to be happy.
Depression	Mood swings, feelings of hopelessness, anxiety, isolation and loneliness are feelings common to sufferers of eating disorders. Bulimics experience a loss of control that leads to depression, whereas anorexics experience depression as a result of gaining weight (Schlundt & Johnson 1990).
Obsession	These adolescents deal with an intense obsession and preoccupation with food, calories, fat grams and weight. Weight becomes their most important and self-defining attribute. Eating disorders are considered addictions in which starvation, bingeing and purging are the addictive behaviours and food is the narcotic (Pipher 1994).
Guilt	Adolescents with eating disorders often feel guilty because they do not think they have met the expectations of others. They are striving for the perfect body and for a sense of control but in this process they start to feel guilty about their habit (Pipher 1994).

Are we right to concentrate on just the individual when looking at factors that influence EDs? The role of the media has increasingly become a contentious one, especially in light of the glorification of 'size zero'. The following piece of research considers the influence of media in the perpetuation of eating disorders. »

EATING DISORDERS AND THE ROLE OF THE MEDIA

McNicholas *et al.* (2009) investigated media influences on eating attitudes in adolescents. The authors note that previous research indicates that a relationship appears to exist between the portrayal of thinness in the media and disordered eating. The authors found that the majority of teens (68.3%) felt the media portrayal was either 'far too thin' or 'a little too thin'. Interestingly, the majority of female respondents felt negatively affected by this portrayal, comparing to 19.9% of males. Further (p.212), 'The fashion industry has also reinforced this unrealistic thin body ideal: 25 years ago the average model was 8% thinner than the average woman – now models are on average 23% thinner.' The research suggests 'that while the media is not always the cause of pathological eating it can interact with other factors in certain cases.'

The authors direct attention to influential research conducted by Becker *et al.* (2002) that evaluated the impact of the advent of television on the island of Fiji. Until its arrival, a more 'rounded' body shape was perceived as the ideal. With the arrival of westernised media, there was a sharp increase in disordered eating, which were hitherto rare. These findings were replicated in research conducted in Tanzania.

These conclusions flag the role the media plays in shaping on our attitudes towards not just eating but a spectrum of topics. While the research isn't saying that the media is directly responsible for EDs, it's apparent that it does play some role. At the end of the chapter, we will delve more into the impact of social media on young people.

LINK

We discussed socialisation in the previous chapter. Here it can highlight the influence of media and the messages it delivers. Using Bronfenbrenner's bio-ecological theory, we can see how media, though a more 'distant' external influence, can nonetheless be a very powerful one.

By now you will be beginning to see the inter-relatedness of the physical, cognitive and socio-emotional areas of development. With the increase in brain growth in adolescence, changes can be seen in the teen's thinking and reasoning capacities.

COGNITIVE DEVELOPMENT

With the increasing activity seen in the brain, one would expect an increase in the cognitive abilities of the adolescent. This growth spurt brings many changes in the way young adults begin to think, such as:

- Better ability to handle more information
- Improved ability to devise mental strategies to help them remember
- Improved ability to organise information
- The growth of the frontal lobe resulting in greater ability in higher reasoning and thinking.

According to Kolb, the growth in the frontal lobe corresponds with Piaget's formal operational stage of thinking, the main features of which are abstract inductive and deductive thinking.

PIAGET'S FORMAL OPERATIONAL STAGE (12 ONWARDS)

The main characteristic of this stage is the growing ability to think in abstract terms and use deductive logic. What does this mean?

First, let's deal with abstract thinking. Up to this stage the child can only think about things that are 'real' or concrete. According to Piaget they are unable to reason about make-believe problems or situations. Concepts such as justice or ethics are abstract terms; you can't touch them or see them. As the adolescent develops **abstract thinking** they also begin to think more logically, they are able to consider hypotheses (educated guesses or explanations) and test them. Think of algebra in school, where letters act as numbers.

In the **third eye experiment**, Shaffer(1999) reports that 12-year-old children, when asked where they'd put a 'third eye', provide more creative justifications than younger children at the concrete level who say they'd put it, between the existing eyes. At this higher level, one responder said they'd put it on their hand so they could use it to see around corners. This answer and the thinking behind it shows their growing cognitive abilities, especially that they can think about their own thoughts.

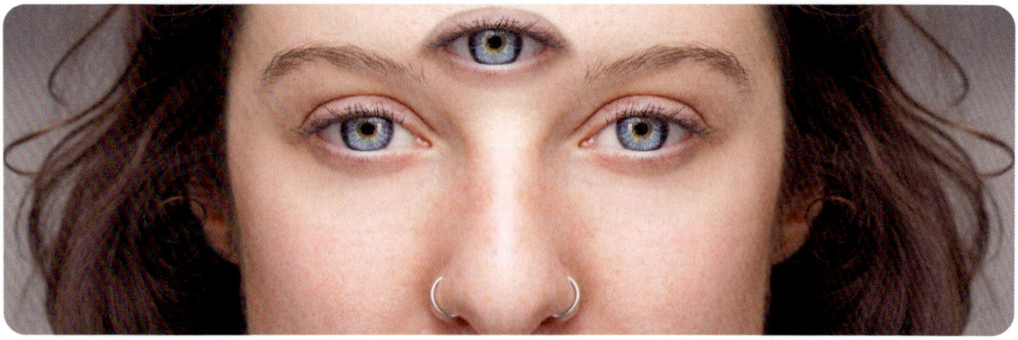

The ability to think **abstractly** gives us great freedom in our thinking as we are no longer confined to the world of 'real' objects, concepts or ideas.

Is Piaget's abstract thinking related to other areas such as:

* **Neurological:** The growth in the prefrontal cortex which is responsible for higher reasoning and thought
* **Moral:** Kohlberg and Piaget believed that the ability to reason morally at higher and more complex levels comes in the early teens
* **Self:** Teens can now think about who they are, their different selves and their possible and future selves, which involves the use of abstract thinking.

Think about it

Do your own research. Ask children, teens and adults of various ages where they would put a third eye and why. Note their answers and especially their reasons for their answer. Do age differences exist?

ELKIND'S ADOLESCENT EGOCENTRISM THEORY

Do you remember ever feeling as a teen that everyone was 'looking at you', of being intensely self-conscious? If this rings true David Elkind has an explanation for this: the **imaginary audience**. This is the belief of an adolescent that others are constantly focusing attention on him or her, scrutinising behaviours, appearance and the like. The adolescent feels as though he or she is continually the central topic of interest to a group of spectators (i.e. an audience) when in fact this is not the case (i.e. it is an imaginary audience). This is an early adolescent construct reflective of acute self-consciousness and is considered an expression of adolescent egocentrism (American Psychological Association (APA) 1994).

As I've got older, I care far less what others think of me than I did when I was younger. Yet adolescents do care, very much so. This is why a pimple on the nose turns into a major crisis as the teen believes everyone will notice, everyone will be looking at them. Elkind refers to this increased self-consciousness seen in adolescents as a form of **egocentrism**.

LINK

We mentioned egocentrism in the early stages of Piaget's cognitive theory. Remember, this is about how we think, not a personality issue such as being self-centred or self-obsessed. Revisit Chapters 2 and 5 to refresh your understanding of the term 'egocentrism' in cognition.

Think about it

How might the role of social media play into the phenomenon of the imaginary audience?

While the imaginary audience forms one part of the social thinking that characterises 'adolescent egocentrism', another aspect of it is the '**personal fable**' (also called the invincibility fable), a belief in one's uniqueness and invulnerability, which is an expression of adolescent egocentrism and may extend further into the lifespan (APA 1994).

Here we see egocentrism at play again. Isn't it interesting that children grow out of one type of egocentrism, developing the ability to recognise that others may have different perspectives, yet here we are in adolescence and 'egocentrism' arises again. But note that it is in a slightly different way. Here the adolescent believes that their experiences are unique.

The kind of egocentrism Elkind speaks of in adolescence feeds into a belief that they are not subject to the rules that govern the rest of the world – which contributes to a sense of invincibility. This belief has been implicated in some of the risk-taking behaviours seen in adolescence. Thus, a teen might take drugs with the belief that they won't become addicted, that it won't happen to them.

While the belief in the 'imaginary audience' is strongest in early teenage years, it declines as the individual moves into later adolescence. The 'personal fable', on the other hand, can persist into early adulthood.

How we think can have a direct impact on how we behave and how we feel. You can see how the 'imaginary audience' thinking described by Elkind could lead to feelings of intense self-consciousness and affect how we interact with others. Adolescence is recognised as a period when young people figure out 'who they are', and the developmental milestone associated with this period is **identity**. We are going to look at this from a historical perspective in psychology. However, we see in this realm the power of societal and cultural changes (recall Bronfenbrenner's bio-ecological theory) where how we think about 'gender' and other aspects of 'identity' is changing rapidly. This highlights the role of culture in our development.

SOCIO-EMOTIONAL DEVELOPMENT

We've seen that Elkind suggests adolescents 'think' differently in this phase of their development. Elkind proposed that risk-taking behaviours witnessed in adolescence can be attributed to 'personal fable', a style of thinking that can lend to beliefs of invincibility or that their 'story' is already written.

Erikson, who is a psychosocial theorist, suggests a different explanation for such behaviours. We saw in Chapter 2 that each of Erikson's stages can have either a negative or positive outcome. In this stage of development the negative outcome for the teen, according to Erikson, is 'role confusion' and this, Erikson says, is responsible for risky behaviours.

ERIKSON'S IDENTITY VS. ROLE CONFUSION

As teens make the transition from childhood to adulthood they face questions of 'who' they are and their future role in life. Erikson's fifth stage reflects this; the major developmental 'crisis' to be resolved is 'identity'. Adolescence , at least in the West, is synonymous with angst about 'Who am I?' and 'What is my role in life?' and those who successfully navigate this period develop their identity. Erikson referred to a **psychological moratorium** – the gap between childhood and adulthood where the teen explores different roles.

By the end of the stage this adolescent will have successfully emerged with a sense of who they are. However, some will be unable to resolve the challenge of emerging identity. According to Erikson they suffer from **role confusion**, resulting in either isolation or a willingness to take on the identity of others. Role confusion has been linked to risk-taking behaviours. For Erikson, the development of self and identity is a major developmental milestone for the teen to accomplish.

Identity is influenced by how the adolescent sees themself and is also based on their relationships with others and how they perceive others see them. Theories have been proposed that try to explain how identity and self-concept emerges. Let's look at another approach to understanding how adolescents characterise self-concept.

Identity is the stable, consistent and reliable sense of who one is and what one stands for in the world. It integrates one's meaning to oneself and one's meaning to others; it provides a match between what one regards as central to oneself and how one is viewed by significant others in one's life.

Identity is not a unitary concept; we can have many aspects:

* Religious identity
* Sexual identity
* Gender identity
* Career identity
* Cultural or ethnic identity.

Who I am in the classroom can be quite different to who I am at home with my son or out with friends. I am Irish, a woman, mother, teacher, friend, daughter and sister.

Think about it

How do you see yourself? List some of your roles and identities.

Historically in psychology, one of the best known theories on the formation of identity in adolescence is found in the work of James Marcia.

MARCIA'S IDENTITY FORMATION

Building on the work of Erikson, James Marcia suggested that identity involves the adoption of ideals and values, sexual orientation and work possibilities. Having considered the possibilities the young person, at the end of adolescence, must make commitments about what to become and what to believe. Marcia used an interview technique to assess identity 'status'. Unlike Erikson, whose theory is a stage-based one, Marcia formulated the idea of status which allowed for a more fluid conception of identity formation.

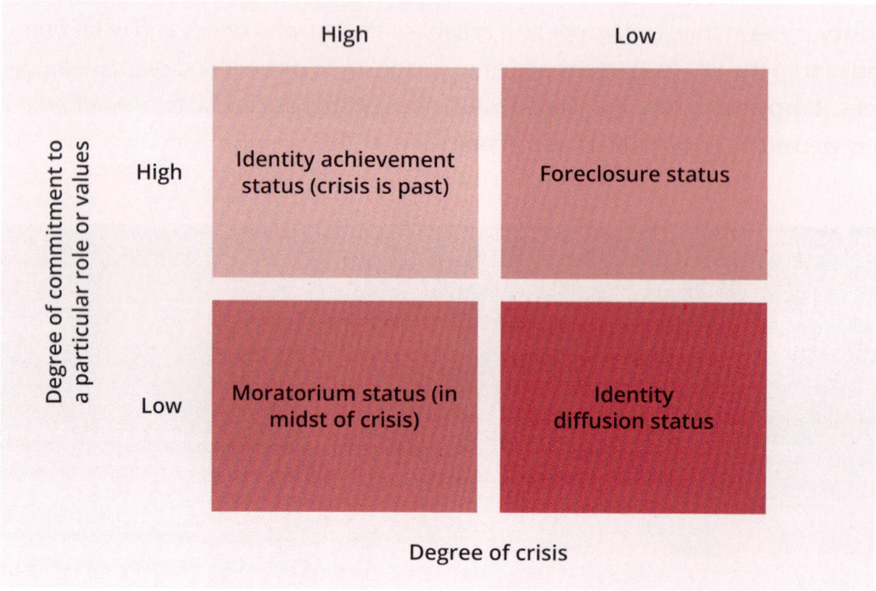

Identity statuses:

* **Moratorium** (in crisis, no commitment): This is marked by intense crisis as the teen searches out possibilities, considering the different roles in their search for identity. No commitment has been made yet.
* **Foreclosure** (no crisis and commitment): This teen might seem like the perfect adolescent who dutifully follows rules and doesn't question orders. This teen has made a commitment to an identity without going through the crisis and exploring alternatives. Instead they have accepted a parentally or culturally defined commitment. Erikson would believe that the teen had not tackled the challenges of this period and instead relied on identification with others.
* **Diffusion** (might have had crisis, no commitment): The main characteristic of this stage is that the teen is not in 'crisis' actively considering possibilities; further, they are avoiding making a commitment. The stereotypical difficult teen watching TV and refusing to talk might be said to be in this state.
* **Achievement** (has had crisis and commitment): The adolescent has come through the 'crisis' and a commitment has been made to ideological, occupational and other goals. They have established a sense of self and identity.

IDENTITY, SELF-CONCEPT AND SELF-ESTEEM

Can we distinguish between identity and self-concept? According to Tap and Sordes-Ader (2012):

* **Identity** consists of representations and feelings and cannot be reduced to a purely cognitive system.
* **Self-concept** focuses on the cognitive dimension of the self.

The American Psychological Association (APA) expands on this definition:

> **Self-concept** is one's description and evaluation of oneself, including psychological and physical characteristics, qualities, skills, roles and so forth. Self-concepts contribute to the individual's sense of identity over time. (APA 1994)

An allied concept is self-esteem, which is, in part, influenced by our self-concept and identity. Harter (1990) defined self-esteem as 'how much a person likes, accepts, and respects [him or herself] overall as a person' (p. 255).

The APA's definition is broader:

> **Self-esteem** is the degree to which the qualities and characteristics contained in one's self-concept are perceived to be positive. It reflects a person's physical self-image, view of his or her accomplishments and capabilities, and values and perceived success in living up to them, as well as the ways in which others view and respond to that person. (APA 1994)

During adolescence self-esteem can be fragile. Remember Elkind's 'imaginary audience' – teens have the potential to judge themselves mercilessly.

Earlier in the chapter we saw that low self-esteem has been implicated in eating disorders. The area of self-esteem has been extensively researched, and the relationship between low self-esteem and low life satisfaction, loneliness, anxiety, resentment, irritability and depression is well documented (Rosenberg 1985).

One research area that has highlighted a relationship between identity and psychological functioning is the experiences of LGBT teens. In the piece of research we're going to look at next, what emerges is how discrimination can impact on the wellbeing of those targeted. (*Note:* this research was carried out in 2009 and the categorisation 'LGBT' reflects that; nowadays the broader LGBTQ+ abbreviation is more commonly used.)

IN FOCUS: LESBIAN, GAY, BISEXUAL AND TRANSGENDER (LGBT) PEOPLE

As we've just seen, identity and self-concept are crucial markers of adolescence. Research can make sense of, or give insight into, our development and how we experience our lives. There is increasing recognition that the lives of LGBT+ people have been overlooked and especially how LGBT+ traverse adolescence in their journey towards identity achievement or integration. There has been a lack of research conducted to better understand their lives and experiences. Like other marginalised groups, LGBT+ people can face discrimination, isolation and, in some cases, rejection » by their families and community. In the past, being gay was classified as a mental illness and categorised as such in the Diagnostic and Statistical Manual of Mental Disorders used by psychologists to categorise mental illness. People in the LGBT+ community have faced, and continue to face, stigmatisation, bullying and discrimination. Those who face such barriers and ostracisation are more vulnerable to depression and, in extreme cases, risk of suicide.

We are going to examine the findings of one notable piece of research which sought to shine a light on the experiences of young LGBT people.

Supporting LGBT Lives (Maycock *et al.* 2009) was a research initiative aimed at better understanding the experiences of LGBT young people. Its findings mirror how different factors impact on burgeoning LGBT identity.

> *The findings highlight the negative effect of stigmatisation and discrimination on mental health and wellbeing implicated is the concept of* ***minority stress*** *(the impact of negative societal reactions). The authors argue their research demonstrates that social and structural factors account for elevated mental health risks among the LGBT population. The findings show that experiences such as homophobic bullying and violence, invisibility and alientation from family and friends are all linked to increased mental health risk and suicidality among Irish LGBT people. The majority of participants in the study reported resilience in their mental health despite their experiences, [while] a 'significant' proportion reported a worrying level of psychological distress and suicidality. (Maycock* et al. *2009)*

The research with LGBT youth captured the experiences of some of the most vulnerable participants. On average, they realised they were LGBT at 14 years of age; they commenced self-harming behaviour at 15.5; they attempted suicide for the first time at 17; and did not come out to others until age 21. The period of concealing their sexual orientation or gender identity appears to coincide with particular mental health vulnerability and distress. The authors conclude that 'this period of vulnerability also coincided with participants' school-going years and their negotiation of early adulthood – a time of critical social and emotion development'.

It is important to stress that the majority of participants had never self-harmed and many reported positive everyday experiences. The authors also caution against any suggestion that it is the experience of being LGBT that is interpreted as causing the mental health challenges; 'It is important to reiterate in this context that a preoccupation with risks – frequently (mis)interpreted as individual deficits – belies the reality of LGBT lives and potentially contributes to a construction of LGBT people as deficient and dysfunctional.'

It is clear that structual and societal attitudes can be very powerful influences on developing LGBT identity, and this emphasises further the absolute necessity to tackle prejudicial, bigoted and discriminatory attitudes in society towards LGBT people and others who are marginalised. In Bronfenbrenner's bio-ecological model, one can see how immediate influences (family support) affect LGBT people but also the role of more distal factors, such as whether anti-discriminatory legislation exists and is enforced. Finally, the **minority stress model**, which is a conceptual framework for understanding the negative impact on health and wellbeing caused by a stigmatising social context, has provided a useful lens through which to view and better understand not just LGBT people's lives but other minorty groups such as the Travelling community.

Think about it

Using this model and the wider ecological approach, you can see how different influences intertwine to affect an individual's mental and physical wellbeing across their lifespan. Using what you have learned, identify other marginalised groups and the different factors that might impact on them.

GENDER

We have looked at research that touches on sexual identity and the experiences of LGBTQ+ teens. Another aspect of identity is gender. We increasingly see challenges to the traditional binary categorisation of male and female which challenge more historical approaches in psychology to capture gender development and identity.

Think about it

Note down some points from this chapter that highlight how changing societal beliefs can be seen in the field of psychology. Using Bronfenbrenner's bio-ecological theory, consider the different factors that might be involved in the development of gender identity.

NON-BINARY GENDER IDENTITIES

It's important to note that terminology and concepts that are situated in binary understandings are contentious and have the potential to be exclusionary. Not all children, adolescents and adults identify or will identify with binary gender categorisations of male or female. Binary gender concepts have been challenged by the LGBTQ+, feminist and other movements.

In non-Western societies, such as the Two-Spirit Community/First Nation Peoples, a third gender is recognised (though not necessarily categorised as non-binary or transgender). There is a lack of research on the experiences of those who do not identify within binary gender categorisations. The limited research that has been conducted suggests non-binary individuals make up between 25% and 35% of transgender populations (Nolan, Kuhner & Dy, 2019). Further, research on the mental health of those with non-binary gender identities (generally only with those who identify as transgender) finds levels of **minority stress**, a concept we came across in the piece on LGBTQ+ teens (Maycock *et al.* 2009).

Recommendations for practice include the following:

* Avoid gender binary assumption
* Understand there is no right way to 'transition' and that not everyone wants to 'transition'
* Practise using singular pronouns such as they/them. (APA)

We've seen in this chapter that adolescence is developmentally understood as a period of identity, as we figure out 'who we are'. We have also seen that it may be a time of vulnerability for some in terms of their mental health functioning. What is apparent is that societal influences can impact on a young person's sense of self and their wellbeing. With this in mind, we are going to end the chapter by looking at one of the most powerful influences in modern times – social media.

IN FOCUS: SOCIAL MEDIA

We saw earlier that media portrayals of body image and accompanying attitudes can impact negatively on young people's self-esteem and self-concept.

Given the phenomenal growth of social media platforms, it's hard to imagine a time before they and 24-hour online access existed.

The brain undergoes significant changes in adolescence and this has been tied into the impact of social media on developing teens. In early adolescence changes in the brain related to 'social rewards' become more apparent. These changes make compliments and positive feedback from peers feel more satisfying. The hormones oxytocin and dopamine ('happy hormones') multiply in a part of the brain called the ventral striatum, making teens particularly sensitive to attention and admiration from others.

Earlier we saw how the media is involved in attitudes to body image. YouTube, TikTok, Snapchat, Facebook and Instagram are all platforms that transmit attitudes regarding body size. Chou *et al.* (2014) report that 'Twitter and Facebook are dominated by derogatory and misogynist sentiment, pointing to weight stigmatization, whereas blogs and forums contained more nuanced comments.'

The influence of media and social media on attitudes among children and young people has been well documented (ESRI & Trinity 2012). What is becoming apparent is the role of **comparison**, which features heavily in social media. Another factor is the increasing numbers of younger individuals who are accessing social media. Ofcom (2017) reports that half of 11- and 12-year-olds have a social media profile, despite most platforms' minimum age being 13. Further, the proportion of 12–15-year-olds who say they have seen hateful content online has increased since 2016.

Instagram is one of the more image-heavy platforms and attracts more than a billion people, with many spending on average 30 minutes per day on the site. Adolescence is a particularly sensitive time for desiring a sense of belonging and connection with peers. It is argued (Abrams 2021) that the app, by design, capitalises on this biological drive for social belonging, and nudges users to keep on scrolling. Studies have linked Instagram to depression, body image concerns, self-esteem issues, social anxiety and other problems.

Abrams (2021) reports that part of the issue is Instagram's 'addictive' nature; it rarely provides 'stopping cues' (cues to the user to stop and participate in a different activity). Instead, it continuously serves up new content, driving users back to the top of their feeds to repeat the descent.

Another issue with social media is the altered experience of social interactions which play out differently from 'in-person' experiences. Measures of popularity and status – such as 'likes, views, and comments – tend to remain visible in perpetuity and can be viewed anytime, anywhere, and often by anyone'. (Abrams, 2021)

Think about it

Summarise what developmental changes you have read in this chapter that might explain why social media can impact much more on adolescents than older people.

Before we write off social media, it is important to look for the nuances. It is rare that a phenomenon is entirely negative – more significant is how it is interacted with. This is certainly true of social media. Research has found that spending hours at a time on Instagram is not of itself harmful – it is the way it is engaged with that appears to impact » on mental health and wellbeing. In the case of Instagram, those who use it for status-seeking or social comparison tend to experience more negative effects. However, using social media for the purposes of connection and intimacy can be positive and rewarding. It is the 'understanding' of how to use social media that is the key to users' experiences.

So we end this chapter with a sage insight – to understand phenomena we need to look carefully at different aspects and factors that are at play. Adolescence is a fascinating time. Yes, it has challenges, but it also represents an opportunity for personal growth and understanding as the individual moves into the adult stage of their life.

CHECK YOUR LEARNING GOALS!

You should be able to:

1. Explain whether adolescence is a synchronous or asynchronous period.
2. Explain what is meant by the reversal of the proximodistal pattern of growth and outline its implications.
3. Identify an area of growth that takes places in the brain during adolescence and describe the associated improved thinking capacities.
4. Define primary and secondary sex characteristics.
5. Explain what is meant by 'pubertal timing', using examples to support your explanation.
6. Summarise, in your own words, what abstract thinking means.
7. Describe the third eye experiment and say why it is important.
8. Describe what is meant by 'adolescent egocentrism'.
9. Summarise in your own words what is meant by 'imaginary audience' and 'personal fable' .
10. Explain a 'psychological moratorium'.
11. List the negative outcome of Erikson's stage and describe its implications for risk-taking behaviours.
12. List Marcia's four identity statuses.
13. Explain the difference between 'crisis' and 'commitment'.
14. Define identity, self-concept and self-esteem.
15. Explain the difference between identity and self-concept.

8

Early and Middle Adulthood (20–65 Years)

In this chapter we will discover:

- Physical development
  - The ageing process
  - The brain in adulthood
  - Menopause
  - Covid and its effects on mental health
  - In Focus: *Our Geels: All-Ireland Traveller Health Study* (2010)
- Cognitive development
  - Postformal thinking
  - Schaie's theory of cognitive development
  - In Focus: Seattle Longitudinal Study
- Socio-emotional development
  - Erikson's isolation vs. intimacy
  - Erikson's generativity vs. stagnation
  - Attachment in adulthood
  - Levinson's seasons of man
  - In Focus: Alcoholism and drug addiction
  - In Focus: Mental health

Early and middle adulthood as a period of development has arguably had less research and interest devoted to it than childhood, adolescence and older age. Why do you think that is? It can be partially explained by the attitude that by adulthood we have become the people we will remain for the rest of our lives. Infancy through to adolescence is a period of tumultuous change when we develop and are shaped; older age is sometimes seen, erroneously, as a time of decline across the different domains; so adulthood is seen as a time of stability marked by relatively little change. We now recognise that this is not true and that adulthood offers an interesting window to track an individual's development as they change, grow and interact with their environment. This chapter, covering early and middle adulthood, will consider the different areas of research that attempt to shine a light upon these changes.

Brim (1992) describes 'midlife' as 'the last uncharted territory in human development', reflecting how middle age has been ignored. Schaie (2010) notes that few comprehensive theories cover the period of adulthood, the main exception being the work of Erik Erikson and Paul Baltes (whose work we will look at in the next chapter). In this chapter we shall look at Schaie's work, which has attempted to rectify this omission, and consider other theories and material that help give some insight into the experiences of people aged between 20 and 65.

PHYSICAL DEVELOPMENT

THE AGEING PROCESS

According to the **wear and tear** approach to ageing, over time the body simply wears out. Hayflick (1980) found that human cells are set to reproduce themselves a fixed or finite number of times, after which they will eventually die. Changes can occur to the cells – we often hear the term '**free radicals**', which are atoms that alter and damage cells. Environmental factors such as pollution and smoking encourage the production of free radicals. Antioxidants such as vitamins A and E, found in fruit and vegetables, can neutralise them. Nonetheless, free radical damage accumulates with age. Increasingly there is recognition of 'healthy ageing' whereby lifestyle choices we make can impact on how we age.

Healthy ageing is the process of optimising opportunities for physical, social and mental health to enable older people to take an active part in society without discrimination and to enjoy an independent, good quality of life. (Healthy Ageing Project, 2006)

LINK

Can you see a link with the nature versus nurture debate? Nature might be your biological ageing process; nurture might include your diet or exercise. As you read this chapter, see what evidence supports this debate.

Factors such as diet, stress and exercise all influence the ageing process – these are called lifestyle factors and can impact on the biological process of ageing.

THE BRAIN IN ADULTHOOD

A second major spurt in the brain occurs at approximately 17 years of age and continues until age 21 or 22. Most of the changes occur in the frontal lobe, which is involved in higher reasoning and emotional control.

It had been suggested that the brain is at its optimum in our late teens and 20s. However, research is increasingly casting doubt on the notion of decline in adult brains in middle age. Phillips (2011) reports that not only does the middle-aged brain retain its capacities, it is capable of acquiring new ones, including the ability to 'rewire' itself well into middle age, with some people having better cognitive abilities than when they were younger. Research suggests that the middle-aged mind is calmer, less neurotic and better able to process social situations. The Seattle Longitudinal Study has been collecting data on thousands of adults for over 60 years, allowing unique insights to be gathered on ageing cognitive abilities. Its results show that middle-aged adults perform better on the majority of cognitive tests than they did in their younger years.

Think about it

The debate about whether early experience affects later development was explored in Chapter 1. Moving into adulthood (later development), what early experiences do you think might contribute towards 'healthy ageing'?

While lifestyle factors can play a part in how we age, we age nonetheless as a matter of biology – as most species do. Below is a table of some of the physical changes that may be witnessed.

Age changes in physical functioning

BODY FUNCTION	AGE AT WHICH CHANGE BEGINS TO BE CLEAR OR MEASURABLE	NATURE OF CHANGE
Vision	Mid-40s	Lens of eye thickens and loses accommodative power, resulting in poorer near vision and more sensitivity to glare
Hearing	50–60	Loss of ability to hear very high and very low tones
Smell	About 40	Decline in ability to detect and discriminate between different smells
Taste	None	No apparent loss in taste discrimination ability »

BODY FUNCTION	AGE AT WHICH CHANGE BEGINS TO BE CLEAR OR MEASURABLE	NATURE OF CHANGE
Muscles	About 50	Loss of muscle tissue, particularly in 'fast twitch' fibres used for bursts of strength or speed
Bones	Mid-30s (women)	Loss of calcium in the bones, called osteoporosis; also wear and tear on bone in joints, called osteoarthritis, more marked after about 60
Heart and lungs	35–40	Most functions (such as aerobic capacity or cardiac output) do not show age changes at rest, but do show age changes during work or exercise
Nervous system	Probably gradual throughout adulthood	Some loss (but not clear how much) of neurons in the brain; gradual reduction in density of dendrites; gradual decline in total brain volume and weight
Immune system	Adolescence	Loss in size of thymus; reduction in number and maturity of T cells; not clear how much of this change is due to stress and how much is primary ageing
Reproductive system	Mid-30s (women) Early 40s (men)	Increased reproductive risk and lowered fertility Gradual decline in viable sperm beginning at about age 40; very gradual decline in testosterone from early adulthood
Cellular elasticity	Gradual	Gradual loss of elasticity in most cells, including skin, muscle, tendon and blood vessel; faster deterioration in cells exposed to sunlight
Height	40	Compression of discs in the spine, with resulting loss of height of 2.5–5 cm (1–2 inches) by age 80
Weight	Nonlinear	In US studies, weight reaches a maximum in middle adulthood and then gradually declines in old age
Skin	40	Increase in wrinkles, as a result of loss of elasticity; oil-secreting glands become less efficient
Hair	Variable	Hair becomes thinner and may grey

Source: Boyd and Bee (2005)

MENOPAUSE

One very clear physical marker of middle age is the menopause, marking the end of the reproductive capacity of women through the cessation of periods. The age range for the menopause is between 40 and 60 years of age. It is considered the most significant physical change experienced by women in middle adulthood.

In the past, little was spoken about the menopause and women suffered the physical effects in silence. Nor was there much interest within psychology as to the psychological effects of this significant physical change. Here again, we see how societal and cultural changes can influence individuals' functioning. The menopause is now being discussed openly and information shared about experiences, which is essential to reduce feelings of isolation and to reassure women that their experiences are normal. Physical symptoms can include sleep problems, tiredness, hot flushes and weight fluctuations. In psychology, there is increasing recognition of the psychological implications for some women; for example, shifts in hormones may cause mood changes. Other symptoms can include:

- Anger and irritability
- Anxiety
- Loss of self-esteem
- Loss of confidence
- Low mood and feelings of sadness or depression
- Poor concentration – often described as 'brain fog'.

As with other aspects of health and wellbeing, it is possible to have a positive experience of menopause and for many women to view it as a transition to the next stage of life, full of possibilities. Research is now being conducted on the menopause and the experiences of women – hopefully this will offer more insight into and understanding of this significant change in women's' lives.

COVID AND ITS EFFECTS ON MENTAL HEALTH

Another area where we have witnessed how the physical domain can impact on other aspects of our functioning is the Covid pandemic. Covid is a virus that physically affects those who contract it to varying degrees, including risk of death. We saw how the effects of the pandemic affected people's wellbeing and social and emotional development. We can understand that its effects might be different for a young child, an adolescent, an adult and elderly person. Later in the chapter we shall examine issues relating to the Covid pandemic and mental health. The example of the pandemic highlights the inter-relatedness of all areas of our development.

SOCIAL FACTORS

Social exclusion, poverty and discrimination are factors that can impact negatively on developmental outcomes. The following research shines a light on how these 'external' factors can affect more than a person's feelings or mood – it can quite literally take years off their life. Men in the Travelling community on average live 15 years less than the average in Ireland.

IN FOCUS: *OUR GEELS: ALL-IRELAND TRAVELLER HEALTH STUDY* (2010)

One very powerful factor that can impact, positively or negatively, on human functioning is socioeconomic status (SES), which shines a light on the relationship between social class and health outcomes and behaviours. Do marginalised groups suffer from poorer health outcomes than the general population?

This following findings on Traveller health (AITHS 2010) indicates that external factors can play a role in physiological health.

Age structure:

- Forty-two per cent of Travellers are under 15 years of age compared with 21% of the general population
- Sixty-three per cent of Travellers are under 25 years compared with 35% of the general population
- Three per cent of Travellers are aged 65 years and over compared with 13% of the general population.

Life expectancy:

- In 1987 the gap in life expectancy between Traveller women and settled women was 12 years. The gap in 2008 was 11 years.
- In 1987 the gap in life expectancy between Traveller men and settled men was 10 years. The gap in 2008 was 15 years.

Mortality:

- Traveller men have four times the mortality rate of the general population.
- Traveller women have three times the mortality rate of the general population.
- If Travellers had the same health status as the general population, the number of deaths expected in the year [2008] would be 54: the actual number of deaths was 188, which means an excess of 134 Traveller deaths.
- Suicide is six times the rate of the general population and accounts for approximately 11% of all Traveller deaths.
- The infant mortality rate for Travellers is 3.5 times the rate of the general population (4 infant deaths per 1,000 in the national population compared to 14 infant deaths per 1,000 in the Traveller population).

Morbidity:

- Over 52% of Travellers aged 40–60 years who were interviewed had been diagnosed with high blood pressure in the last year, compared to 35% of the general population.
- Over 42% of Travellers were diagnosed with high cholesterol in the last year compared to 30% of the general population.

Main causes of death:

- Heart disease and stroke – 25%
- Cancer – 19%
- Lung disease – 13%

Causes of the gap in levels of morbidity and mortality among Travellers:

Both Travellers and health service providers interviewed acknowledged that social determinants were the main cause of the poor health status of Travellers.

These social determinants include: accommodation, education, employment, poverty, discrimination, lifestyle and access and utilisation of services.

For more information, see: https://www.paveepoint.ie/wp-content/uploads/2013/10/AITHS-Booklet-Sep.12.pdf

According to the *All-Ireland Traveller Health Study*, the key health issues for Travellers identified during the consultation process were:

- Environment and poor living conditions
- Issues related to equality of access to, participation in and outcome of service provision
- Right of Travellers to appropriate access to services based on culture and way of life
- Lifestyle issues
- Lack of culturally appropriate provision
- Lack of data on Traveller health and health needs
- Lack of recognition of Traveller culture and identity
- Individual- and institutional-level racism
- Social exclusion (AITHST 2010, p.36.)

This report into the health outcomes of the Travelling community powerfully demonstrates how factors such as poverty, lack of access and poor living conditions can adversely affect wellbeing. It demonstrates the relationship between nature and nurture, where innate characteristics within an individual do not, in of themselves, determine life expectancy or health outcomes. Increasingly we are beginning to understand how 'nurture' and external factors can shape a person's life, not just psychologically but physically.

The full report can be viewed at:

www.gov.ie/en/publication/b9c48a-all-ireland-traveller-health-study/

Think about it

We saw in Chapter 7 that LGBTQ+ young people can suffer from higher levels of mental health challenges due to discrimination – the concept of minority stress was offered as a possible explanation. Here we see that members of the Travelling community suffer far higher rates of physical and mental health issues. Can you identify other groups who are marginalised and might experience poorer outcomes as a result?

COGNITIVE DEVELOPMENT

From a cognitive perspective it can be argued that middle age differs from both youth and old age in the following ways:

Cognitive development

In **younger** years, our cognitive development is strongly influenced by formal training, for example schooling and our peer group.

In **middle** adulthood, cognitive performance is influenced by individual environments, for example different job environments impact on the development of cognitive skills; a librarian and an accountant will develop different cognitive skills. This differs from schooling in younger years that is more similar than individualised.

In **older** age, influences on cognition are impacted more by physical factors such as sensory and sensorimotor functioning.

Development potential

In **young** age, supports are needed to aid natural maturation and academic achievement and to prepare for job demands.

In **middle** age, cognitive potential is typically used to develop job-specific skills, thus contributing to the development of highly job-specific and individualised change trajectories.

In **older** age, cognitive training may serve to prevent consequences of age-associated decline, although effects are typically small.

In addition, the effects of and transfer from cognitive training are likely to be higher in midlife than in young or old age, and different biological or hormonal changes may influence cognition in middle compared with young and old age.

There are two approaches generally used in the study of cognitive development in midlife:

1. Focusing on whether groups at risk of decline in early old age can be identified, which would allow for preventive measures such as cognitive training.
2. Recognising that middle adulthood is characterised by high levels of cognitive performance and intellectually demanding activities.

In studying this period, researchers hope to see how and if demanding cognitive activities and interests may protect adults from cognitive decline in later years.

While more attention is being paid to cognitive development, interest still lags behind the study of cognition in both young and older people. Piaget's theory of cognition ended at the beginning of puberty. One of the criticisms of his theory is that it implies that our cognition is in place and unchanging immediately after childhood. Several theories have emerged that include cognition in adulthood. Let's start with a follow-up to Piaget's work.

POSTFORMAL THINKING

It has been argued that there is a fifth stage after Piaget's formal operational stage (see Chapter 7). Rather than the mere acquisition of mental structures, the individual is now able to apply this new level of thinking to problem-solving and reasoning.

> **Postformal thought** incorporates the ability to recognise that the correct answer to a problem requires reflective thinking and may vary from situation to situation.

Adolescents tend to think in a dualistic manner, e.g. right or wrong; adults recognise that there are shades of grey and that each situation or problem is unique.

While the addition of this stage is a positive move forward it still doesn't offer a comprehensive overview of cognitive change across the lifespan, but the work of Schaie does.

SCHAIE'S THEORY OF COGNITIVE DEVELOPMENT

K. Warner Schaie (2000) offers a theory of cognitive development across the lifespan, beginning with 'acquisition' and ending, towards the end of life, with 'legacy creating'. We will examine each stage of his theory within its age specificity.

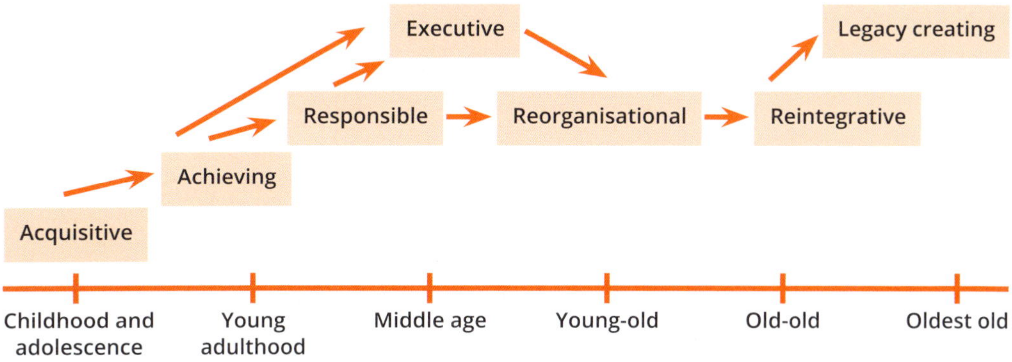

Schaie's theory of cognitive development

* **Acquisition** (childhood and adolescence): This stage involves the acquisition of mental structures, information and skills in order to gain understanding of the world.
* **Achieving** (late teens to early twenties): Young adults use their knowledge to pursue a career, choose a lifestyle and solve personal dilemmas.
* **Responsibility** (middle adulthood): Individuals use their abilities to solve problems related to their responsibilities to others, for example family members.
* **Executive** (middle adulthood): This stage reflects a concern for the welfare of the broader social system. People deal with complex relationships on multiple levels.
* **Reorganisation** (end of middle adulthood to the beginning of late adulthood): This stage is marked by retirement. Cognitive tasks involve the reorganisation of life around new interests and pursuits.
* **Reintegrative** (late adulthood): Older adults look back over their lives to make sense of it. The older person learns to be selective in using more limited energies.
* **Legacy creating** (advanced old age): This is the final stage of Schaie's theory and represents attempts by the older person to ensure that some part of them will continue after they are gone, that they leave a legacy. This includes activities such as making a will or funeral arrangements.

Schaie's theory is stage-based, concentrating on developmental changes across the span of adulthood into old age. The strength of this theory is its specificity. Schaie's theory emerged from his frustration with the lack of data and measurements of adult functioning. In response, he established a longitudinal study (researching individuals over a long period of time) to remedy this.

IN FOCUS: SEATTLE LONGITUDINAL STUDY

Schaie set up this longitudinal study of cognitive functioning in adults in 1956. Originally, five hundred participants were recruited, ranging in age from their early 20s to their late 60s. The study has run for over fifty years and the age range of current participants is 22 years to 101 years.

Below is a brief summary of the main questions they wished to study and the findings that emerged.

QUESTION	FINDINGS
Does intelligence change uniformly through adulthood, or are there different life course ability patterns?	Our studies have shown that there is no uniform pattern of age-related changes across all intellectual abilities.
At what age is there a reliably detectable decrement in ability, and what is its magnitude?	Decreases in such abilities do not occur prior to age 60, but there is some evidence for such decreases for all abilities by 74 years of age. »

QUESTION	FINDINGS
What accounts for individual differences in age-related change in adulthood?	The variables that have been implicated in reducing risk of cognitive decline in old age have included: (a) absence of cardiovascular and other chronic diseases; (b) a favorable environment mediated by high socioeconomic status; (c) involvement in a complex and intellectually stimulating environment; (d) flexible personality style at midlife; (e) high cognitive status of spouse; and (f) maintenance of high levels of perceptual processing speed.
Can intellectual decline with increasing age be reversed by educational intervention?	Findings from the cognitive training studies conducted with our participants suggested that observed decline in many community-dwelling older people might well be a function of disuse and is clearly reversible for many. Indeed, cognitive training resulted in approximately two-thirds showing significant improvement; and about 40% of those who had declined significantly over 14 years were returned to their pre-decline level.

Source: Adapted from Schaie & Willis (2010)

Schaie (2010) reports that 'some genetically and environmentally disadvantaged individuals show decline in the late 40s or early 50s.'

Think about it

What do you think Schaie means by 'environmentally disadvantaged'? Reflect on some of the risk factors we have identified as being 'outside' the person (in their environment), such as poverty or poor housing. Do you think this is another example of how these factors can negatively impact an individual's development?

SOCIO-EMOTIONAL DEVELOPMENT

ERIKSON'S ISOLATION VS. INTIMACY (20–30 YEARS)

In this stage Erikson proposes a positive outcome – intimacy – and a negative one – isolation. Intimacy relates to forming an intimate or love relationship and committing to it. Erikson suggested that isolation reflects an individual's hesitation to form a relationship, possibly due to a fear of losing identity or to self-absorption.

ERIKSON'S GENERATIVITY VS. STAGNATION

Generativity is related to the verb 'to generate' and Erikson envisaged this stage as offering the opportunity to the individual to reach out to others and guide the younger generation. This can be seen particularly in child-rearing but also in more civic-minded activities such as coaching or community involvement. Here the focus lies beyond the self and towards others. If this does not occur the individual is faced with feelings of stagnation, where they place their needs above challenge and sacrifice. They are self-indulgent, displaying little interest in work productivity or involvement with younger people.

ATTACHMENT IN ADULTHOOD

As we saw in Chapter 2, attachment is considered one of the most important concepts in psychology. It highlights the importance of early experiences for later development. We have already observed how attachment works in childhood, but does it really affect us in later life, colouring our choice of romantic partner? Mary Ainsworth developed a measuring tool (the strange situation) to assess attachment styles in young children by removing their primary attachment figure and charting their reaction. Since we can't replicate the strange situation, how do we measure attachment style in an adult?

A method called the 'adult attachment interview' (AAI) was developed. This questions adults' recollections of their childhood and rates their responses. From this adults can be classified as being either securely or insecurely attached.

Four patterns of adult attachment have been observed, based on responses to the AAI:

1. **Autonomous – secure:** Persons who can recall their own earlier attachment-related experiences objectively and openly, even if these were not favourable. These adults openly expressed their valuing of relationships.
2. **Dismissing – detached:** Persons who dismissed attachment relationships as of little concern, value or influence; they gave brief accounts, had few childhood memories and often idealised their childhood without being able to provide any supporting evidence.
3. **Preoccupied – entangled:** Persons who seem preoccupied with dependency on their own parents and still actively struggle to please them; they gave inconsistent accounts of their childhood. The conflicts they described were often unresolved and still an ongoing issue with them.
4. **Unresolved – disorganised:** Individuals who had experienced traumatic separation from the attachment figure and had not worked through the mourning process; or who had experienced severe neglect or abuse.

Reviewing research on attachment styles in adulthood, Crowell and Treboux (1995) discovered the following:

> *The avoidant group scored lowest on a scale of love and endorsement of a romantic ideal. Ambivalent subjects were characterised by emotional dependency, preoccupation, having ideas of all-encompassing love, and low scores on friendship. Secure subjects scored highest in self-confidence, avoidant subjects highest on avoidance of intimacy, and ambivalent subjects had the highest scores on neurotic love and lowest scores on circumspect love. Love styles were examined in another study of college students in which secure and ambivalent subjects endorsed romantic ideas and avoidant subjects endorsed logical ideas about love.*

WHY ARE RELATIONSHIPS IMPORTANT?

According to Clulow (2007), Bowlby believed that relationships allow us to 'discover not only our sense of security as human beings but also the kernel of our personal identity, an identity that is essentially relational'. Does this identity and model of relationships carved out in our early lives impact on our adult years? Clulow writes:

> *[E]stablished adult romantic relationships [are] potential containers of and for attachment behaviour, and contemporary thinking seeks to understand intimacy in adult life as the interweaving of attachment, care-giving and sexual systems of behaviour activated by specific triggers and assuaged by specific responses. Threats to the couple that might activate attachment behaviour come from both internal and external sources. Predictable changes (like the arrival of children) and unpredictable crises (like an affair or serious illness) are filtered through the lens of each partner's internal working models to constitute meaning and register any challenges to 'felt security'.*

Relationships allow for two separate identities (me and you) to create an 'us' which gives a space for partners to test out and develop their dearly held assumptions about themselves and each other in ways that hold real potential for affective and cognitive learning to take place.

In terms of a lifespan and ecological approach, these relationships are crucial for social and emotional development, affecting our ability to parent, which has consequences for the next generation. As both 'safe haven' and 'secure base', partnerships provide a refuge from the pressures of the outside world and a platform from which adults can contribute to life beyond the concerns of the immediate family.

LEVINSON'S SEASONS OF MAN

Daniel Levinson (1986) devised a theory that attempts to capture the lifespan of being an adult. It extends over the entire lifespan but pays particular attention to the 'nature' of adult development. Central to his theory is the idea of four 'seasonal cycles':

- pre-adulthood
- early adulthood
- middle adulthood
- late adulthood.

The scheme was initially based on interviews with forty men. Levinson later interviewed women and found they proceeded through the same eras (life cycles) in a similar manner to men. Levinson did find, though, that women's lives are more closely linked to the family cycle.

Underlying Levinson's theory are two important concepts:

* **Life structure:** The underlying pattern of an individual's life at a given time. It is shaped by their social and physical environment, primarily family and work, although other factors such as religion and economic status are often important.
* **Life cycle:** Relates to the underlying order spanning adult life, consisting of a sequence of eras. The move from one era to another is not smooth; there are cross-era **periods of transition**, which last for about five years.

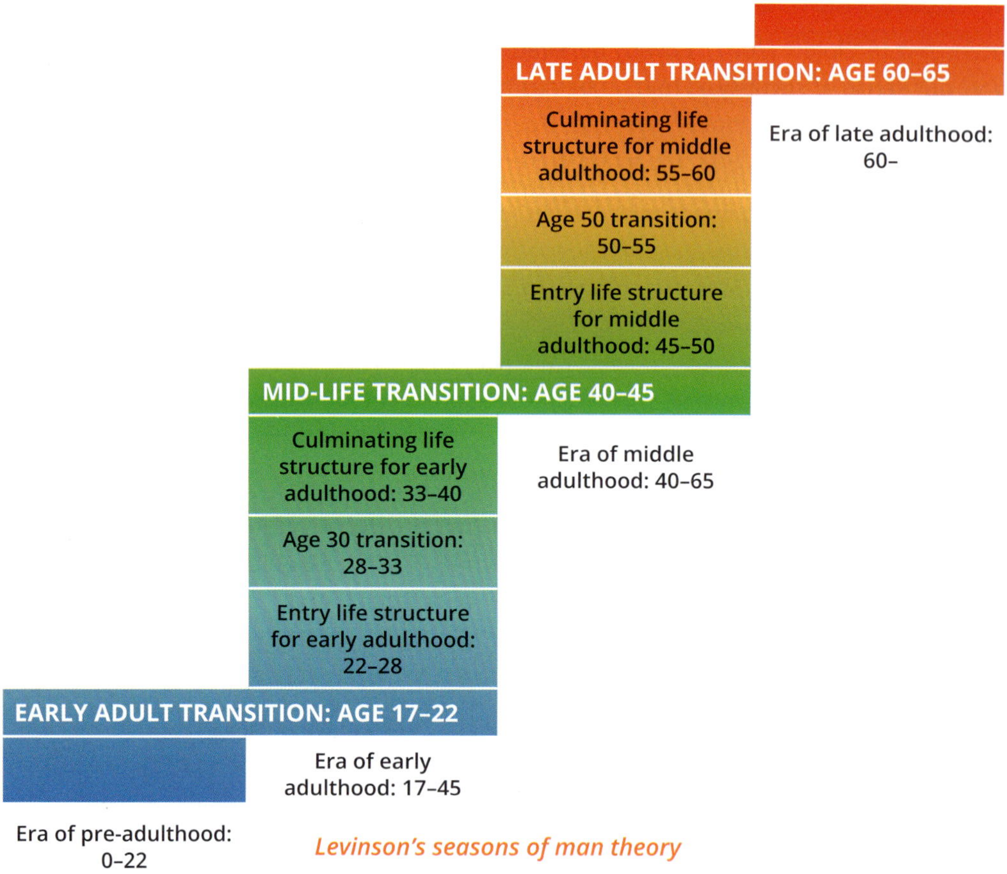

Levinson's seasons of man theory

Source: Levinson (1986, p.7)

Levinson's developmental periods

Early adult transition (17–22)	A developmental bridge between pre-adulthood and early adulthood
Entry life structure for early adulthood (22–28)	The time for building and maintaining an initial mode of adult living
Age 30 transition (28–33)	An opportunity to reappraise and modify the entry structure and to create the basis for the next life structure
Culminating life structure for early adulthood (33–40)	The vehicle for completing this era and realising our youthful ambitions
Midlife transition (40–45)	Another cross-era shift, serving both to terminate early adulthood and to initiate middle adulthood
Entry life structure for middle adulthood (45–50)	Provides an initial basis for life in a new era
Age 50 transition (50–55)	Offers a mid-era opportunity for modifying and perhaps improving the entry life structure
Culminating life structure for middle adulthood (55–60)	The framework with which we conclude this era
Late adult transition (55–60)	A boundary period between middle and late adulthood, separating and linking the two eras. The transition to late adulthood marks an opportunity to reflect upon successes and failures and enjoy the rest of life.

As we can see, starting careers and families marks the beginning of early adulthood. Around age 30, an evaluation occurs and people begin to settle down and also work towards career advancement. Another transition begins at age 40 with the realisation that not all the ambitions and goals that we set will be achieved. (I have included Levinson's final stage here although it falls into late adulthood, otherwise termed 'older age', which we shall deal with in the next chapter.)

Think about it

Applying critical thinking skills to Levinson's theory, what would you identify as some of the possible criticisms of his theory? Think of criticisms of other stage theories such as Piaget's or Erikson's – do individuals pass neatly from one stage to the next in a predictable pattern, for example? Levinson wrote his theory over forty years ago when men's and women's roles were more rigid – might that be a weakness in his theory? Make a note of some of the criticisms that you can think of. Are there any strengths to this theory?

The final part of this chapter explores addiction and mental health. Mental health affects not just adults but teens and, increasingly, children. Addiction is a serious issue that affects not just the individual but also their families and communities. Here we look at it from a psychological perspective.

IN FOCUS: ALCOHOLISM AND DRUG ADDICTION

WHAT IS ADDICTION?

There are two types of drug abuse: habitual or chronic use, and recreational or experimental abuse.

Addiction, or **dependence**, is 'a cluster of three of more symptoms listed below occurring at any time in the same 12-month period' (APA 1994, p.176).

Symptoms of addiction are:

1. Tolerance, or needing more and more of a substance to achieve the same effect
2. Withdrawal, which involves unpleasant symptoms when the body is deprived of the substance, resulting in more frequent use to alleviate the negative symptoms
3. Taking the substance for a longer period of time or in larger amounts than originally intended
4. Unsuccessful desire to minimise use of the substance
5. Much time spent to obtain, use, or recover from the effects of the substance
6. Social, occupational or recreational activities are missed because of substance abuse
7. Substance use is continued despite knowledge of causing a problem
8. If neither tolerance nor withdrawal are present, then at least three of the remaining symptoms must be present (APA 1994).

Did you know?

- One in 15 children will become alcoholic in their lifetime because of genetic predisposition (Weber & McCormick 1992).
- Children from alcoholic families are four to six times more likely to become alcoholic than children raised in a non-alcoholic home (Weber & McCormick 1992).
- By their mid-20s, nearly 80% of young adults have used an illicit drug.

Think about it

We've examined debates in psychology, including nature versus nurture and early experiences affecting later development. How might either of these debates shine a light on the statistics above? Do you think genetics alone explains addiction, or are other aspects, such as early experiences, important?

CAUSES OF DRUG ABUSE

Carr lists seven categories of theories which seek to explain drug abuse:

> **First**, *biological theories of drug abuse focus on specific genetic factors; on temperamental attributes that are known to be strongly genetically determined; and on the role of physiological mechanisms in the development of tolerance, dependence and withdrawal.*
>
> **Second**, *intrapsychic deficit theories point to the importance of personal psychological vulnerabilities in the development of drug-using behaviour patterns.*
>
> **Third**, *cognitive-behavioural theories underlie the significance of certain learning processes in the genesis of drug problems.*
>
> **Fourth**, *family systems theories emphasise the importance of parental drug-using behaviour, parenting style and family organisation patterns in the causation and maintenance of drug abuse.*
>
> **Fifth**, *the role of societal factors such as social disadvantage, neighbourhood norms concerning drug use and abuse, and drug availability are the central concerns of sociological theories of drug abuse.*
>
> **Sixth**, *multiple-risk factor theories highlight the roles of factors at biological, psychological and social levels in the aetiology of drug abuse.*
>
> **Finally**, *change-process theories offer explanations for how recovery and relapse occur. (Carr 2003, p.590)*

Addiction doesn't just affect the individual; it can also impact on interpersonal relationships. Carr observes that 'within the family, drug abuse often leads to conflict' and that the individual may become isolated or break ties with friends who don't abuse; there is potential impact on the community, where 'drug-related antisocial behaviour such as aggression, theft and selling drugs may bring youngsters into contact with the juvenile justice system'; finally, drug-related health problems and drug dependency may bring people into contact with the health service (2003, p.589). »

CAN ADDICTION BE TREATED?

There are several successful treatments for addiction. It goes without saying that the earlier the addiction is treated, the easier it will be to control. Some of the most effective treatments for addiction are 12-step programmes such as Alcoholics Anonymous (Weber & McCormick 1992). Other treatments include individual and family therapy, group therapy, educational programmes, and self-esteem building and anger management workshops.

EMCDDA NATIONAL REPORT: IRELAND

In Ireland each year a report is compiled and presented to the European Monitoring Centre for Drugs and Drug Addiction (EMCDDA). Below are some of the findings of the 2006 report regarding the prevalence of drug use in Ireland.

Prevalence and trends

- Drug use has become more common among the adult general population aged 15–64 years in Ireland over recent years.
- Fewer than 2 in 10 adults reported use of any illicit drug during their lifetime in 2002–03, but this figure increased to approximately 3 in 10 in 2014–15.
- Similarly, last year and last month prevalence of use of any illicit drug has increased since the 2011 survey.
- Cannabis remains the most commonly used illicit drug, followed by MDMA/ecstasy and cocaine.
- Illicit drug use is more common among males and younger age groups.
- Among young adults (aged 15–34 years), the numbers using cannabis and MDMA have increased whereas the use of cocaine has remained stable.
- In 2014, more than half of opioid users were aged 35 years or older, compared with less than one third in 2006, suggesting that this high-risk population is ageing.
- Data from the specialised drug treatment centres indicate that opioids (mainly heroin) remain the most common primary drug among those entering treatment. Between 2006 and 2010, heroin was the main drug reported by first-time entrants, but this was superseded by cannabis in 2011, and this remained the case in 2017.

Think about it

Why do you think there has been an increase in drug-taking? Research prevention approaches. What other interventions (based on your understanding of external factors) might reduce the risk of falling into addiction?

If you do your own additional research you will find a relationship between mental health challenges and addiction. 'Multiple national population surveys have found that about half of those who experience a mental illness during their lives will also experience a substance use disorder and vice versa', the most commonly seen mental health disorders being anxiety and depression (National Institutes on Drug Abuse, April 2021).

Stressors in our early experiences and in our lives, such as poverty, discrimination or a pandemic, can affect individuals' mental health.

IN FOCUS: MENTAL HEALTH

Mental health is a challenge we can all encounter at any stage of our lives. The Covid pandemic, research suggests, placed a greater burden on people's wellbeing, with many experiencing anxiety. We shall explore some factors involved in mental health and take a closer look at how anxiety is understood in psychology.

Mental health is 'a state of wellbeing in which the individual realises his or her own abilities, can cope with the normal stresses of life, can work productively and fruitfully, and is able to make a contribution to his or her community' (WHO).

It has been argued that mental health is more than the absence of mental illness alone.

Think about it

What do you think is meant by the statement 'Mental health is more than the absence of mental illness'? With a friend, discuss how you define mental health. Is it solely focused on mental 'illness' or should it be broader in its understanding and include concepts such as resilience? Write down your thoughts and as well as your own definition of what mental health is.

In psychology we often focus more on when people are struggling than flourishing; later we shall look at concepts such as resilience and how to support positive mental wellbeing.

The following table, developed by the WHO, outlines the different risk and protective factors that influence mental health. »

Mental health risk factors

LEVEL	ADVERSE FACTORS	PROTECTIVE FACTORS
Individual attributes	▪ Low self-esteem ▪ Cognitive/emotional immaturity ▪ Difficulties in communicating ▪ Medical illness, substance use	▪ Self-esteem, confidence ▪ Ability to solve problems and manage stress or adversity ▪ Communication skills ▪ Physical health, fitness
Social circumstances	▪ Loneliness, bereavement ▪ Neglect, family conflict ▪ Exposure to violence/abuse ▪ Low income and poverty ▪ Difficulties or failure at school ▪ Work stress/unemployment	▪ Social support of family and friends ▪ Good parenting/family interaction ▪ Physical security and safety ▪ Economic security ▪ Scholastic achievement ▪ Satisfaction and success at work
Environmental factors	▪ Poor access to basic services ▪ Injustice and discrimination ▪ Social and gender inequalities ▪ Exposure to war and disaster	▪ Equality of access to basic services ▪ Social justice, tolerance, integration ▪ Social and gender equality ▪ Physical security and safety

LINK

Revisit Chapter 1 where both risk and protective factors are explained. As you read this section, make a note of the factors you think are important and why. In relation to the Covid pandemic, see if you can identify the risk factors from the table.

We can see from the table that factors aren't just located within the individual themselves – influences outside the person can have a significant impact, either positive or negative. This aligns with Bronfenbrenner's bio-ecological theory and reminds us that to gain understanding of a person we need to recognise the different layers of influences in their life.

One of the most common mental health conditions is anxiety. It was one of the most common conditions before Covid, but the pandemic experience led many more to experience it.

ANXIETY DISORDERS

Anxiety is a painful emotional experience resulting from internal or external stimulation.

Anxiety disorders are recognised in the DSM-V. Anxiety is an emotion characterised by feelings of tension, worried thoughts and physical changes, such as increased blood pressure.

People with anxiety disorders usually have recurring intrusive thoughts or concerns. They may avoid certain situations out of worry. They may also have physical symptoms such as sweating, trembling, dizziness or a rapid heartbeat. Anxiety disorders differ from normal feelings of nervousness.

Untreated anxiety disorders can push people into avoiding situations that trigger or worsen their symptoms. People with anxiety disorders are likely to suffer from depression, and they may also abuse alcohol and other drugs in an effort to gain relief from their symptoms. Job performance, schoolwork and personal relationships can also suffer.

Can you see the different areas of development involved in the overview of anxiety?

- Feelings (emotional domain) – feelings of worry
- Thinking (cognitive domain) – intrusive thoughts
- Behaviour (physical domain) – rapid heartbeat.

If we look at other mental health conditions or at our development in general we can see the interplay of all these different areas and influences. When trying to understand human functioning it's important to be aware of all aspects that feed into it.

Types of anxiety disorder:

- Panic disorder
- Generalised anxiety disorder phobias
- Post-traumatic stress disorder
- Obsessive-compulsive disorder.

Anxiety disorders are the most common of the 'emotional' disorders. In the USA they affect 40 million adults aged 18 and older, or 18.1% of the population, every year.

Let's take a look at some of the symptoms associated with one of the more common anxiety disorders, generalised anxiety disorder (GAD). »

SYMPTOMS OF GENERALISED ANXIETY DISORDER (GAD)

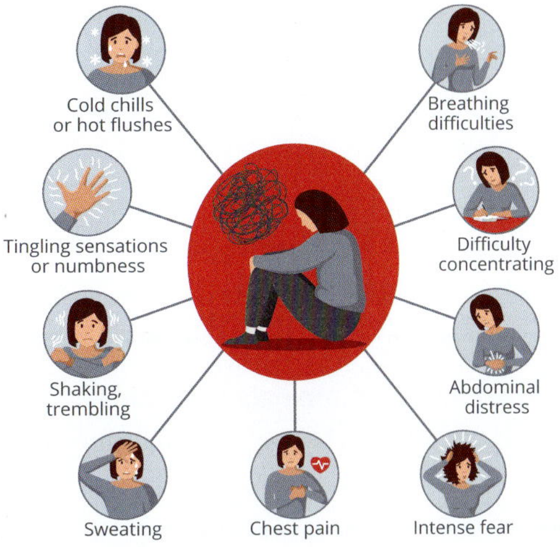

We have seen how our thoughts, feelings and behaviour interact in mental health conditions such as anxiety. One common approach to supporting and treating anxiety is **cognitive behavioural therapy** (CBT). CBT is a therapeutic approach that recognises the relationship between thinking patterns or systems (cognitive) and behaviour or action. In Chapter 1 we briefly examined behaviourism, principles of reinforcement and learned behaviour and mentioned the application of behaviourism to changing individual behaviour in the form of applied behavioural analysis (ABA). CBT is an umbrella term for therapies that use behavioural and cognitive techniques. To define CBT very simply, how we think about ourselves and situations determines how we feel, act and behave. Maladaptive or dysfunctional behaviour is the result of cognitive distortions or maladaptive thinking. CBT emphasises the ability of people to make changes in their lives without having to understand why the change occurs. This differs from the psychodynamic approach which delves into the 'why'. With CBT, clients are given 'homework' to help them change. The popularity of CBT lies in its effectiveness but also in the brevity of treatment, which makes it less costly than some other therapies.

Albert Ellis introduced an early form of this approach – rational emotive behaviour therapy (REBT). Though Ellis was originally a psychoanalyst he became convinced that irrational thought process, not unconscious forces, are responsible for maladaptive behaviour. Ellis believed that in challenging these irrational thoughts one could effect change and restore the person to healthy functioning. He devised an ABCD model in which his theory is reflected:

A	Activating event – the trigger
B	Belief that is activated by A
C	Consequences that follow this belief; these can be emotional and behavioural
D	Disputing or challenging the belief system to change the maladaptive consequences

Dryden (1999) outlines that rational and irrational beliefs lie at the heart of REBT. Rational beliefs are associated with healthy psychological functioning. The aim is to enable clients to change their irrational beliefs to rational ones. The four basic types of irrational belief are:

- Demands
- 'Awfulising' or catastrophising beliefs
- Low frustration tolerance (LFT) beliefs
- Beliefs where the self, others and/or life conditions are depreciated.

Irrational beliefs are defined through their inconsistency with reality. They are illogical, and this leads to unhealthy results for the individual. The role of the therapist is to challenge the irrational beliefs.

Too often in psychology, the focus is on the negatives or 'when things go wrong'. **Positive psychology** is beginning to push back against that trend by examining how people overcome adversity or show resilience.

Resilience, which may be defined as 'unusually good adaptation in the face of severe stress' (Beardslee 1989, p.267), has been applied to a wide spectrum of domains, from psychology to social work to education. Within the domain of psychology resilience has been explored in issues ranging from psychopathology to child development, elderly populations and individuals with disabilities. In applied practice this has led to the popularity of using a strengths-based approach to support others (or yourself!).

According to Saleebey (2009), six guiding assumptions underpin the strengths perspective:

1. Every individual, group, family and community has strengths.
2. Trauma, abuse, illness and struggle may be injurious, but they may also be sources of challenge and opportunity.
3. Assume that you do not know the upper limits of the capacity to grow and change and take individual, group and community aspirations seriously.
4. We best serve clients by collaborating with them.
5. Every environment is full of resources.
6. Caring, caretaking and context – all are essential to human wellbeing.

How can we build resilience within ourselves and take a strengths-based approach? One starting place is to look at some factors that promote resilience:

- caring relationships
- high expectation messages
- opportunities for participation and contribution.

Think about it

Using the idea of these factors, what initiatives could an individual take to build their resilience? Research initiatives that promote opportunities for participation and meeting others (volunteering might be one idea).

So we end this chapter with hope and the recognition that initiatives that support people can be protective. Our wellbeing doesn't just rest within us; it can also be fostered and nourished in relationship with others and in our wider community.

CHECK YOUR LEARNING GOALS!

You should be able to:

1. Outline what is meant by the 'wear and tear' approach to ageing.
2. Define 'healthy ageing'
3. Summarise the main changes seen in the brain during adulthood.
4. List some of the symptoms of the menopause.
5. Explain how post-formal thought differs from Piaget's formal operational stage.
6. List and explain the stages of Schaie's theory of cognition.
7. Outline the main findings of the Seattle Longitudinal Study and explain why it is important to the study of cognitive change in adulthood.
8. Outline the positive and negative outcomes of Erikson's psychosocial stages associated with adulthood.
9. Describe the 'adult attachment interview'.
10. Outline, with reference to theories or other material, why relationships are important.
11. Explain the difference between 'life structure' and 'life cycle' in Levinson's theory.
12. Use Levinson's stages to critically evaluate the usefulness of 'stage' theories.

9

Older Age

In this chapter we will discover:

* Physical development
  - Theories of ageing
  - Physical changes
  - The ageing brain
  - Disability
  - In Focus: Disabilities and ageing
* Cognitive development
  - Baltes' dual-process model
  - Fluid and crystallised intelligence
* Socio-emotional development
  - Erikson's integrity vs. despair
  - Social isolation and loneliness
  - In Focus: Dementia and *Creating Excellence in Dementia Care* (2012)
* End of life
  - Terminology
  - Phases of dying
  - Awareness and interaction model of dying
  - Kübler-Ross's stages of dying
  - Bereavement

In the past, scant regard or interest was paid to the psychological changes that occur in older age, and when it was it was firmly rooted in a deficit model approach. In recent times, more attention is being paid to older age. Increasing life expectancy and the growing needs of this group are shining a light on a complex period of development. In this chapter we will chart the changes of later life: physical, cognitive and socio-emotional.

You will have an opportunity to discover the building body of research focusing on greater understanding of the elderly. At the end of the chapter, we will examine 'end of life', including concepts and theories of dying and death, and reactions to bereavement.

Late adulthood is the period from 65 years onwards. As we are living longer, we must give more attention to understanding and supporting this period of development. In Ireland, for example, a longitudinal study researching the lives of older people (TILDA) aims to gather information from a nationally representative survey which will become the foundation for policy formation and implementation to enable successful ageing. The study will provide an accurate picture of the needs and contributions of older people. We have seen the importance of having accurate data so as to understand changes in human development. Over the course of the book, we have also encountered the role factors can play, positively and negatively, in developmental outcomes. These factors can become very apparent in older age; we have already seen them implicated in life expectancy in the Travelling community and in cognitive outcomes in adults in the Seattle Longitudinal Study (Chapter 8).

Think about it

As you read this chapter, see what material you might use to argue for the nature versus nurture and early experiences/later development debates.

PHYSICAL DEVELOPMENT

* **Young-old**: Appear physically young for their actual age.
* **Old-old:** Appear physically frail and show signs of decline.

We touched on healthy ageing in the previous chapter. Can you see how it might be implicated here?

There are many theories of ageing, but first we need to understand the distinction between primary and secondary ageing.

* **Primary ageing** is the gradual age-related changes that we have no control over, reflecting the biological aspects of ageing that affect everyone. Changes include greying hair and deterioration in hearing and vision.
* **Secondary ageing** is more individual in that it is influenced by lifestyle and environmental factors such as lack of exercise, smoking, alcohol consumption and obesity. Disease is also a factor in secondary ageing.

THEORIES OF AGEING

Damage-based theories suggest that ageing results from a continuous process of damage which accumulates throughout the entire lifespan. This approach argues that ageing is predominantly a result of interactions with the environment.

Programmed theories of ageing suggest that ageing is not a result of random processes but rather that it is predetermined and occurs on a fixed schedule.

PHYSICAL CHANGES

Senescence is the deterioration of bodily functions that accompanies aging in a living organism. The following changes are witnessed during old age, but individual variation must be taken into account as lifestyle and other factors can determine the rate of ageing and the magnitude of its effects.

* Loss of brain weight increases after 60 years of age
* Neurons (nerve cells) are lost in visual, hearing and motor areas of the brain
* Vision and hearing become increasingly impaired
* Heart rate slows, as does blood flow
* Sleep patterns change; less sleep is needed
* Appearance of the skin continues to change; age spots develop
* Loss of weight and height after 60
* Muscle strength declines; there is less flexibility.

THE AGEING BRAIN

According to Carter:

> *[T]he natural degeneration of the brain and the nervous system is not caused by disease, and so should not be confused with the pathology of dementia, which is associated with a pattern of specific brain changes. Recent research shows that most neurons actually remain healthy until you die, but brain volume and size decrease 5–10 per cent from the age of 20–90. (Carter 2009, p.206)*

The ageing brain is a relatively recent phenomenon in human history. In the past many people did not live beyond the age of fifty, so the issue was not relevant.

NEUROPSYCHOLOGY OF AGEING

The biggest threat to successful ageing is loss of mental function – memory, thinking, concentration, learning, problem-solving, alertness, error-proneness, vulnerability to crime/ deception, etc. Changes in these mental abilities occur because the brain changes as we get older, and these alterations may accelerate in our fifties and sixties. In an unfortunate minority of people, they accelerate into dementia. Such difficulties are also linked to other common problems of age – depression, falls and social isolation.

MALNUTRITION

Malnutrition is 'a state of nutrition in which a deficiency or excess (or imbalance) of energy, protein, and other nutrients causes measurable adverse effects on tissue/ body form and function, and clinical outcome'. (Stratton, 2019)

Medical and social factors that increase the risk of malnutrition in older people include:

* Acute illness/disease
* Dementia
* Depression
* Decreased mobility, inability to go out shopping
* Social isolation, bereavement, loss of spouse
* Economic hardship
* Alcohol consumption and smoking.

Think about it

How would 'social isolation' be a factor in reduced appetite or consumption of food?

Biologically based changes in the body, such as changes in the ability to taste and smell, can also have an impact on food consumption. Issues with joint problems and movement might make it difficult to prepare food while reduced gastrointestinal functions might make it more difficult to digest food (NCAOP — National Council on Ageing & Older People).

Think about it

We can clearly see here the interaction of nature-based factors (biological/body) and external ones (nurture). As you read this chapter, use Bronfenbrenner's bio-ecological theory to identify the different factors at play. Summarise your reflections as an example of the nature–nurture debate and how the bio-ecological theory helps us understand the interaction of factors in outcomes.

DISABILITY

Disability, as we saw in Chapter 3, can occur at conception or birth; and disabilities can also be acquired through accidents, illness or ageing. Therefore, as we age our likelihood of becoming disabled increases.

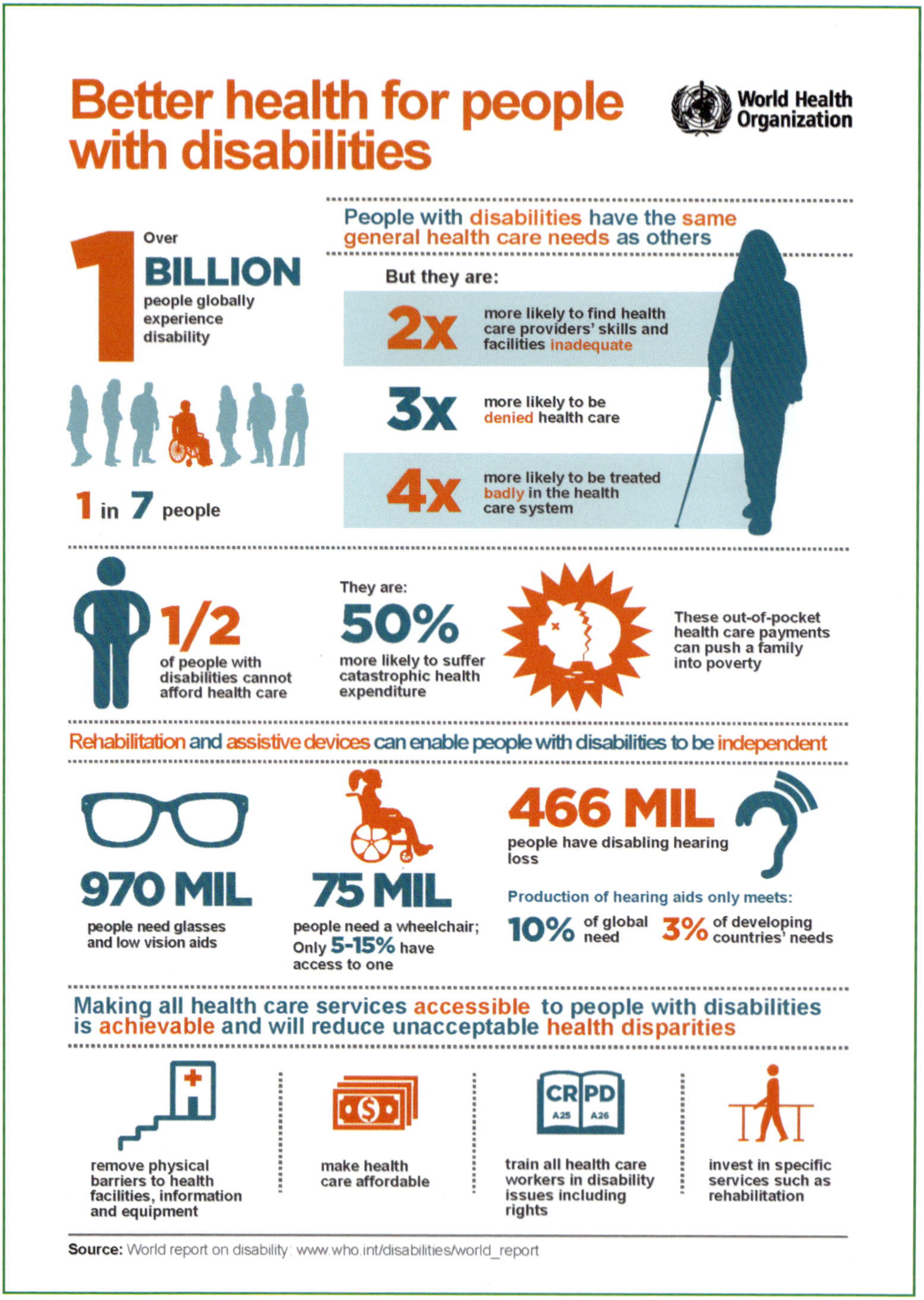

WHO Better health for people with disabilities infographic

IN FOCUS: DISABILITY AND AGEING

There are many definitions of 'disability', and the issue of definition has proven to be one of the most contentious issues facing the delegates of the United Nations committee on a Comprehensive and Integral International Convention on Protection and Promotion of the Rights and Dignity of Persons with Disabilities. In 2006, the following definition was suggested:

> '**Disability** results from the interaction between persons with impairments, conditions, or illnesses and the environmental and attitudinal barriers they face. Such impairments, conditions, or illnesses may be permanent, temporary, intermittent, or imputed, and those that are physical, sensory, psychosocial, neurological, medical or intellectual.' (United Nations, 2006)

This definition captures the three dimensions of disability – the body, the individual and society. It increases inclusivity and encompasses the full range and diversity of disability experience.

PHYSICAL DISABILITIES

Kirk *et al.* (2000, p.485) suggests that there are two categories of physical disability: physical disability and health impairment.

> A **physical disability** is 'a condition that interferes with a person's ability to use his or her body'.

This highlights that most physical disabilities involve difficulties with skeletal, muscular or nervous systems.

> A **health impairment** is 'a condition that requires ongoing medical attention'.

Physical disabilities are either congenital or acquired.

- Congenital disability: The disability is present at birth (it may or may not have been present earlier in utero but it must be present at birth, though the condition might sometimes show itself soon after). Congenital disabilities can span from mild to severe and include cerebral palsy, epilepsy, neural tube disorders (spina bifida) and muscular dystrophy.
- Acquired disability: Physical impairment that develops, usually though an accident or illness, after a period of typical development.

»

O'Donovan and Doyle (2009) report that the top three diagnostic categories in the age groups 16–65 are as follows:

- 16–24 years: Cerebral palsy, cystic fibrosis, congenital deafness
- 25–44 years: Multiple sclerosis, cerebral palsy, head injury
- 45–65 years: Multiple sclerosis, diabetes 1, stroke/hemiplegia.

ACQUIRED BRAIN INJURY

Acquired brain injury (ABI) is an umbrella term that refers to any injury to the brain that occurs after birth and is caused by trauma or disease.

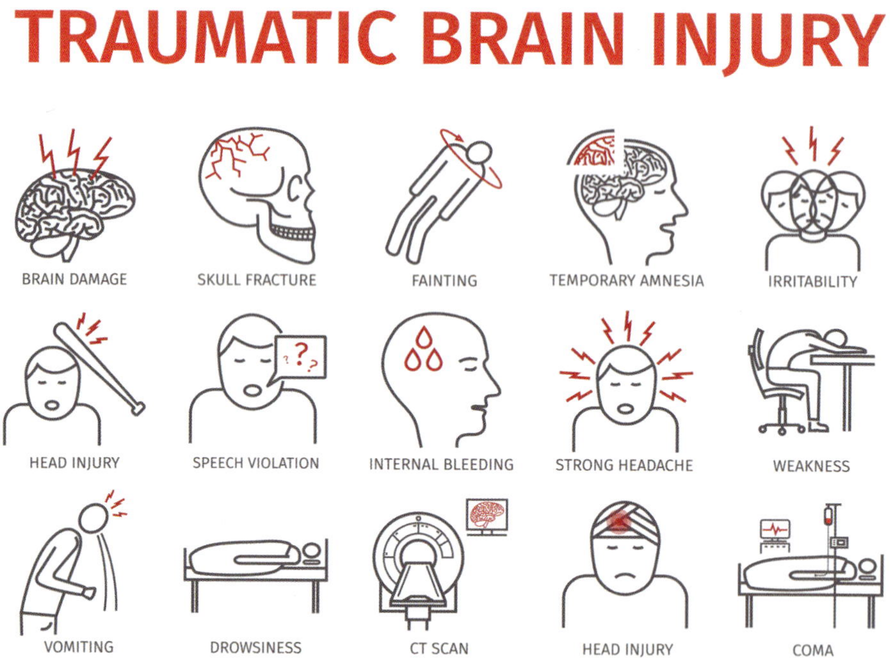

Traumatic brain injury (TBI) is a form of ABI that is due to a sudden blow or jolt to the brain from an accident, fall or assault. Other forms of ABI include infection, tumour and stroke. Rehabilitation depends on many factors, from social support network to the severity of the damage. ABI can affect an individual at any stage across the life span and is one of the most common causes of disability. As we saw earlier, the brain is involved in all aspects of functioning, from physical, intellectual and social to emotional; therefore, ABIs can affect physical ability, speech, memory and thought processes, and psychological functioning and behaviour.

Think about it

Could the age at which a brain injury is acquired determine the impact on the individual and their families? For instance, if I acquire a brain injury at 41 or 67 or 82, would the effects of that differ in terms of impact on my life and those around me? Research has suggested that differences exist, including in relation to family and financial outcomes. Compare a 58-year-old mum of two who works full time and acquires a brain injury with an 80-year-old living alone. Will their brain injury impact on their lives and those around them differently? Draw up a list of the different areas of life affected and implications for support.

INTELLECTUAL DISABILITY

The longitudinal study on ageing included adults with an intellectual disability (ID) and looked at their experiences of ageing.

Intellectual disability is 'a disability characterised by significant limitations both in intellectual functioning and in adaptive behaviour, which covers many everyday social and practical skills. This disability originates before the age of 18' (American Association on Intellectual and Developmental Disability, 2009).

An ID may be the result of a genetic, chromosomal or congenital condition or acquired before the age of 18. Challenges facing those with ID can be long-term or lifelong. The demands of ordinary life (social, educational, domestic, safety, communication) can create ongoing challenges to people with even mild ID. Understanding the experiences of ageing in older adults with ID is crucial; we cannot assume that their experiences and life path matches those without ID.

The Intellectual Disability Supplement to the Irish Longitudinal Study on Ageing (IDS-TILDA) is a large-scale nationally representative study of people with an ID. This study is the first of its kind in Europe, and the only study with the potential to compare the ageing of people with ID directly with the general ageing population. It is a wide-ranging report covering a variety of aspects. We will consider some of its findings here, including health service needs and social inclusion. »

Key areas for understanding the ageing of persons with intellectual disability suggested by the international literature include:

(1) their physical and psychological health status,

(2) their use of health services,

(3) their social networks and supports including living arrangements and income available, and

(4) their experience of personally defined quality of life. (p.17)

LIFE EXPECTANCY

The life expectancy of persons with intellectual disability in Ireland remains less than that of the general population, with the average age of death in an Irish population with ID reported at 46 years. Longevity in Ireland is also less compared to cohorts of persons . with ID identified in international reports, e.g. 66 years for New York State, and 58 to 74 years depending on level of disability in the UK. (p.17)

HEALTH SERVICE NEEDS

There has been controversial evidence in other countries that the experience of poor health and early mortality among people with intellectual disability may be related to the location and to the types and quality of healthcare services people with intellectual disability receive. It has also been reported that:

- *People with intellectual disability are more likely to lead unhealthy lifestyles which contribute to the development of physical ailments in later life.*
- *People with intellectual disability do not access health promotion and health screening services to the same extent as peers without disability.*
- *Health promotion programmes are seldom targeted at people with ID yet they have been shown to increase disease prevention and case finding.*

PSYCHOLOGICAL HEALTH

Among the population of adults with intellectual disability, there is a reported high point prevalence (more than one third) rate of mental health problems.

In a review of available studies, it was reported that ... 20–40% of older persons with intellectual disability have a mental health problem.

It has also been found that older people with ID have significantly higher levels of psychiatric issues than younger adults with ID. Social, cultural, environmental and development factors have been implicated, including over-medication and lack of review of medications in this group. The report noted this has a 'significant' impact on psychiatric and behavioural disorders.

LONELINESS AND SOCIAL INCLUSION

While those living in community settings had higher levels of engagement than those in residential centres, the report still found low levels of engagement. This suggests that society has done a better job of increasing the community presence of people with an ID than facilitating them to actually live within the community. Consequently, as we move people to more community-based accommodation it is not good enough to be simply happy with a 'presence'. Instead, there is an urgent need to develop sound polices and to support actions to facilitate people with an ID to participate in the life of their communities. This is not unique to Ireland and has been reported in other countries.

> *In terms of day-to-day life, it was encouraging to find that most adults with an ID had a hobby, went on holidays or day trips, engaged in regular daytime activity and leisure pursuits and had social contacts with others. However, adults with an ID reported that they seldom engaged in social activities with friends outside their home; almost 80% of respondents relied on staff support and companionship when it came to social activities and a majority reported being dependent on others for transportation and other assistance to access community options.*
>
> *It is of particular concern that older people with severe levels of ID appeared to have increased risk of social isolation. Additionally, and in contrast to the general population, a range of findings related to both social connectedness and social participation by adults with an ID. They included the following:*
>
> - *One in four adults reported meeting their family once a year or less.*
> - *Over three-quarters of adults with an ID reported that they never wrote, texted, emailed or used multimedia such as Facebook to contact their family or friends.*
> - *Less than 60% used the telephone to make such contact.*
> - *Most adults with an ID identified a staff member as their confidant and their principal source of social interactions.*
>
> *These findings highlight the growing challenges faced by people with an ID in making connections with others. They also show that opportunities for social networks can shrink as people with an ID age. In particular, the very limited role of families in the lives of many adults with an ID is of concern. This is especially so when we consider that, for the general population, family represents both a central source of social engagement and an important provider of support for adults as they age. (pp. 63–4)*

Think about it

The report mentions social isolation in different forms. Do you think that some groups in society are at higher risk of being or becoming socially isolated? List them and your reasoning as to why they're at higher risk. Is being reliant on a care staff member for your social interactions problematic?

COGNITIVE DEVELOPMENT

As we saw in the previous chapter, cognitive development is influenced not just by the ageing process but also by lifestyle factors. Data from the Seattle Longitudinal Study shows that it is possible to maintain healthy cognitive function in old age. External factors such as diet, smoking or positive brain training and engagement can make a difference to the health of the brain and consequently to cognition. It's a complex picture. The following theory by Paul Baltes captures the concept of both deterioration and improvement as we enter older age.

BALTES' DUAL-PROCESS MODEL

Paul Baltes (1939–2006), a leading researcher in the field of ageing, contributed enormously to our understanding of this area. Baltes proposed a dual-process model (1997) of cognitive functioning.

The **dual-process model** attempts to measure what aspects of intelligence are likely to improve or deteriorate with age.

Papalia *et al.* distinguish between the mechanics of intelligence and the pragmatics of intelligence (2005, p.654).

Mechanics of intelligence are the brain's neurophysiological 'hardware' – information-processing and problem-solving function independent of any particular content. This dimension, like fluid intelligence, often declines with age.

Pragmatics of intelligence are culture-based 'software' – practical thinking, application of accumulated knowledge and skills, specialised expertise, professional productivity and wisdom. This area, which may continue to develop until very late adulthood, is similar to, but broader than, crystallised intelligence and includes information and know-how garnered from education, work and life experience.

So this theory differentiates two aspects of thinking: the 'structures' of thinking that link closely to the brain and may be impacted by the ageing process; and the 'content' of thinking, the things we learn and experiences we accumulate. The second kind of thinking, according to Baltes, is less affected by ageing.

Another theory that differentiates between different types of thinking or cognition is Horn and Cattell's theory of fluid and crystallised intelligence.

FLUID AND CRYSTALLISED INTELLIGENCE

John Horn and Raymond Cattell proposed that general intelligence is not a singular thing but instead a grouping of about a hundred abilities all working together. These numerous abilities are separated into two strands or abilities (fluid and crystallised) that have quite different developmental pathways across the lifespan.

Fluid Intelligence

- Global capacity to reason
- Ability to learn new things
- Think abstractly and solve problems

Crystalised Intelligence

- Prior learning and past experiences
- Based on facts
- Increases with age

Fluid intelligence drives the individual's ability to think and act quickly and to solve problems. Fluid intelligence is grounded in biological efficiency and is thus relatively independent of education or cultural influences (Horn & Cattell 1967). Many studies have demonstrated that fluid intelligence peaks in early adulthood and then declines, gradually at first and then more rapidly as old age sets in after about 70 years of age.

Crystallised intelligence stems from learning and cultural influences, and is reflected in tests of knowledge, general information, use of language (vocabulary) and a wide variety of acquired skills. Personality factors, motivation and educational and cultural opportunity are central to its development. Crystallised abilities continue to improve as individuals age. Crystallised intelligence can be thought of as wisdom which the individual accumulates as they progress through life.

Research by Bergman and Almkvist (2013) suggests that physical health is directly involved in 'fluid' but not 'crystallised' intelligence. In studying how cognitive abilities were predicted by differences in physical health, they conclude that improving physical health can play an important role in improving cognition and reducing its demise.

Again, we can see the web of connectedness between different areas of development and how lots of factors, both within the person and external to them, are involved. The issue of isolation and its effect on physical and mental wellbeing has been highlighted. If we needed any proof of the importance of social connection, the Covid pandemic showed us just how vital connection is to all aspects of our wellbeing.

Let's take a look at some theories that explore social and emotional development in older age.

SOCIO-EMOTIONAL DEVELOPMENT

ERIKSON'S INTEGRITY VS. DESPAIR

The final stage of Erikson's theory of psychosocial development is characterised by integrity or despair. The former represents a positive outcome and is associated with a feeling of satisfaction with one's life and achievements. The individual feels content and at peace, reflecting psychosocial maturity. However, if the outcome of this stage is despair, the individual believes that they have made many mistakes in their life and that it is too late to correct them, which manifests in bitterness and anger. An individual in 'despair' may not be accepting of death.

SOCIAL ISOLATION AND LONELINESS

Covid has shone a light on the importance of social connection and our relationships with others. However, long before the pandemic, conversations were already being had regarding the increasing levels of loneliness and isolation being experienced in Irish society. But is loneliness really increasing or, as Novotney (2019) asks, 'Are we becoming lonelier or just more inclined to recognise and talk about the problem?'

This is a hard question to answer because historical data regarding social isolation and loneliness is scant. Still, some research suggests that both are increasing.

Social isolation is an objective lack of social contact.

Loneliness is the subjective feeling of being lonely; you can be alone without feeling lonely (Clay 2020).

According to the National Council on Ageing and Older People (Murphy *et al.*, 2007):

> *[T]he importance of family and kinship to quality of life has been generally recognised in social gerontological studies ... social interaction with people, including connectedness to family and friends, is usually beneficial and a positive influence on quality of life. People who are not connected to others often experience loneliness, which detracts from quality of life.*

The importance of social relationships for quality of life has been noted in several studies, yet relationships are not without their difficulties; they can detract from quality of life as much as add to it. Issues such as family disputes, difficulties maintaining contact or family members not having enough time to visit were raised by older people as an obstacle to their happiness. Thus loneliness and reduced social contact can have a detrimental impact on an older person's wellbeing. This piece highlights the importance of a good social support network enveloping the older person, which is a protective factor in old age.

During the pandemic, given the higher risk associated with becoming ill, older people were encouraged to limit their social interactions and contacts, which significantly amplified the problems of social isolation and loneliness.

Clay (2020) reports that both isolation and loneliness are associated with an increase in heart disease, dementia and other health problems. It has been suggested that social isolation has a mortality risk similar to other risk factors such as smoking, obesity and lack of physical activity, and yet little recognition is given to the connection between social relationships and health (Novotney 2019).

Think about it

What other knock-on effects do you think the pandemic may have had? Are there other groups, apart from the elderly, who are more vulnerable to its impact? How would you explain your answer with reference to psychological theories (e.g. bio-ecological theory) and other information (such as factors)? Remember, in psychology you must support your answers with reference to theories, studies or other information.

Social isolation and loneliness have been implicated in the risks for developing dementia. Here we take an in-depth look at dementia – a condition that continues to afflict the elderly as life expectancy increases.

IN FOCUS: DEMENTIA AND *CREATING EXCELLENCE IN DEMENTIA CARE* (2012)

> *A woman in her early 50s was admitted to a hospital because of increasingly odd behavior. Her family reported that she had been showing memory problems and strong feelings of jealousy. She also had become disoriented at home and was hiding objects. During a doctor's examination, the woman was unable to remember her husband's name, the year, or how long she had been at the hospital. She could read but did not seem to understand what she read, and she stressed the words in an unusual way. She sometimes became agitated and seemed to have hallucinations and irrational fears.*

This account relates to the first known case of dementia, presented in the early 1900s. Dementia is an umbrella term for a collection of symptoms resulting from a number of disorders that affect the brain. Those with dementia have significantly impaired cognitive (intellectual) functioning, with this impairment impacting on relationships and daily activities. Symptoms can include:

- An inability to solve problems
- Personality changes such as agitation, emotional control and hallucinations
- Memory loss, though this feature alone is not enough to warrant a diagnosis of dementia.

»

Doctors diagnose dementia only if two or more brain functions – such as memory, language skills or perception – or cognitive skills – including reasoning and judgement – are significantly impaired without loss of consciousness.

- Currently more than 55 million people live with dementia worldwide, and there are nearly 10 million new cases every year.
- Over 64,000 people are living with dementia in Ireland, with the number expected to be in excess of 104,000 by 2036 unless there is a medical breakthrough.
- Dementia can affect younger people; currently approximately 4,000 people in Ireland under the age of 65 have younger onset dementia.
- Alzheimer's disease is the most common form of dementia and may contribute to 60–70% of cases.
- Dementia is currently the seventh leading cause of death among all diseases and one of the major causes of disability and dependency among older people globally.

Alzheimer's disease is the most common cause of dementia in people aged 65 and older. In most people, symptoms of Alzheimer's disease appear after age 60. However, there are some early-onset forms of the disease, usually linked to a specific gene defect, which may appear as early as age 30. Alzheimer's disease usually causes a gradual decline in thinking abilities, usually during a span of seven to ten years. Nearly all brain functions, including memory, movement, language, judgement, behaviour and abstract thinking, are eventually affected. Different types of dementia cause characteristic patterns of memory loss because they attack different parts of the brain. In Alzheimer's disease the first area to go tends to be the hippocampus where personal memories are stored. The hippocampus is also involved in remembering one's way around, which is why people with Alzheimer's type dementia often get lost (Carter 1998).

Alzheimer's disease is characterised by two abnormalities in the brain: amyloid plaques, which are clumps of protein found in the tissue between the nerve cells; and neurofibrillary tangles, bundles of twisted filaments found within neurons. These tangles are largely made up of a protein called tau.

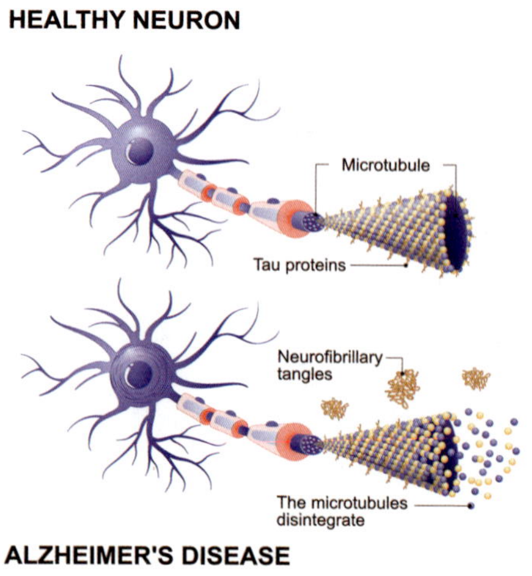

In healthy neurons, the tau protein helps the functioning of microtubules, which are part of the cell's structural support and deliver substances throughout the nerve cell. However, in Alzheimer's disease, tau is changed in a way that causes it to twist into tangles. When this happens, the microtubules cannot function correctly and they disintegrate. This collapse of the neuron's transport system may impair communication between nerve cells and cause them to die.

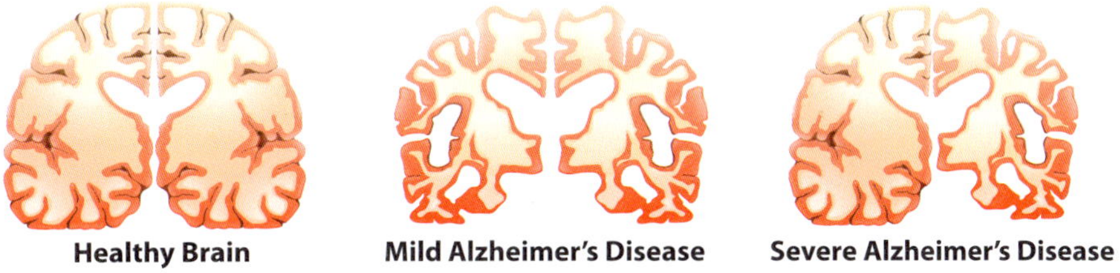

In the early stages of Alzheimer's disease, patients may experience memory impairment, lapses of judgement and subtle changes in personality. As the disorder progresses, memory and language problems worsen and patients begin to have difficulty performing activities of daily living. They may become disoriented about places and times, may suffer delusions (such as the idea that someone is stealing from them or that their spouse is being unfaithful), and may become short-tempered and hostile.

Symptoms of Alzheimer's disease

»

During the late stages of the disease, patients begin to lose the ability to control motor functions such as swallowing, or lose bowel and bladder control. They eventually lose the ability to recognise family members and to speak. As the disease progresses it begins to affect the person's emotions and behaviour and they develop symptoms such as aggression, agitation, depression, sleeplessness or delusions. On average, patients with Alzheimer's disease live for 8 to ten years after they are diagnosed. However, some people live as long as twenty years.

CREATING EXCELLENCE IN DEMENTIA CARE REPORT

This report (Cahill ***et al.*** 2012) was funded by Atlantic Philanthropies to provide evidence-based research for the purpose of supporting the development of a national dementia strategy, which was published two years later in 2014 by the Department of Health. It is a comprehensive overview of dementia encompassing, among other topics, the economic and social costs of dementia and community-based health services. Here we'll look at two aspects of the report: psychosocial interventions; and the physical environment.

PSYCHOSOCIAL INTERVENTIONS

The following extract outlines the variety of psychosocial interventions that can be used in the care of those with dementia:

> *There are a whole range of psychosocial approaches or non-pharmacological interventions that can be used by trained staff to promote wellbeing and improve quality of life for people with dementia living in residential care. These include: reality orientation, which uses rehearsal and physical prompts to improve cognitive function related to personal orientation; cognitive stimulation therapy, which focuses on information processing; reminiscence therapy, which involves discussion of past experiences and activities individually or in a group; music therapy, aromatherapy, doll therapy, Snoozelins and validation therapy. Many of these approaches have been the subject of extensive systematic reviews and there is emerging evidence demonstrating that several such approaches yield positive outcomes at least in the short-term. Other psychosocial approaches used in long-stay care facilities include pet therapy, creative therapies, structured activity/interaction programmes, and exercise. The latter have also been found to have positive effects, as has sensory stimulation programmes. Dementia care mapping, an approach where a trained practitioner spends dedicated time (minimum of 6 hours) in a residential care setting observing and recording instances of wellbeing and ill-being of residents with dementia, is a further example of a dementia-specific intervention designed to improve quality of care. For over 20 years in Ireland, Sonas aPc has been hosting training workshops focusing on sensory stimulation and communication in both public and private long-stay facilities. A preliminary evaluation of the Sonas method has shown that the intervention may significantly improve quality of life and quality of care in residential and community settings. Sonas aPc has also developed spirituality programmes for long-stay residents of all faiths. (p.116)*

PHYSICAL ENVIRONMENT

People with dementia are particularly sensitive to their built and psychosocial environment and need a stable, consistent, familiar environment easy for them to negotiate and one that ideally reinforces their identity. Accordingly, it is not surprising why an admission to hospital can cause them enormous distress and can aggravate their disorientation and precipitate or aggravate challenging behaviours. The hospital environment complete with multiple and competing stimuli including noises (such as call bells, moaning, swinging doors, discordant television and radio, trolleys clattering), ward rounds, visitors coming and going, staff changeovers, cluttered ward layouts and poor signage are far from ideal for a persons with a cognitive impairment and can be experienced as frightening and hostile. Even cognitively impaired people who were functioning well in their home environment prior to hospitalisation often become extremely confused and unsettled in a general hospital setting. (p.95)

There is an international consensus about the features and principles of good design for dementia care. There is also some emerging evidence from the international and national literature demonstrating the benefits of small-scale group dwellings both for the person with dementia, their family caregivers and for staff. Our review has shown that in Ireland few people with dementia gain access to specialist care units and even when they do, the size of these units (average of 18 to 19 residents) does not conform with best practice models. We need to develop incentives for people to design more appropriate long-term care alternatives for people with dementia, rather than merely restricting them to accommodation in nursing homes. We can learn from the experience of other countries where National Dementia Strategies have targeted plans for designing more customised purpose built buildings. (p.115)

BEST PRACTICE IN DEMENTIA CARE

There is international consensus on design features that underpin best practice in dementia care:

- Small scale
- Familiar, domestic, homely in style
- Plenty of scope for ordinary activities (unit kitchens, washing lines, garden sheds)
- Unobtrusive concern for safety
- Different rooms for different functions
- Age-appropriate furniture and fittings
- Safe outside space
- Single rooms big enough for lots of personal belongings
- Good signage and multiple cues where possible, e.g. sight, smell, sound
- Use of objects rather than colour for orientation
- Enhanced visual access
- Controlled stimuli, especially noise. (p. 111)

CASE STUDY: HOGEWEY – AN INNOVATION IN DEMENTIA CARE

The *Creating Excellence in Dementia Care* report highlights the relationship between the physical environment and its potential impact on those with dementia. This relationship has been underscored with an innovative development in dementia care. Archer (2012) introduces us to Hogewey, a 'village' in the Netherlands:

> *[I]t's a step back into the 1950s boasting pretty, manicured streets, a grocery, café, coffee shop, restaurant and even a beauty salon and barber shop. There are 152 residents in Hogewey, and all have something in common – dementia. You see, Hogewey is not a real village; it is a treatment facility for dementia and Alzheimer's patients. Those who are lucky enough to live there do so in a time gone by, a time when many were in their prime. It is set in the 1950s because the dementia patient's long term memory is preserved much more vividly than short term. Thus they can relate to things from their younger days, which gives a feeling of familiarity, safety and comfort. Dementia waxes and wanes; with times of clarity interspersed with periods of confusion and memory loss. It's during those moments of clarity that Hogewey becomes priceless. Instead of a nursing home, with cold steel, linoleum floors, the smell of antiseptic and staff members wearing white, they live in a neighborhood. Patients come and go as they please, because the village, which takes up a city block, is staffed by 'villagers' who are really trained geriatric nurses and specialists, all there to help the residents when needed. Patients are free to take a buggy and walk to the supermarket, go grab a coffee or get a meal in the café. If they forget their wallet, no problem. If they get lost, there's always a 'villager' to help them get home ... Hogewey officials say that after a few weeks, residents improve dramatically, require less medication, become calmer.*

This revolutionary development marks a step forward in the care of those with dementia and particularly in terms of 'independent living'. The physical environment has been tailored to reflect the difficulties faced by those with dementia and to maximise their strengths. For example, longer-term memory is less affected than short-term so the village is designed to mirror the inhabitants' earlier lives. The staff do not wear 'medicalised' uniforms and blend into their surroundings yet still offer the same level of care when needed. This development marks a new way of thinking about how we care for those with dementia.

Think about it

Does this 'village' strike you as a positive step forward in independent living or do you feel there are any disadvantages in this approach?

END OF LIFE

Coming towards the end of life is the final developmental task we will all face. Not only does the individual face it, those around them also have to come to terms with the end-of-life stage, and losing those we love is a difficult and painful process. In this section we will look at models of dying including Kübler-Ross's theory. Bereavement reactions will also be considered.

TERMINOLOGY

Kastenbaum (2000) remarks that the following terminology has evolved, as more direct terms such as 'death' and 'dying' are 'too plain spoken ... for some tastes' (p.200).

Life-threatening condition may be used where some possibility for recovery exists.

End of life issues refers to any decisions regarding the end of life, from medical directives to funeral arrangements.

The phases of dying are identified as follows:

Agonal phase comes from the Greek *agon*, meaning struggle. Muscles may jerk and breathing becomes difficult as the body can no longer support life.

Clinical death is when breathing and heartbeat have ceased, though resuscitation may be possible.

Death occurs when all activity in the brain and brain stem has stopped, resulting in brain death which is irreversible.

Perspectives on end of life can be personal or role-specific:

The **personal perspective** acknowledges that each of us has our own views on dying and death. This perspective is shaped by our life experiences, family, cultural and religious beliefs and even the mass media. Our personal perspective influences our reactions to and perceptions of death.

The **role-specific perspective** is 'influenced by education, role, and responsibility ... the clergyperson's personal perspective on dying is expected to function within the established framework of theology and custom' (Kastenbaum 2000, p.210). Others with this perspective include nurses, doctors and trained counsellors who have specific roles within the process of death and dying. They are influenced by their role and its responsibilities.

AWARENESS AND INTERACTION MODEL OF DYING

David Sudnow, in *Passing On: The Social Organization of Dying* (1967), found that the attention people receive in life or death situations is 'significantly influenced by hospital staff perception of their age, present ability and social situation' (cited in Kastenbaum 2000, p.212). Discrimination and prejudice continue right until the end of life; this highlights the interaction of socioeconomic factors in influencing an individual's outcome.

Barney Glaser and Anselm Strauss (1966, 1968, cited in Kastenbaum 2000) wrote two pieces based on their observations of interactions in several hospitals. From these observations they identified that different types of 'awareness and interaction' patterns exist. 'Awareness and interaction' refers to awareness on the part of the patient and the communication (interaction) pattern with another (family or medical professional).

They identified four basic types of awareness and interaction:

- Closed awareness
- Suspected awareness
- Open awareness
- Mutual pretence.

CLOSED AWARENESS

The dying person does not realise that he or she is dying and the care provider or the interaction partner is not going to tell them. This is a keeping-the-secret context of the communication (or, rather, noncommunication). It is of great psychological interest because of the tension involved in trying to interact positively with a dying person while at the same time avoiding a disclosure that one fears would be devastating.

SUSPECTED AWARENESS

The patient surmises that he or she is not being told the truth, all the truth, and nothing but the truth. There is an effort to check out one's growing belief that the progress of the disease cannot be reversed or halted. The other interactant may or may not suspect that the patient is suspecting, but in any case, is resolved not to let the truth slip out.

OPEN AWARENESS

Both the patient and others are willing and able to share their knowledge and concerns. This does not necessarily mean that they have extensive discussions of dying and death. Rather, it means that everybody involved feels free to bring up the subject whenever it seems necessary or useful to do so. The open awareness context is almost invariably accompanied by less tension and conflict than either of the first two noted.

MUTUAL PRETENCE

This is perhaps the most subtle and certainly the most discussed type of interaction context. The patient knows he or she is dying. The visitor knows the patient is dying. Both pretend that they don't know. Furthermore, both may be aware that the other person is pretending, too. The mutual pretence act is difficult to sustain; one or the other person may be caught off guard or under pressure and let the horrifying truth escape (cited in Kastenbaum 2000 pp.214–15).

KÜBLER-ROSS'S STAGES OF DYING

Elisabeth Kübler-Ross's book *On Death and Dying*, first published in 1969, proved to be a seminal one. The area had been ignored and Kübler-Ross used her work as a doctor in American hospitals to shine a light on it. She recounted how in her homeland she, as a child, and other neighbours visited a local farmer as he lay dying at home. Dying and death seemed far more 'natural' than the medicalised environment and approach that appeared to dominate in American hospitals. She believed that a fear of death was strong in American culture, maybe due to the fact that death had been made cold, sterile, impersonal and mechanised. Kübler-Ross noted that the American view of death was one of abhorrence and avoidance; in other cultures it is treated as part of a normal transition.

Based on her observations and work with dying patients she devised the following five stages of dying:

The stages of dying

First stage: Denial and isolation	'No, not me. It cannot be true'	The first response derives from a temporary state of shock. This stage is characterised by isolation; sometimes dying people withdraw. Others can occasionally withdraw from them.
Second stage: Anger	'Life is not fair! Why me?'	When denial can no longer be maintained it is replaced by anger, rage, envy and resentment. The anger may extend in all directions and the person may feel a loss of control. Life is a constant reminder of death.
Third stage: Bargaining	'If you'll just let me live until my grandchild is born ...'	Seeking the chance that one will be rewarded for good behaviour – but really it represents an attempt to postpone the death.
Fourth stage: Depression	'What difference does it make anyway?'	Bargaining is replaced by a sense of loss at the inevitable. This may represent a preparatory grief as the person prepares for death. Other behaviours that might be seen are reactive depression, loss of self-esteem and guilt.
Fifth stage: Acceptance	'I've lived a good life, I'm ready to go'	If the patient has enough time, they will become neither depressed nor angry, neither happy nor sad, but void of feelings ('all felt out'). Dying patients find peace and acceptance, their circle of interests diminishes and they prefer fewer visits and distractions.

There are individual differences: some patients fight to the end; others just give up.

The best forms of support for dying patients include encouragement, maintenance of dignity and independence.

CRITICISMS OF THE THEORY

* Not all individuals go through the same sequence.
* Some individuals may struggle to the end.

BEREAVEMENT

Colin Murray Parkes (1998, p.200) outlines three responses common to those bereaved.

THE TRAUMA RESPONSE

* An alarm reaction – anxiety, restlessness and the physiological accompaniments of fear.
* Anger and guilt, including outbursts directed at those who press the bereaved person towards premature acceptance of the loss.
* Post-traumatic stress disorder, the specific pathological response and the less specific anxiety states and panic syndromes.

THE GRIEF RESPONSE

* An urge to search for and to find the lost person in some form.
* Relocating the lost person, including identification phenomena – adopting traits, mannerisms or symptoms of the lost person, with or without a sense of that person's presence within the self.
* Pathological variants of grief, i.e. the reaction may be excessive and prolonged or uninhibited and inclined to emerge in distorted form.

THE PSYCHOSOCIAL RESPONSE

* A sense of dislocation between the world that is and the world that should be, often expressed as a sense of mutilation or emptiness which reflects the individual's need to relearn their internal model of the world.
* A process of realisation, i.e. the way in which the bereaved moves from denial or avoidance of recognition of the loss towards acceptance and the adoption of a new model of the world.
* This process may be impaired by the feelings of helplessness and hopelessness which characterise depression.

CHECK YOUR LEARNING GOALS!

You should be able to:

1. Describe, with examples, the difference between primary and secondary ageing.
2. Outline the two theories of ageing.
3. Define 'senescence'.
4. Describe the changes in the brain commonly witnessed in older age.
5. List the factors that can impact on brain health.
6. Describe the difference between mechanics and pragmatics of intelligence.
7. Describe Horn and Cattell's theory of fluid and crystallised intelligence and explain which type of intelligence deteriorates with age.
8. Say which psychosocial stage is associated with this stage of life, according to Erikson, and outline its main features.
9. Explain the difference between social isolation and loneliness.
10. Explain why social isolation and loneliness is considered a serious threat to physical and mental wellbeing.
11. Outline the phases of dying.
12. Explain the 'awareness and interaction' model of dying and briefly summarise the four different types.
13. Describe the five stages in Kübler-Ross's stages of dying.
14. List two criticisms of Kübler-Ross's theory.
15. Outline the three common responses to bereavement, according to Murray Parkes.

We have now come to the end of our journey from conception to death. It is difficult to capture the complexity of the many different aspects of development in a single book – I'm not sure any number of books would be able to capture it! In truth, we know relatively little about how we become the person we are – we are still at the early stages in our understanding of such things. Through this book, however, I hope you have come to know and to an extent understand the myriad of factors that shape the development of the person. Good luck with your journey!

Bibliography

Abrams, Z. (2021). *How can we minimize Instagram's harmful effects?* <https://www.apa.org/monitor/2022/03/feature-minimize-instagram-effects>

Ainsworth, M. D. S., Blehar, M. C., Waters, E. and Wall, S. (1978) *Patterns of Attachment: A Psychological Study of the Strange Situation*. Hillsdale, NJ: Erlbaum.

AITHST (All Ireland Traveller Health Study Team) (2010) *Our Geels: All Ireland Traveller Health Study*. Dublin: School of Public Health, Physiotherapy and Population Science, University College Dublin. Available at: <https://www.gov.ie/en/publication/b9c48a-all-ireland-traveller-health-study>.

American Association on Intellectual and Developmental Disability (2009). *Definition of Intellectual and Development Disabilities.* Available at: <https://www.operationhousecall.com/wp-content/uploads/2016/12/AAIDD_definition_of_ID-DD_2009.pdf>

Andrews, A., Ben-Arieh, A., Carlson, M., Damon, W., Dweck, C., Earls, F., Garcia-Coll, C., Gold, R., Halfon, N., Hart, R., Lerner, R. M., McEwen, B., Meaney, M., Offord, D., Patrick, D., Peck, M., Trickett, B., Weisner, T. and Zuckerman, B. (Ecology Working Group) (2002) *Ecology of Child Well-Being: Advancing the Science and the Science-Practice Link*. Georgia: Centre for Child Well-Being.

APA (American Psychiatric Association) (1994) *Diagnostic and Statistical Manual of Mental Disorders* (4th edn). Washington, DC: American Psychiatric Press.

Archer, D. (2012) 'Stepping back in time: Help for Alzheimer's', *Psychology Today* 12 April.

Aslin, R. N. (1987) 'Motor Aspects of Visual Development in Infancy' in N. P. Salapatek and L. Cohen (eds), *Handbook of Infant Perception*, Vol. 1: *From sensation to Perception*, pp. 43–113. Orlando: Academic Press.

Baltes, P. B. (1997) 'On the incomplete architecture of human ontogeny: Selection, optimization, and compensation as foundation of developmental theory', *American Psychologist* 52: 366–80.

Barnes, P. (2002) *Personal, Social and Emotional Development of Children*. Open University; Blackwell.

Barrett, A., Savva, G., Timonen, V. and Kenny, R. A. (eds) (2011) *Fifty Plus in Ireland 2011: First Results from the Irish Longitudinal Study on Ageing (TILDA)*. Dublin: TILDA. Available at: <www.tcd.ie/tilda/assets/pdf/glossy/Tilda_Master_First_Findings_Report.pdf>.

Baumrind, D. (1966) 'Effects of authoritative parental control on child behavior', *Child Development*, 37(4), 887–907.

Beardslee, W. R. (1989) 'The role of self-understanding in resilient individuals: The development of a perspective', *American Journal of Orthopsychiatry*, 59, 266–278

Beck, A. T. (1976) *Cognitive Therapy of Depression*. Guildford Press.

Becker, A., Burwell, R., Herzog, D. and Hamburg, P. (2002) 'Eating behaviours and attitudes following prolonged exposure to television among ethnic Fijian adolescent girls', *British Journal of Psychology* 180: 509–14.

Becker, E. (1997) *The Denial of Death*. New York: Free Press.

Belsky, J. (1984) 'The determinants of parenting: a process model', *Child Development* 55: 83–96.

Belsky, J., Steinberg, L. and Draper, P. (1991) 'Childhood experience, interpersonal development, and reproductive strategy: an evolutionary theory of socialization', *Child Development* 62: 647–70.

Bennett, M. (2005) 'Socialisation', in B. Hopkins (ed.), *The Cambridge Encyclopedia of Child Development*. Cambridge University Press.

Benson, N. (2003) *Introducing Psychology*. England: Icon Books.

Bergman, I. and Almkvist, O. (2013) 'The effect of age on fluid intelligence is fully mediated by physical health', *Archives of gerontology and Geriatrics* 57(1): 100–9 <https://doi.org/10.1016/j.archger.2013.02.010>.

Best, D., Day, E., McCarthy, T., Darlington, I. and Pinchbeck, K. (2008) 'The Hierarchy of Needs and care planning in addiction services: What Maslow can tell us about addressing competing priorities', *Addiction Research and Theory* 16(4): 305–7.

Bogle, V. and Sykes, C. (2011) 'Psychological interventions in the treatment of childhood obesity: what we know and need to find out', *Journal of Health Psychology* 16(7): 997–1014.

Bowlby, J. (1951) 'Maternal care and mental health', World Health Organization monograph (Serial No. 2).

Boyd, D. and Bee, H. (2005) *Lifespan Development* (4th edn). New York: Allyn & Bacon.

Brim, O. G. (1992) *Ambition: How We Manage Success and Failure Throughout Our Lives*. New York: Basic Books.

Bronfenbrenner, U. (1979) *The Ecology of Human Development*. Cambridge, MA: Harvard University Press.

Bronfenbrenner, U. (2005) *Making Human Beings Human: Bioecological Perspectives on Human Development*. London: Sage.

Brooks-Gunn, J., Petersen, A. C. and Eichorn, D. (1985) 'The study of maturational timing effects in adolescence', *Journal of Youth and Adolescence* 14(3): 149–61.

Bruch, H., Czyzewski D. and Suhr, M. A. (1988) *Conversations with Anorexics*. Basic Books.

Bushnell, I. W. R., Sai, F., and Mullin, J. T. (1989) 'Neonatal recognition of the mother's face', *British Journal of Developmental Psychology* 7: 3–15.

Buss, A. H. and Plomin, R. (1984) *Temperament: Early Developing Personality Traits*. Hillsdale, NJ: Erlbaum.

Cahill, S., O'Shea, E., Pierce, M. (2012) *Creating Excellence in Dementia Care: A Research Review for Ireland's National Dementia Study*. Dublin: Department of Health.

Carr, A. (2003) *The Handbook of Clinical and Adolescent Clinical Psychology: A Contextual Approach*. New York: Brunner-Rutledge.

Carter, R. (1998) *Mapping the Mind*. London: Phoenix.

Carter, R. (2009) *The Brain Book*. London: Dorling Kindersley.

Chomsky, N., Hauser, M. and Tecumseh Fitch, W. (2002) 'The faculty of language: what it is, who has it, and how did it evolve?', *Science* 298: 1569–79.

Chou, W., Prestin, A., & Kunath, S. (2014). 'Obesity in social media: A mixed methods analysis'. *Translational Behavioral Medicine*, 4(3), 314–323.

Cianciolo, A. T. and Sternberg, R. J. (2004) *Intelligence: A Brief History*. Malden, MA: Blackwell.

Clarke, A. M. and Clarke, A. D. B. (1976) *Early Experiences: Myth and Experience*. London: Open Books.

Clarke, A. M. and Clarke, A. D. B. (1999) 'Early Experience and the Life Path', in S. Ceci and W. Williams (eds), *The Nature–Nurture Debate: The Essential Readings*. Oxford: Blackwell.

Clay, R. (2020) 'COVID-19 isn't just a danger to older people's physical health', *APA News*, 18 March <https://www.apa.org/news/apa/2020/covid-19-danger-physical-health>.

Clulow, C. (2007) 'Marriage, partnership and adult attachment', *Sexual and Relationship Therapy* 22(3): 291–94.

Cohen, D. and Volkmar, F. (1997) *Autism and Pervasive Developmental Disorders* (2nd edn). New York: John Wiley & Sons.

Colby, A., Kohlberg, L., Gibbs, J. and Lieberman, M. (1983) 'A longitudinal study of moral judgment', *Monographs of the Society for Research in Child Development* 48(1–2), serial no. 200.

Connolly, G. Conroy, R. Byrne PJ. & Kennelly S. (1998) 'Teenage pregnancy in the Rotunda Hospital'. *Irish Medical Journal*, 91 (6), pp. 209-12

Crain, W. C. (1985) *Theories of Development: Concepts and Applications*. London: Prentice- Hall.

Crockett, L. and Petersen, A. (1987) 'Pubertal Status and Psychological Development: Findings from Early Adolescence Studies', in R. M. Lerner and T. T. Foch (eds), *Biological-Psychosocial Interactions in Early Adolescence: A Lifespan Perspective*. Hillsdale, NJ: Erlbaum.

Crowell, J. A. and Treboux, D. (1995) 'A review of adult attachment measures: Implications for theory and research', *Social Development* 4: 294–327.

Croft, C., O'Connor, T.G., Keaveney, L., Groothues, C., Rutter, M. & the ERA team (2001) 'Longitudinal change in parenting associated with developmental delay and catch-up', *Journal of Child Psychology and Psychiatry* 42(5): 649–59.

Curtiss, S. (1977) *Genie: A Psycholinguistic Study of a Modern Day 'Wild Child'*. London: Academic Press.

Daichman, L. S. (2005) 'Elder abuse in developing countries' in M. Johnson (ed.), The Cambridge Handbook of Age and Ageing. Cambridge: Cambridge University Press.

Daniel, B., Wassell, S and Gilligan, R (2010) *Child Development for Child Care and Protection Workers 2nd edition*, London: Jessica Kingsley Publishers.

De Brún, A., McCarthy, M., McKenzie, K. and McGloin, A. (2014) 'Weight stigma and narrative resistance evident in online discussions of obesity', *Appetite* 72: 73–81, doi: 10.1016/j.appet.2013.09.022.

De Wolff, M. S. and van Ijzendoorn, M. H. (1997) 'Sensitivity and attachment: A meta- analysis on parental antecedents of infant attachment', *Child Development* 68: 571–91.

Deacon, T. (1997) *The Symbolic Species*. London: Allen Lane.

DeCasper, A. J. and Spence, M. J. (1986) 'Prenatal maternal speech influences newborns' perception of speech sounds', *Infant Behaviour and Development* 9: 133–50.

Dekovic, M. and Janssens, J. M. (1992) 'Parents' child-rearing style and child's sociometric status', *Developmental Psychology* 28(5): 925–32.

DoH (Department of Health) (2018) *Estimating Prevalence of Autism Spectrum Disorders* <https://assets.gov.ie/10707/ce1ca48714424c0ba4bb4c0ae2e510b2.pdf>.

DoHC (Department of Health and Children) (2006) *A Vision for Change: Report of the Expert Group on Mental Health Policy*. Dublin: Government Publications Office.

DoHC and Centre for Health Promotion Studies, NUI Galway (1998, 2002, 2007) *Survey of Lifestyle, Attitudes and Nutrition* (Slán). Available at: <www.dohc.ie/publications/slan07_report.html>.

Dryden, W. (1999) 'Some reflections on rational beliefs' in M. Neenan and W. Dryden, *Rational Emotive Behaviour Therapy: Advances in theory and practice*, London: Whurr.

Dubas, J. S., Graber, J. A. and Petersen, A. C. (1991) 'The effects of pubertal development on achievement during adolescence', *American Journal of Education* 99: 444–60.

Elkind, D. (1967) 'Egocentrism in adolescence', *Child Development* 38: 1025–33.

Elkins, D. (2009) 'Why humanistic psychology lost its power and influence in American psychology: Implications for advancing humanistic psychology', *Journal of Humanistic Psychology*, 49 (3), 267–91.

Erikson, E. H. (1963) *Childhood and Society* (2nd edn). New York: Norton.

Erikson, E. H. (1980) *Identity and the Lifecycle*. New York: Norton.

ESRI (Economic and Social Research Institute) (2012) *Perinatal Statistics Report 2010*. Dublin: Health Research and Information Division, ESRI. Available at: <www.esri.ie/health_information/nprs/nprs_reports/Perinatal_Statistics_Report_ 2010.pdf>.

ESRI and Trinity College Dublin (various dates) *Growing Up in Ireland: National Longitudinal Study of Children*. Dublin: Department of Children and Youth Affairs <www.growingup.ie>.

European Monitoring Centre for Drugs and Drug Addiction (EMCDDA) (2006) 'National Report (2005 Data) to the EMCDDA' by the Reitox National Focal Point Ireland. *New developments, trends and in-depth information on selected issues*.
<https://www.drugsandalcohol.ie/6062/1/3029-3227.pdf>

Fantz, R. L. (1961) 'The origin of form perception', *Scientific American* 204(5), 66–72.

Favaro A, Caregaro L, Tenconi E, Bosello R, Santonastaso P (2009). 'Time Trends in Age of Onset of Anorexia Nervosa and Bulimia Nervosa'. *J Clin Psychiatry*: 70 (12): 1715-21.

Field, H. and Domangue, B. (1987) *Eating Disorders Throughout the Lifespan*. Greenwood Press.

Freud, S. (1964) 'An outline of psychoanalysis', in J. Strachey (ed. & trans.), *The Standard Edition of the Complete Psychological Works of Sigmund Freud* (Vol. 22). London: Hogarth.

Frith, U. (1996) *Autism: Explaining the Enigma*. Oxford: Blackwell Press.

Garcia-Moro, C. and Hernandez, M. (1990) 'Changes in age at menarche in Spain, 1909–1965', *International Journal of Anthropology*, 5(2), 117–24.

Gardner, H. (1983) *Frames of Mind: The Theory of Multiple Intelligence*. New York: Basic Books.

Garhart Mooney, C. (2000) *Theories of Childhood: An Introduction to Dewey, Montessori, Erickson, Piaget and Vygotsky*. Minnesota: Redleaf Press.

Gibson, E. J. and Walk, R. D. (1960) 'The "visual cliff"', *Scientific American* 202: 64–71.

Giedd, J. (2004) 'What makes teens tick?', *Time*, 10 May.

Greene, S. (2007) ' Children's recovery after early adversity: Lessons from inter-country adoption'. Available at: <www.tcd.ie/childrensresearchcentre/index.php?id=129>.

Griffin, S. and Shevlin, M. (2007) *Responding to Special Educational Needs: An Irish Perspective*. Dublin: Gill & Macmillan.

Gross, R. (2009) *Psychology: The Science of Mind and Behaviour* (6th edn). London: Hodder Education.

Hadhazy, A. (2021) 'Women's risk for depression during pregnancy doubled during the COVID-19 pandemic', Stanford study, *Standford News*, 1 June. https://news.stanford.edu/2021/06/01/stress-pregnancy-doubled-pandemic/

Hall, C. (1962) *A Primer of Freudian Psychology*, London: George Allen & Unwin.

Hall, D. (1985) 'Technical note: Extreme deprivation in early childhood', *Journal of Child Psychology and Psychiatry* 26(5): 825.

Harlow, H. F. (1961) 'The development of affectional patterns in infant monkeys', in B.M. Foss (ed.), *Determinants of Infant Behaviour*, pp. 75–97. London: Methuen.

Harrison, K., Bost, K. K., McBride, B. A., Donovan, S. M., Grigsby-Toussaint, D. S., Kim, J., Liechty, J. M., Wiley, A., Teran-Garcia, M. and Costa Jacobsohn, G. (2011) 'Toward a developmental conceptualisation of contributors to overweight and obesity in childhood: the Six-Cs Model', *Child Development Perspectives* 5(1): 50–8.

Harter, S. (1990) 'Causes, Correlates and the Functional Role of Global Self-worth: A Life-span Perspective', in R. J. Sternberg and J. Kolligian (eds), *Competence Considered*. New Haven: Yale.

Hayflick, L. (1980) 'The cell biology of human aging', *Scientific American* 242: 56–65.

Healthy Ageing Project (2006), *Healthy Ageing- a Challenge for Europe*, © The Swedish National Institute of Public Health R 2006:29, ISSN: 1651-8624,ISBN: 91-7257-481-X, p. 16, Available at: <http://ec.europa.eu/health/ph_projects/2003/action1/docs/2003_1_26_frep_en.pdf>

Herbert, M. (2006) *Typical and Atypical Development: From Conception to Adolescence*. Oxford: BPS Blackwell.

Hetherington, E. M. and Parke, R. D. (1999) *Child Psychology: A Contemporary Viewpoint* (5th edn). New York: McGraw-Hill.

Hinman, N. G., Burmeister, J. M., Kiefner, A. E., Borushok, J. and Carels, R. A. (2015) 'Stereotypical portrayals of obesity and the expression of implicit weight bias', *Body Image* 12: 32–5 <https://doi.org/10.1016/j.bodyim.2014.09.002>.

Horn, J. L. and Cattell, R. B. (1967) 'Age differences in fluid and crystallized intelligence', *Acta Psychologica* 26: 107–29.

HSE (Health Service Executive) (2011) *A Practical Guide to Newborn Bloodspot Screening in Ireland*. Dublin: HSE. Available at: <www.hse.ie/eng/services/healthpromotion/ newbornscreening/newbornbloodspotscreening/PracticalGuide.pdf>.

HSE (2018). Eating Disorders Service: *HSE Model of Care for Ireland*. Available at <https://www.hse.ie/eng/services/list/4/mental-health-services/national-clinical-programme-for-eating-disorders/ed-moc.pdf>

Irish College of Psychiatrists (2005) 'A better future now: Position statement on psychiatric services for children and adolescents in Ireland'. Available at: <www.rcpsych.ac.uk/files/pdfversion/op60.pdf>.

Irish Focal Point (2010) *2011 National Report (2010 data) to the EMCDDA by the Reitox National Focal Point. Ireland: New developments, trends and in-depth information on selected issues*. Dublin: Health Research Board. Available at: <https://www.drugsandalcohol.ie/30621/>.

James, W. (1890) *The Principles of Psychology*. Dover Publications.

Jeon, Yongwoog & Hale, Brent & Knackmuhs, Eric & Mackert, Michael. (2018). 'Weight Stigma Goes Viral on the Internet: Systematic Assessment of YouTube Comments Attacking Overweight Men and Women'. *Interactive Journal of Medical Research*. 7. e6. 10.2196/ijmr.9182.

Jones, J., Duffy, M., Coull, Y. and Wilkinson, H. (2009) *Older People Living in the Community – Nutritional Needs, Barriers and Interventions: A Literature Review*. Edinburgh: RBS Centre for the Older Person's Agenda, Queen Margaret University.

Kagan, J., Reznick, J. S. and Snidman, N. (1988) 'Biological basis of childhood shyness', *Science* 240(4849): 167–71.

Kastenbaum, R. (2000) *The Psychology of Death* (3rd edn). New York: Springer.

Kelly, C., Gavin, A., Molcho, M. and Nic Gabhainn, S. (2012) *The Irish Health Behaviour in School-Going Children (HBSC) Study 2010*. Galway: Health Promotion Research Centre, National University of Ireland, Galway.

Kernan, M. (2007) *Play as a Context for Early Learning and Development: A Background Paper*. National Council for Curriculum and Assessment.

King, L.S., Feddoes, D.E., Kirshenbaum, J.S., Humphreys, K.L. and Gotlib, I.H. (2021) 'Pregnancy during the pandemic: The impact of COVID-19-related stress on risk for prenatal depression', *Psychological Medicine* 1(11), doi:10.1017/S003329172100132X.

Kirk, S., Gallagher, J. J., Coleman, M. R. and Anastasiow, N. (2000) *Educating Exceptional Children*. Boston: Houghton Mifflin.

Kitwood, T. (2007) *Dementia Reconsidered: The Person Comes First*. Oxford: Oxford University Press.

Kohlberg, L. (1976) 'Moral Stages and Moralisation: The Cognitive Developmental Approach' in T. Lickona (ed.), *Moral Development and Behaviour: Theory, Research and Social Issues*, pp. 31–53). New York: Holt.

Kravtsov, G. G. and Kravtsov, E. E. (2010) 'Play in L.S. Vygotsky's nonclassical psychology', *Journal of Russian and East European Psychology* 48(4): 25–41.

Kübler-Ross, E. (2005) *On Death and Dying*. London: Routledge.

Kuhn, D., Nash, S. C. and Brucken, L. (1978) 'Sex role concepts of two- and three-year-olds', *Child Development* 49.

Latner, J. D., Rosewall, J. K. and Simmonds, M. B. (2007) 'Childhood obesity stigma: Association with television, videogame, and magazine exposure', *Body Image* 4(2): 147–55 <https://doi.org/10.1016/j.bodyim.2007.03>.

LeClerc, G., 'The self-actualization concept: A content validation', *Journal of Social Behaviour and Personality*, 13(1) (1998), 69–84.

Levine, S. (2005) 'Developmental determinants of sensitivity and resistance to stress', *Psychoneuroendocrinology* 30:939–46.

Levinson, D. (1986) 'A conception of adult development', *American Psychologist* 41(1): 3–13.

Lewis, C. (2005) 'Parenting and the Family', in B. Hopkins (ed.), *The Cambridge Encyclopedia of Child Development*, pp. 340–3. Cambridge: Cambridge University Press.

McAvoy, H., Sturley, J., Burke, S. and Balanda, K. (2006) *Unequal at Birth: Inequalities in the Occurrence of Low Birthweight Babies in Ireland*. Institute of Public Health in Ireland. Available at: <www.publichealth.ie/index.asp?locID=489&docID=689>.

McCarron, M., Swinburne, J., Burke, E., McGlinchey, E., Mulryan, N., Andrews, V., Foran S. and McCallion, P. (2011) *Growing Older with an Intellectual Disability in Ireland 2011: First Results from the Intellectual Disability Supplement of the Irish Longitudinal Study on Ageing*. Dublin: School of Nursing and Midwifery, Trinity College Dublin. Available at: <www.hrb.ie/uploads/media/Growing_Older_with_an_Intellectual_Disability_in_Ireland_2011.pdf>.

MacFarlane, A. J. (1975) 'Olfaction in the development of social preferences in the human neonate', *Ciba Foundation Symposium* 33: 103–17.

McGivern, Y. (ed.) (2006) *Nutrition and Older People in Residential and Community Care Settings: Proceedings of the 2006 Health Ageing Conference. Report No. 96, National Council on Ageing and Older People*. Available at: <www.ncaop.ie/publications/ research/reports/96_Nutrition_procs.pdf>.

McGovern, M. (2011) 'Still unequal at birth: birth weight, socioeconomic status and outcomes at age 9', UCD Centre for Economic Research, Working Paper Series 25. Retrieved from <www.ucd.ie/t4cms/WP11_25.pdf> (accessed 12 August 2012).

McNicholas, F., Lydon, A., Lennon, R. and Dooley, B. (2009) 'Eating concerns and media influences in an adolescent context', *European Eating Disorders Review* 17: 208–13.

Maccoby, E. E. and Martin, J. A. (1983) 'Socialization in the Context of the Family: Parent–Child Interaction', in P. H. Mussen and E. M. Hetherington (eds), *Handbook of Child Psychology* Vol. 4: *Socialization, Personality, and Social Development*, pp. 1–101. New York: Wiley.

Madden, D. (2012) 'The relationship between low birthweight and socioeconomic status in Ireland', UCD Centre for Economic Research Working Paper Series 14. Retrieved from <www.ucd.ie/t4cms/WP12_14.pdf> (accessed 12 August 2012).

Magnusson, D., Stattin, H. and Allen, V. L. (1985) 'Biological maturation and social development: a longitudinal study of some adjustment processes from mid adolescence to adulthood', *Journal of Youth and Adolescence* 14(4): 267–83.

Malina, R. M., Bouchard, C. and Bar-Or, O. (2004) *Growth, Maturation and Physical Activity* (2nd edn). Human Kinetics Europe.

Marcia, J. (1980) 'Identity in Adolesence', in J. Adelson (ed.), *Handbook of Adolescent Psychology*. New York: Wiley.

Maslow, A. (1970) *Motivation and Personality*, 3rd ed., New York: Harper & Row.

Maslow, A. (1943) 'A theory of human motivation', *Psychological Review*, 50, 370–96.

Maycock, P., Bryan, P., Carr, N. and Kitching, K. (2009) *Supporting LGBT Lives: A Study of Mental Health and Well-being of Lesbian, Gay, Bisexual and Transgender People*. Dublin: Gay and Lesbian Equality Network (GLEN) and BeLonG To Youth Services.

Meggitt, C. (2006) *Child Development: An Illustrated Guide* (2nd edn). Oxford: Heinemann Educational.

Meltzoff, A. (1988) 'Infant imitation and memory: Nine month olds in immediate and deferred tasks', *Child Development* 59: 217–25.

Meltzoff, A. and Moore, M. (1977) 'Imitation of facial and manual gestures by human neonates', *Science* 198: 75–8.

Miller, P. (2002) *Theories of Developmental Psychology*, 4th ed., New York: Worth Publishers.

Mishra, P.S., Sinha, D., Kumar, P. *et al.* (2021) 'Newborn low birth weight: Does socio-economic inequality still persist in India?' *BMC Pediatrics* 21: 518 <https://doi.org/10.1186/s12887-021-02988-3>

Mitchell L, Bel-Serrat S, Stanley I, Hegarty T, McCann L, Mehegan J, Murrin C, Heinen M, Kelleher C (2020). *The Childhood Obesity Surveillance Initiative (COSI) in the Republic of Ireland – Findings from 2018 and 2019*. Available at: <https://www.hse.ie/eng/about/who/healthwellbeing/our-priority-programmes/heal/childhood-obesity-surveillance-initiativecosi/childhood-obesity-surveillance-initiative-report-2020.pdf>.

Moody, H. (2005) 'Ethical Dilemmas in Old Age Care' in M. Johnson (ed.), *The Cambridge Handbook of Age and Ageing*. Cambridge: Cambridge University Press.

Murphy, K., O'Shea, E., Cooney, A. and Casey, D. (2007) *The Quality of Life of Older People with a Disability in Ireland* (Report No. 99). Dublin: National Council on Ageing and Older People.

Murray Parkes, C. (1998) *Bereavement*. London: Penguin.

Music, G. (2011) *Nurturing Natures: Attachment and Children's Emotional, Sociocultural and Brain Development*. London: Psychology Press.

National Children's Office (2004) *Ready, Steady, Play*. Dublin: Stationery Office.

National Institute on Drug Abuse (NIDA) (2021), *The Connection Between Substance Use Disorders and Mental Illness*, April 13. Part 1. Retrieved from <https://nida.nih.gov/publications/research-reports/common-comorbidities-substance-use-disorders/part-1-connection-between-substance-use-disorders-mental-illness> on 2022, July 22.

National Institute for Neurological Disorders and Stroke (2012) *Dementia: Hope through Research*. Bethesda, MD: NINDS. Available at: <https://www.ninds.nih.gov/health-information/patient-caregiver-education/hope-through-research/dementias-hope-through-research>.

NDA (n.d.) *National Disability Study Pilot Report*. Available at: <https://nda.ie/Policy-and-research/Research/Research-publications/National-Disability-Study-Pilot-Report/Chapter-4-The-WHO-s-ICF/Chapter-4-The-WHO-s-ICF.html>

Nic Gabhainn, S. and Sixsmith, J. (2005) 'Children's understandings of well-being'. Available at: <https://www.researchgate.net/profile/Saoirse-Gabhainn/publication/235642816_Children's_Understandings_of_Well-being/links/0c960528cf4b7d2624000000/Childrens-Understandings-of-Well-being.pdf>.

Nixon, E. and Halpenny, A.M. (2010) *Children's Perspectives on Parenting Styles and Discipline: A Developmental Approach*, Office for the Minister of Children and Youth Affairs. Dublin: Stationery Office. Retrieved from <https://www.tcd.ie/tricc/assets/pdfs/crc-archive/2010-Nixon-Halpenny-Childrens-perspectives-on-parenting-styles.pdf>.

Nolan IT, Kuhner CJ, Dy GW. (2019) *Demographic and temporal trends in transgender identities and gender confirming surgery*. Transl Androl Urol. 2019 Jun;8(3):184-190. doi: 10.21037/tau.2019.04.09. PMID: 31380225; PMCID: PMC6626314. <https://www.ncbi.nlm.nih.gov/pmc/articles/PMC6626314/>

Novotney, A. (2019) 'The risks of social isolation', *Monitor on Psychology* 50(5): 33–7 <https://doi.org/https://www.apa.org/monitor/2019/05/ce-corner-isolation>.

O'Brien, E. (2011) *Psychology for Social Care*. Dublin: Gill & Macmillan.

O'Donovan, M.-A. and Doyle, A. (2010) 'Measure of activity and participation (MAP): Participation and ageing: The experience of people on the NPSDD', *MAP Bulletin* 4 (January).

Ofcom (2017). *Children and parents: media use and attitudes report*. <https://www.ofcom.org.uk/research-and-data/media-literacy-research/childrens/children-parents-2017>

Papalia, D. E., Olds, S. W. and Feldman, R. D. (2005) *Human Development* (10th edn). New York: McGraw-Hill.

Passer, M. and Smith, R. (2001) *Psychology: Frontiers and Applications*. New York: McGraw-Hill.

Passer, M. and Smith, R. (2007) *Psychology: The Science of Mind and Behavior* (3rd edn). New York: McGraw-Hill.

Pearson, E. and Podeschi, R. (1999) 'Humanism and individualism: Maslow and his critics', *Adult Education Quarterly* 50(1), Fall: 41–55.

Perry, B. (2008) *The Boy who was Raised as a Dog*. Basic Books.

Pesonen, A. K. and Räikkönen, K. (2012) 'The lifespan consequences of early stress', *Physiology and Behaviour* 105(6): 722–7.

Phillips, M. L.(2011) 'The mind at midlife', *Monitor on Psychology* 42(4): 38 <https://www.apa.org/monitor/2011/04/mind-midlife#:~:text=The%20adult%20brain%20seems%20to,even%20have%20improved%20cognitive%20abilities>.

Pipher, M. (1994) *Reviving Ophelia: Saving the Selves of Adolescent Girls*. New York: Ballantine Books.

Puder, J. J. and Munsch, S. (2010) 'Psychological correlates of childhood obesity', *International Journal of Obesity* 34: 37–43.

Radke-Yarrow, M., Cummings, E. M., Kuczinsky, L. and Chapman, M. (1985) 'Patterns of attachment in two- and three-year-olds in normal families and families with parental depression', *Child Development* 56: 884–93.

Robertson, I. H., & Dockree, P. M. (2020). Aging and attention. In K. M. Heilman & S. E. Nadeau (Eds.), *Cognitive changes and the aging brain* (pp. 140–152). Cambridge University Press. https://doi.org/10.1017/9781108554350.010

Rochat, P. (2001) *The Infant's World*. Cambridge, MA: Harvard University Press.

Rosenberg, M. (1985) 'Self-concept and Psychological Well-being in Adolescence', in R.L. Leahy (ed.), *The Development of the Self*, pp. 205–46. Orlando, FL: Academic Press.

Rutter, M. (1989) 'Pathway from childhood to adult life', *Journal of Child Psychology and Psychiatry* 30: 23–51.

Rutter, M., Bailey, A., Simonoff, E. and Pickles, A., (1997) 'Genetic influences in autism' in D. J. Cohen and F. R. Volkmar, eds, *Handbook of Autism and Pervasive Developmental Disorders*, 2nd ed., New York: Wiley.

Rutter, M. and Bartak, L. (1973) 'Special education treatment of autistic children: A comparative study: I. Follow-up findings and implications for services', *Journal of Child Psychology and Psychiatry* 14: 241–70.

Rutter, M. and the English and Romanian Adoptees (ERA) Study Team (1998, online 2000) 'Developmental catch-up, and deficit, following adoption after severe global early privation', *Journal of Child Psychology and Psychiatry* 39(4): 465–76.

Sacks, O. (1985) *The Man Who Mistook his Wife for a Hat*. Summit.

Saleebey, D. (2009) *The Strengths Perspective in Social Work*, New York: Allyn & Bacon.

Sameroff, A. J. (1983) *Handbook of Child Psychology: formerly Carmichael's Manual of Child Psychology*, P. H. Mussen (ed.). New York: Wiley.

Schaffer, H.R. (1996) *Social Development*. Oxford: Blackwell.

Schaie, K. W. and Willis, S. L. (2000) 'A Stage Theory Model of Adult Cognitive Development Revisited', in B. Rubinstein, M. Moss and M. Kleban (eds), *The Many Dimensions of Aging: Essays in Honor of M. Powell Lawton*, pp. 175–93. New York: Springer.

Schaie, K. W. and Willis, S. L. (2010) 'The Seattle Longitudinal Study of Adult Cognitive Development', *ISSBD Bulletin* 57(1): 24–9 <https://www.ncbi.nlm.nih.gov/pmc/articles/PMC3607395>.

Schaie, K.W. (2010) 'Adult cognitive development from a lifespan developmental perspective', Annual Report, Meiso University, Tokyo 28: 21-36 <https://sls.psychiatry.uw.edu/wp-content/uploads/2020/03/Adult-Cognitive-dev-from-lifespan.2010.pdf>.

Schlundt, D. G. and Johnson, W. G. (1990) *Eating Disorders, Assessment and Treatment*. Boston: Allyn and Bacon.

Selman, R. and Schultz, L. (1990) *Making a Friend in Youth: Developmental Theory and Pair Theory*. University of Chicago Press.

Shaffer, D. R. (1999) *Developmental Psychology: Childhood and Adolescence* (4th edn). Pacific Grove, CA: Brooks/Cole Publishing Company.

Shaver, P. and Mikulincer, M. (2010) 'New directions in attachment theory and research', *Journal of Social and Personal Relationships* 27(2): 163–72.

Skuse, D. (1984a) 'Extreme deprivation in early childhood — I. Diverse outcomes for three siblings from an extraordinary family', *Journal of Child Psychology and Psychiatry* 25(4): 525–41.

Skuse, D. (1984b) 'Extreme deprivation in early childhood — II. Theoretical issues and a comparative review', *Journal of Child Psychology and Psychiatry* 25(4).

Skuse, D. (1985) 'Technical note: Extreme deprivation in early childhood: A reply', *Journal of Child Psychology and Psychiatry* 26(5): 827–8.

Smith, P., Cowie, H. and Blades, M. (2003) *Understanding Children's Development* (4th edn). London: Blackwell.

Sroufe, L. A. (2005) 'Attachment and development: A prospective, longitudinal study from birth to adulthood', *Attachment and Human Development* 7(4): 349–67.

Steiner, Jean-François (1966) *Treblinka*, New York: Plume Publishers.

Sternberg, R. J. (1988) *The Triarchic Mind: A New Theory of Human Intelligence*. New York: Viking.

Stratton, R. (n.d.) (2019) 'Malnutrition'. In Gandy, J.(ed). *Manual of Dietetic Practice*. John Wiley &; Sons, Inc. <https://www.bda.uk.com/uploads/assets/cc187a3f-9df7-4613-98c1d9398fbec2eb/Manual-of-Dietetic-Practice-Chapter-62-Malnutrition.pdf>

Sudnow, D. (1967) *Passing On: The Social Organization of Dying*. Prentice Hall.

Sunderland, M. (2006) *The Science of Parenting*. London: Dorling Kindersley.

Tap, P. and Sordes-Ader, F. (2012) 'Soi, identités et adaptation', in M. Karwowski and J. C. Kaufman (eds, 2017), *The Creative Self: Effect of Beliefs, Self-efficacy, Mindset, and Identity*. Elsevier, Academic Press.

Tedstone Doherty, D., Moran, R. and Kartalova-O'Doherty, Y. (2008) *Psychological Distress, Mental Health Problems and Use of Health Services in Ireland* (HRB Research Series 5). Dublin: Health Research Board.

Thomas, A. and Chess, S. (1977) *Temperament and Development*. New York: Brenner/Mazel.

Thomas, A. and Chess, S. (1986) 'The New York Longitudinal Study: From Infancy to Early Adult Life', in R. Plomin and J. Dunn (eds), *The Study of Temperament: Changes, Continuities and Challenges*. Hillsdale, NJ: Erlbaum.

Unicef (2004) *Low Birthweight: Country, Regional and Global Estimates*. New York: Unicef.

United Nations (UN) (2006) Seventh Session of the Ad Hoc Committee on a Comprehensive and Integral International Convention on Protection and Promotion of the Rights and Dignity of Persons with Disabilities, 16 January–3 February. Available at: <www.un.org/esa/socdev/enable/rights/ahc7.htm>.

Valentino, K., Cicchetti, D., Toth, S. and Rogosch, F. (2011) 'Mother–child play and maltreatment: a longitudinal analysis of emerging social behaviors from infancy to toddlerhood', *Developmental Psychology* 47(5): 1280–94.

Vygotsky, L. S. (1978) *Mind and Society: The development of higher psychological processes*, Cambridge, MA: Harvard University Press.

Walker, J. (2008). 'Communication and social work from an attachment perspective', *Journal of Social Work Practice* 22(1): 1–22.

Weber, J. A. and McCormick, P. (1992) 'Alateen members' and non-members' understanding of alcoholism', *Journal of Alcohol and Drug Education* 37(3): 74–84.

Wermter, A. K., Laucht, M., Schimmelmann, B., Banaschweski, T., Sonuga-Barke, E., Rietschel, M. and Becker, K. (2010) 'From Nature versus Nurture, to gene x environment interaction in mental disorders', *European Child and Adolescent Psychiatry* 19: 199–210.

WHO (World Health Organisation) (2011) *World Health Statistics 2011* <www.who.int/whosis/whostat/EN_WHS2011_Full.pdf>.

WHO (2012) *Risks to Mental Health: An Overview of Vulnerabilities and Risk Factors*, background paper by the WHO Secretariat for the development of a comprehensive mental health action plan.

WHO (2016) *Physical Activity Strategy for the WHO European Region 2016–2025* <https://www.euro.who.int/__data/assets/pdf_file/0014/311360/Physical-activity-strategy-2016-2025.pdf> (accessed 15 June 2022).

Index

B

C

E

N

O

Q

R

S